LAND'S END TO JOHN O'GROATS

Andrew McCloy is Information Officer for the Ramblers' Association and is a keen long-distance walker of many years' experience.

LAND'S END TO JOHN O'GROATS

a choice of footpaths for walking the length of Britain

Andrew McCloy

CORONET BOOKS
Hodder and Stoughton

First published in Great Britain in 1994 by Hodder & Stoughton
A division of Hodder Headline PLC
First published in paperback in 1995 by Hodder & Stoughton

A Coronet paperback

10 9 8 7 6 5 4 3 2 1

British Library Cataloguing in Publication Data
McCloy, Andrew
Land's End to John O'Groats: Choice of Footpaths for Walking the Length of Britain
I. Title
914.104

ISBN 0 340 63750 1

Printed and bound in Great Britain by
Cox & Wyman Ltd, Reading, Berkshire

Hodder and Stoughton
A division of Hodder Headline PLC
338 Euston Road
London NW1 3BH

For Katherine

Contents

Photographic Credits

The author and publishers would like to thank A. F. Kersting for supplying the pictures of Land's End rocks; Glastonbury Tor; Chapel Porth; Woolacombe Sands; Greylake; Vicars' Close; Beeston Castle; Langdale Pikes; Buachaille Etive Mor; Dartmoor; Widecombe in the Moor; Salcombe; Start Point; Beer and Coldingham Bay; Cheshire County Council for the picture of Tegg's Nose; Terry Marsh for his pictures of Bleaklow; High Force and Windy Gyle; Hamish MacInnes for his picture of the Lairig Ghru; Derek G. Widdicombe of Worldwide Photographic Library for the picture of Lowick Bridge; Chris Bonington for the picture of High Pike; Lorne Gill of the Scottish National Heritage for the picture of Rannoch Moor; Ian Johnson for supplying the pictures of Robin Hood's Bay and Whitby, and English Heritage for their picture of Dunstanburgh Castle. All other photographs were taken by the author.

Maps were drawn by Jeremy Ashcroft.

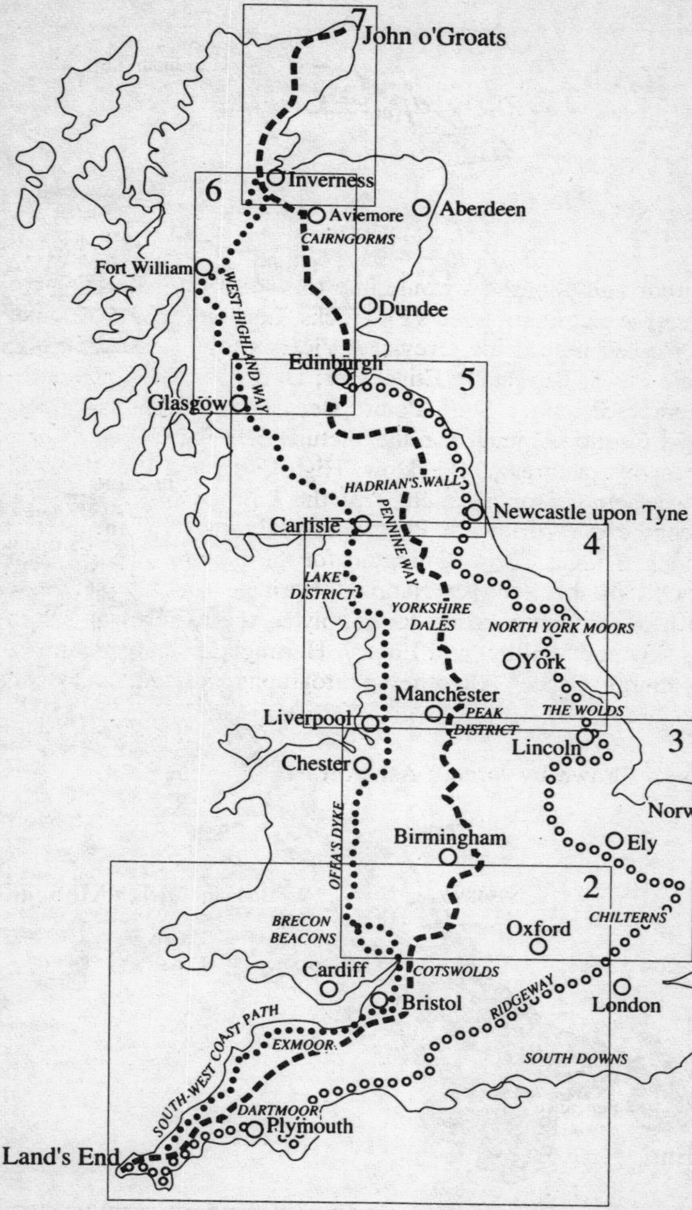
7
John o'Groats
Inverness
6
Aviemore
Aberdeen
CAIRNGORMS
Fort William
WEST HIGHLAND WAY
Dundee
Edinburgh
5
Glasgow
HADRIAN'S WALL
PENNINE WAY
Newcastle upon Tyne
Carlisle
4
LAKE DISTRICT
YORKSHIRE DALES
NORTH YORK MOORS
York
Manchester
PEAK DISTRICT
THE WOLDS
Liverpool
Lincoln
3
Chester
Norwich
OFFA'S DYKE
Birmingham
Ely
2
CHILTERNS
BRECON BEACONS
Oxford
Cardiff
COTSWOLDS
Bristol
London
RIDGEWAY
SOUTH-WEST COAST PATH
EXMOOR
SOUTH DOWNS
DARTMOOR
Plymouth
Land's End

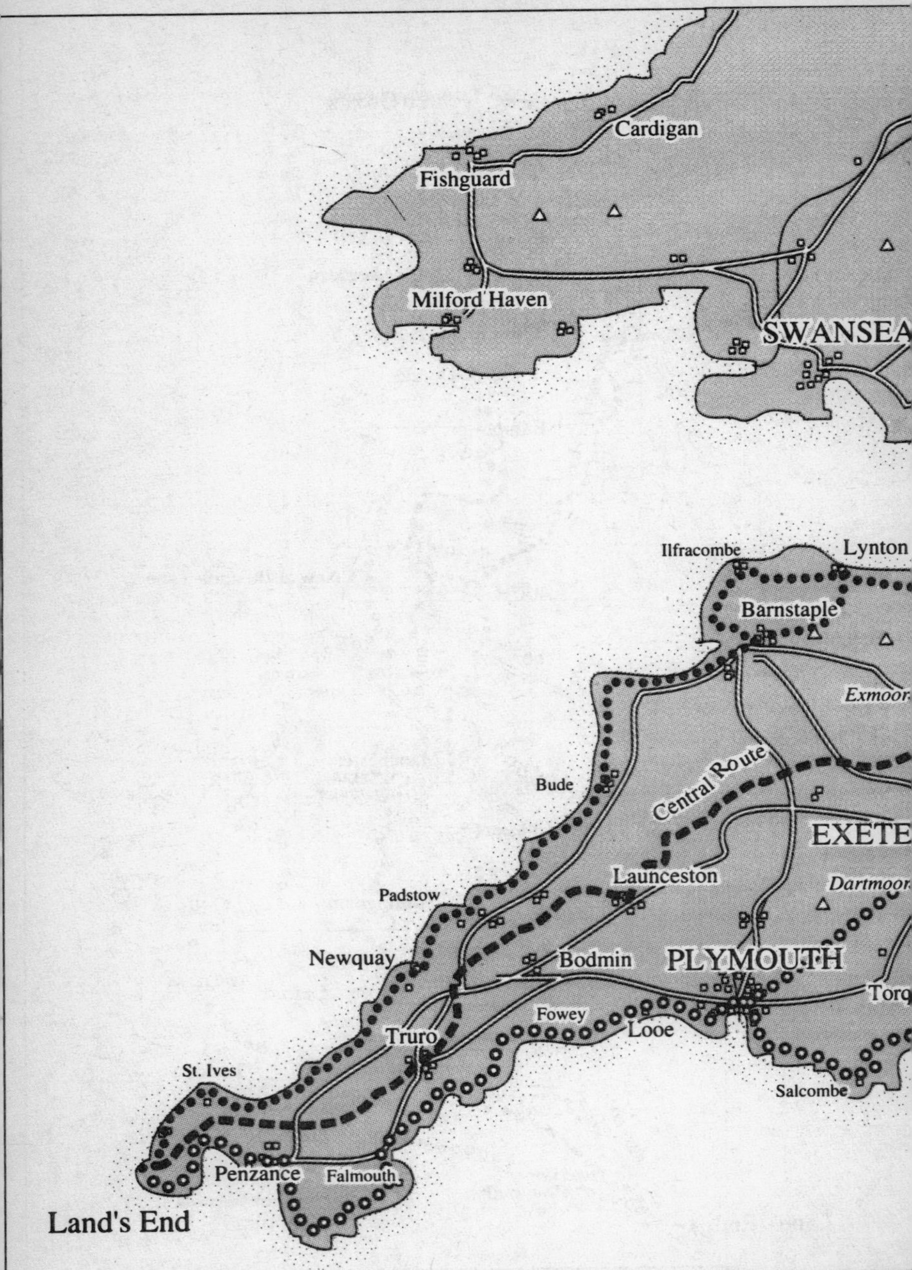
Cardigan
Fishguard
Milford Haven
SWANSEA
Ilfracombe
Lynton
Barnstaple
Exmoor
Central Route
Bude
EXETE
Launceston
Dartmoor
Padstow
Newquay
Bodmin
PLYMOUTH
Torq
Fowey
Looe
Truro
St. Ives
Salcombe
Penzance
Falmouth
Land's End

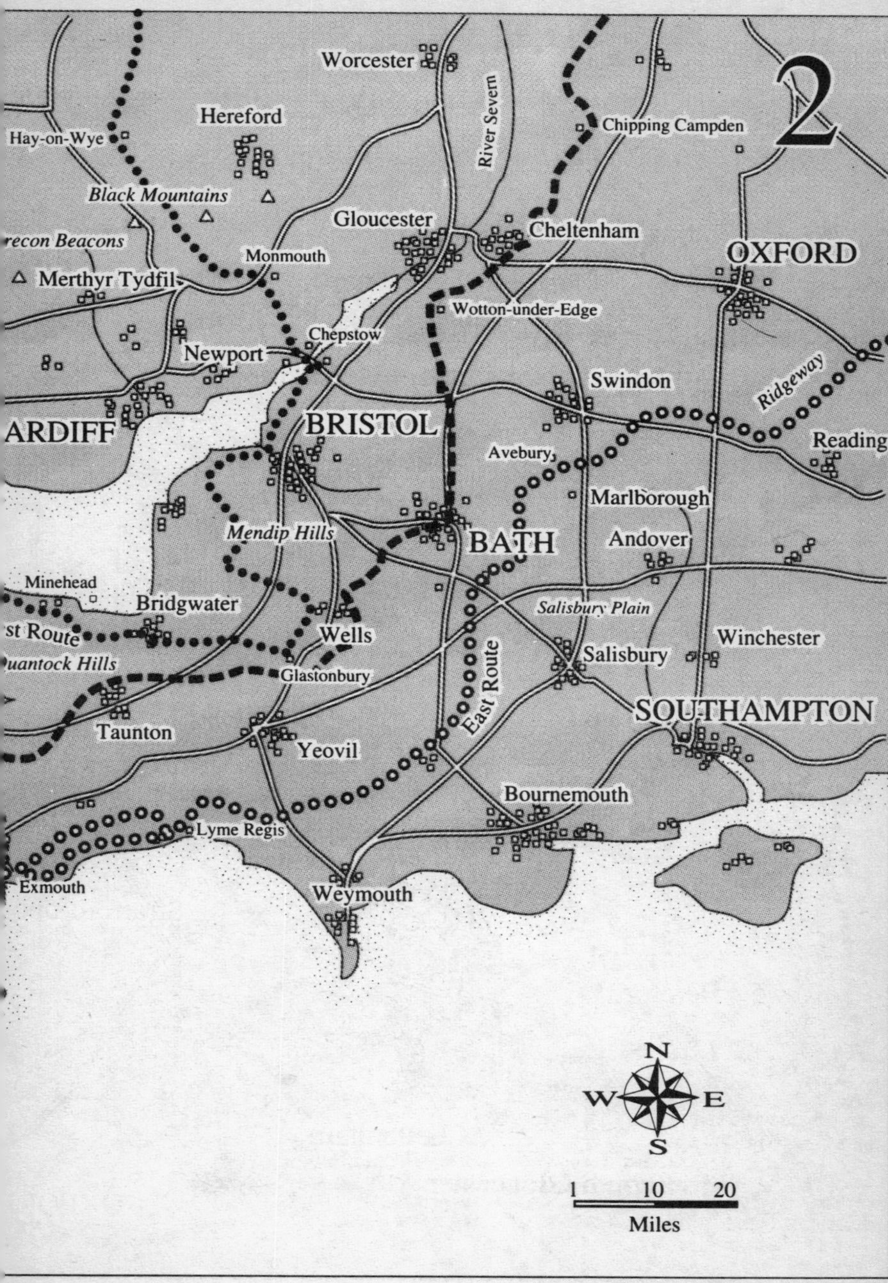
2
Worcester
Hereford
Hay-on-Wye
River Severn
Chipping Campden
Black Mountains
recon Beacons
Gloucester
Cheltenham
OXFORD
Monmouth
Merthyr Tydfil
Wotton-under-Edge
Chepstow
Newport
Swindon
Ridgeway
ARDIFF
BRISTOL
Reading
Avebury
Marlborough
Mendip Hills
BATH
Andover
Minehead
Bridgwater
Salisbury Plain
st Route
Wells
Winchester
uantock Hills
Salisbury
Glastonbury
East Route
SOUTHAMPTON
Taunton
Yeovil
Bournemouth
Lyme Regis
Exmouth
Weymouth
N
W
E
S
1
10
20
Miles

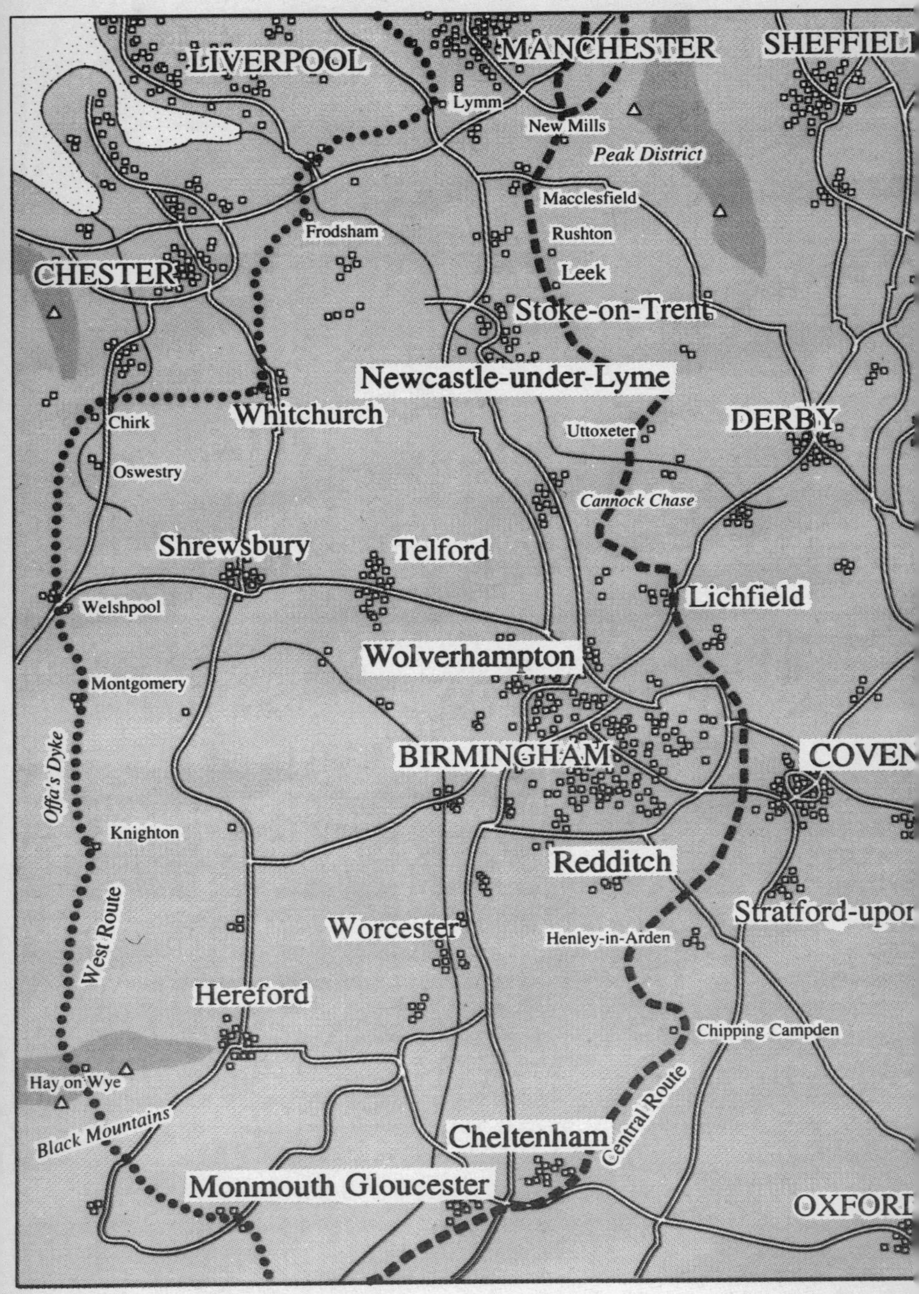

LIVERPOOL
MANCHESTER
SHEFFIEL
Lymm
New Mills
Peak District
Macclesfield
Frodsham
Rushton
CHESTER
Leek
Stoke-on-Trent
Newcastle-under-Lyme
Whitchurch
Chirk
Uttoxeter
DERBY
Oswestry
Cannock Chase
Shrewsbury
Telford
Lichfield
Welshpool
Wolverhampton
Montgomery
BIRMINGHAM
COVEN
Offa's Dyke
Knighton
Redditch
West Route
Worcester
Henley-in-Arden
Stratford-upon
Hereford
Chipping Campden
Hay on Wye
Black Mountains
Central Route
Cheltenham
Monmouth
Gloucester
OXFORD

3
Lincolnshire Wolds
Market Rasen
LINCOLN
Skegness
Horncastle
Newark-on-Trent
Boston
OTTINGHAM
Grantham
King's Lynn
Oakham
Stamford
Peterborough
EICESTER
East Route
Thetford
Huntingdon
Ely
Northampton
Bedford
Newmarket
CAMBRIDGE
N
W
E
S
Milton Keynes
Luton
Stevenage
1
10
20
Miles
Aylesbury
Dunstable

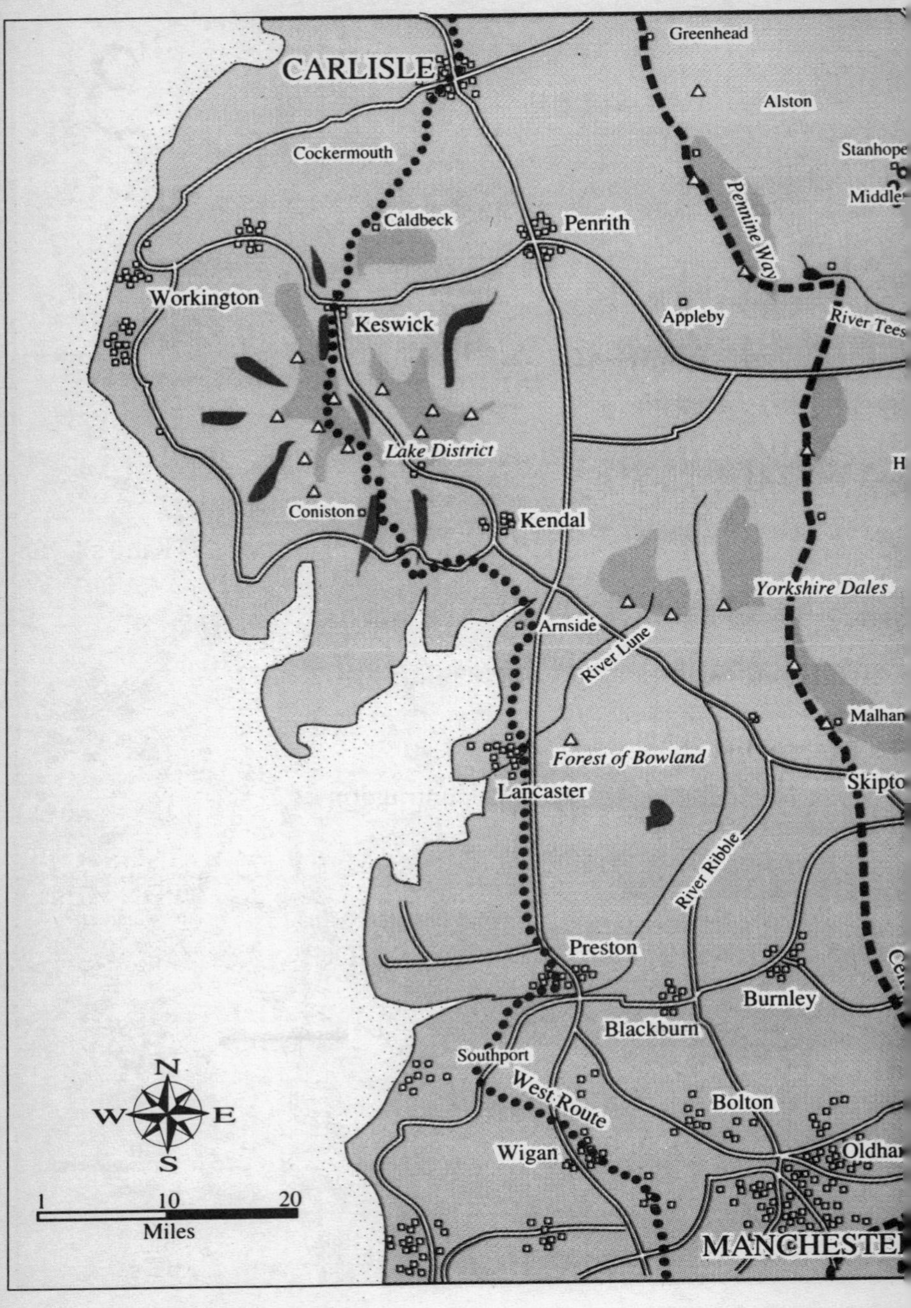
CARLISLE
Greenhead
Alston
Stanhope
Middle
Cockermouth
Caldbeck
Penrith
Pennine Way
Workington
Keswick
Appleby
River Tees
Lake District
Coniston
Kendal
Yorkshire Dales
Arnside
River Lune
Malham
Forest of Bowland
Skipto
Lancaster
River Ribble
Preston
Burnley
Blackburn
Southport
West Route
Bolton
Wigan
Oldha
MANCHESTE
N
W
E
S
1
10
20
Miles

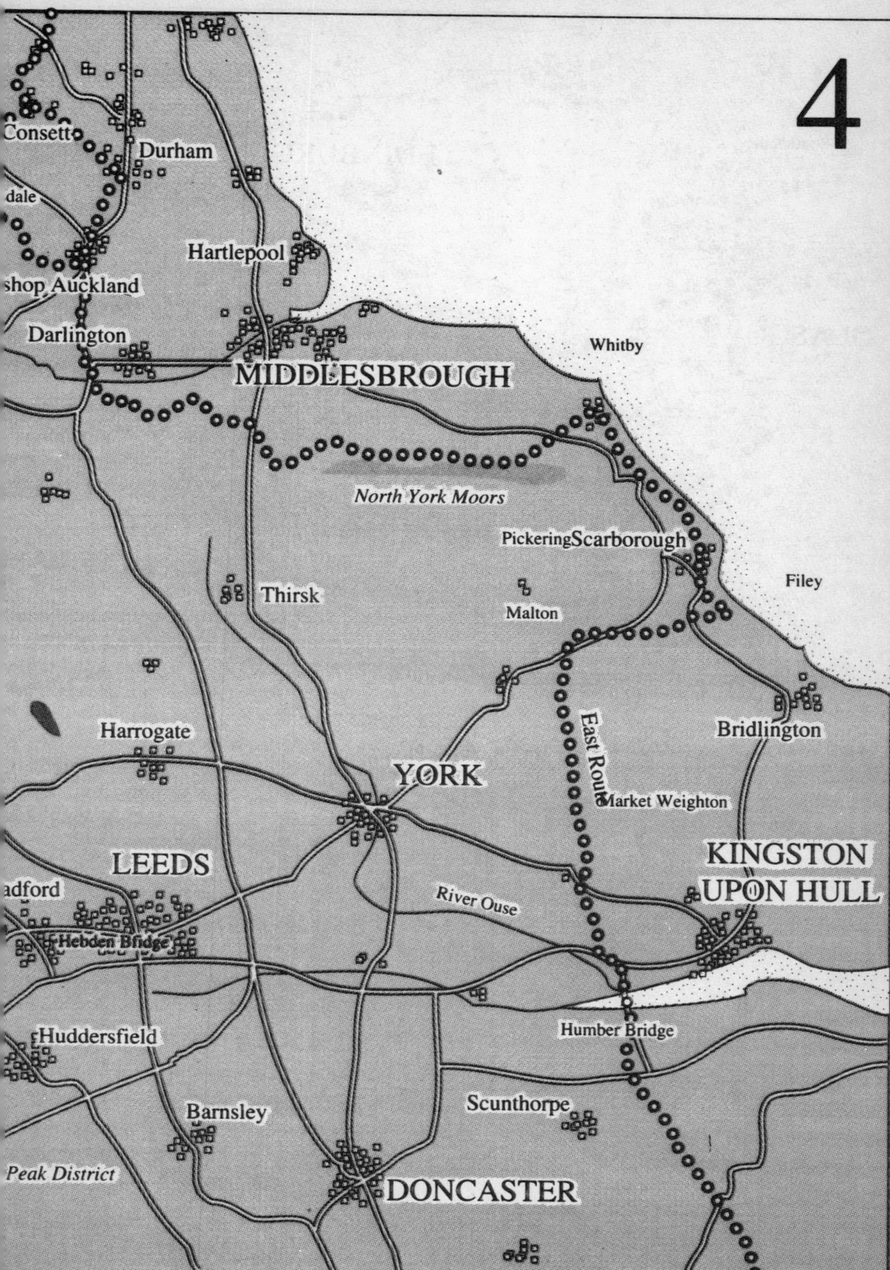
4
Consett
Durham
dale
Hartlepool
shop Auckland
Darlington
Whitby
MIDDLESBROUGH
North York Moors
Pickering
Scarborough
Filey
Thirsk
Malton
Harrogate
Bridlington
YORK
East Route
Market Weighton
LEEDS
KINGSTON UPON HULL
adford
River Ouse
Hebden Bridge
Humber Bridge
Huddersfield
Scunthorpe
Barnsley
Peak District
DONCASTER

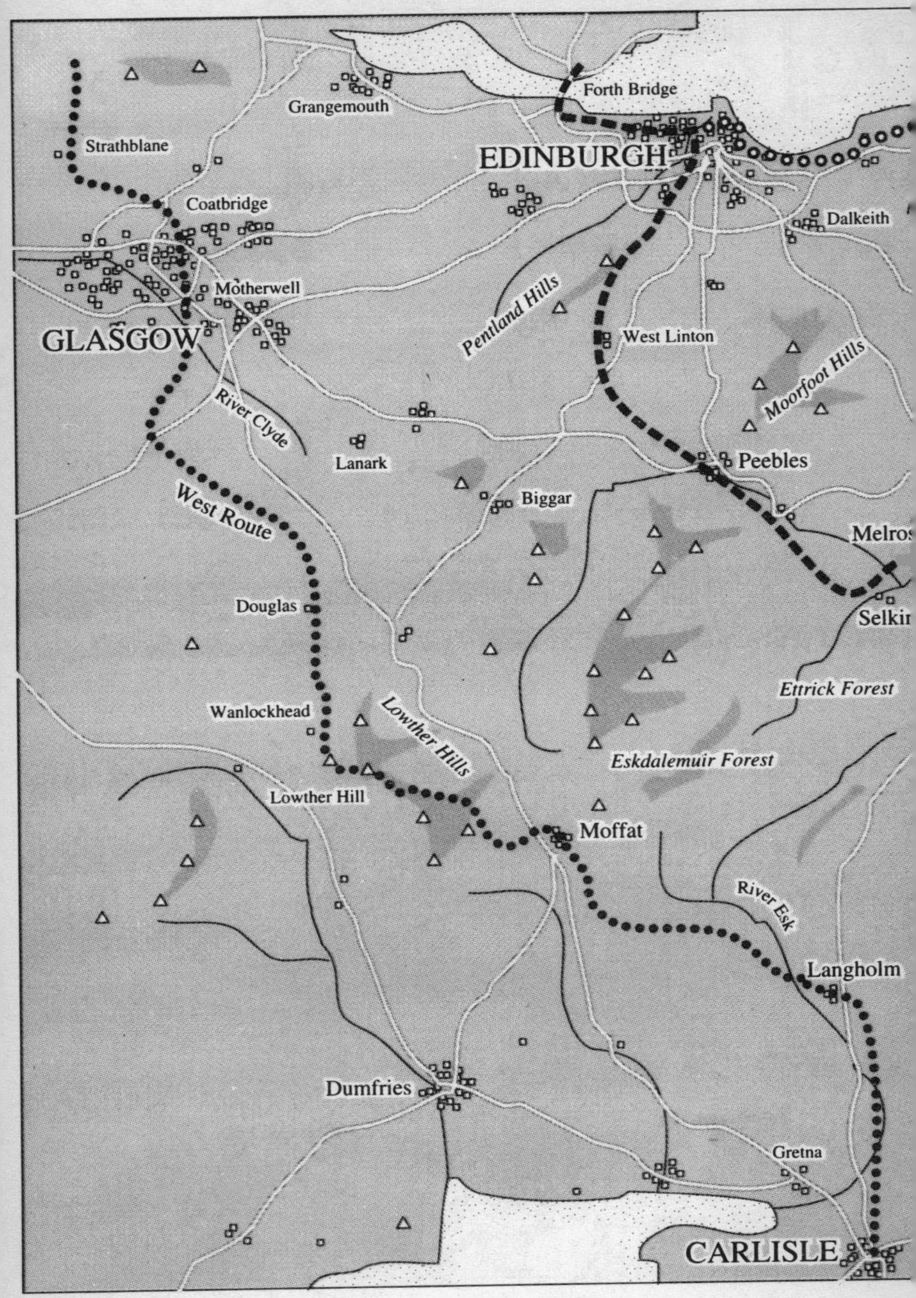
Forth Bridge
Grangemouth
Strathblane
EDINBURGH
Coatbridge
Dalkeith
Motherwell
Pentland Hills
West Linton
GLASGOW
Moorfoot Hills
River Clyde
Lanark
Peebles
West Route
Biggar
Melros
Douglas
Selkir
Ettrick Forest
Wanlockhead
Lowther Hills
Eskdalemuir Forest
Lowther Hill
Moffat
River Esk
Langholm
Dumfries
Gretna
CARLISLE

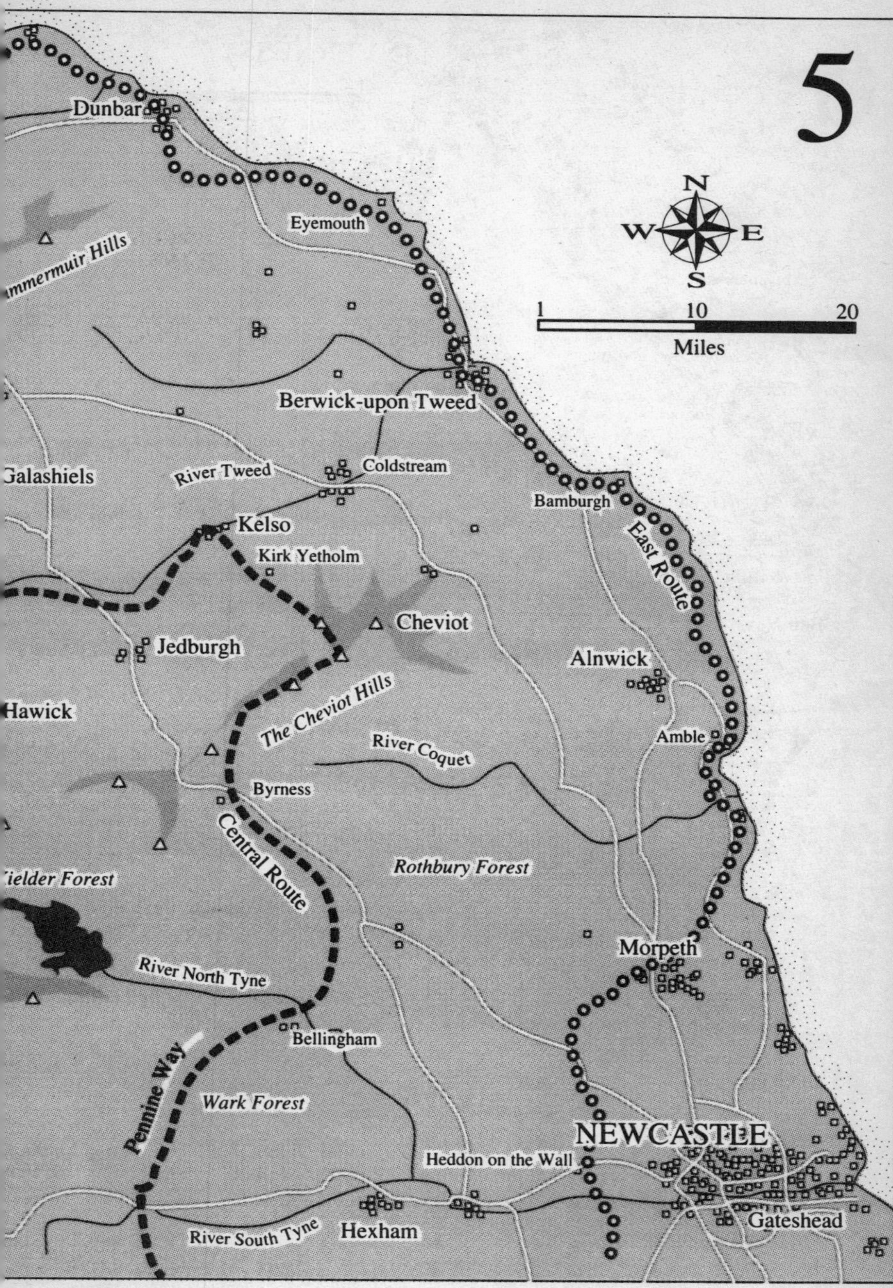
5
N
W
E
S
1
10
20
Miles
Dunbar
Eyemouth
mmermuir Hills
Berwick-upon Tweed
Galashiels
River Tweed
Coldstream
Bamburgh
Kelso
Kirk Yetholm
East Route
Cheviot
Jedburgh
Alnwick
The Cheviot Hills
Hawick
River Coquet
Amble
Byrness
Central Route
Rothbury Forest
ielder Forest
Morpeth
River North Tyne
Bellingham
Pennine Way
Wark Forest
NEWCASTLE
Heddon on the Wall
Gateshead
River South Tyne
Hexham

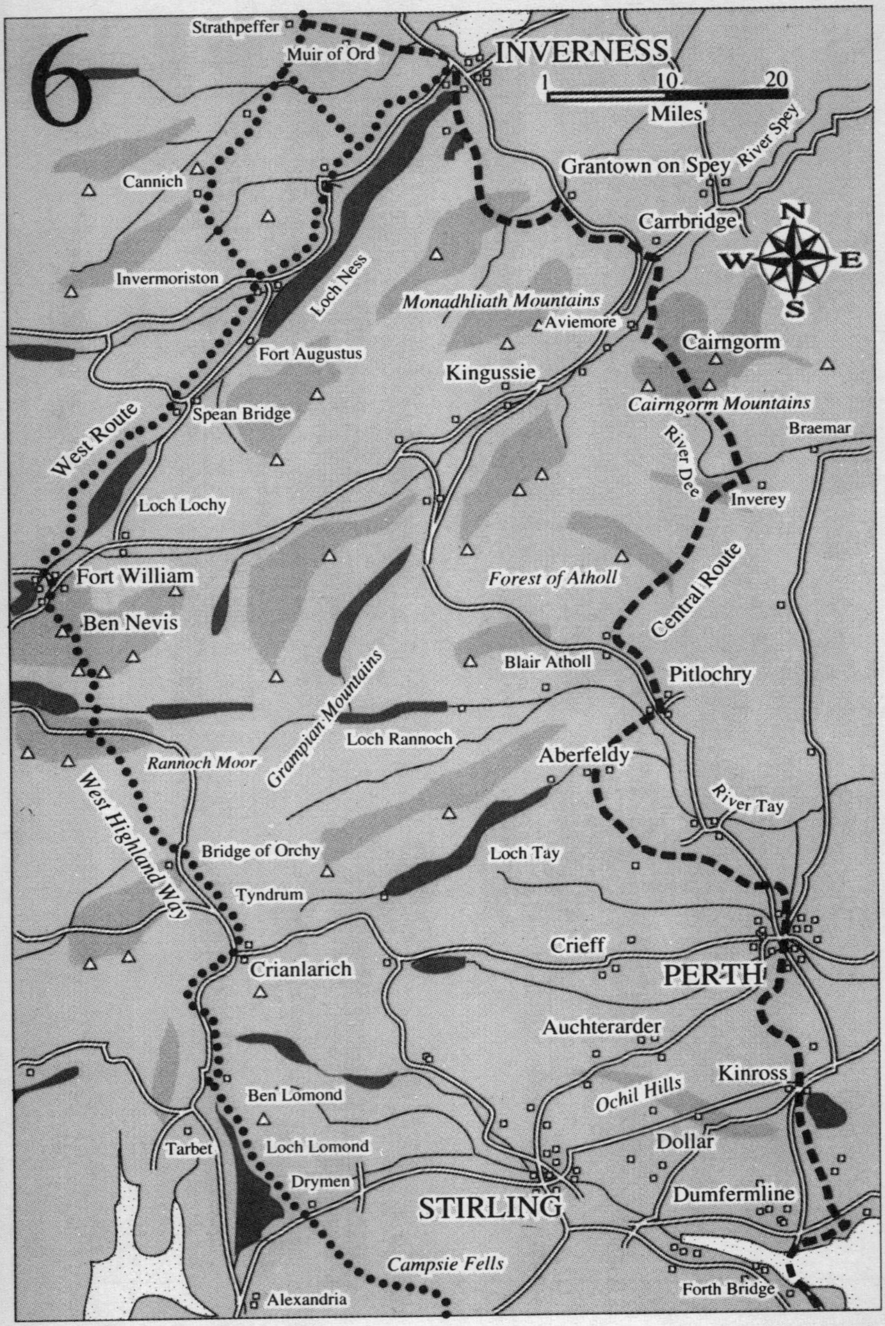
6
INVERNESS
1
10
20
Miles
Strathpeffer
Muir of Ord
Cannich
Invermoriston
Loch Ness
Grantown on Spey
River Spey
Carrbridge
N
W
E
S
Monadhliath Mountains
Aviemore
Cairngorm
Fort Augustus
Kingussie
Cairngorm Mountains
Spean Bridge
West Route
Braemar
River Dee
Inverey
Loch Lochy
Central Route
Fort William
Forest of Atholl
Ben Nevis
Blair Atholl
Pitlochry
Grampian Mountains
Loch Rannoch
Aberfeldy
Rannoch Moor
West Highland Way
River Tay
Bridge of Orchy
Loch Tay
Tyndrum
Crieff
PERTH
Crianlarich
Auchterarder
Kinross
Ochil Hills
Ben Lomond
Dollar
Tarbet
Loch Lomond
Drymen
Dumfermline
STIRLING
Campsie Fells
Forth Bridge
Alexandria

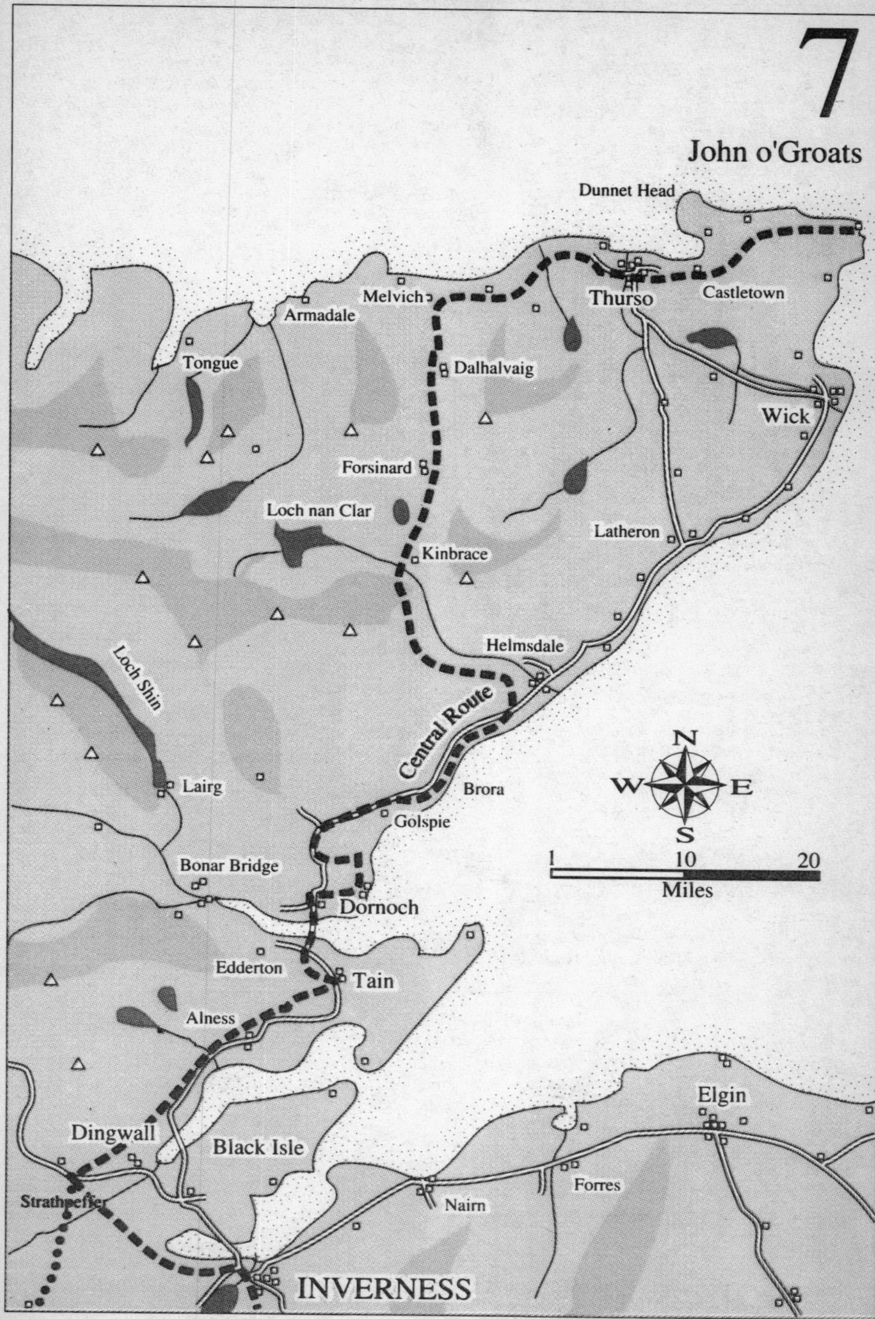
7
John o'Groats
Dunnet Head
Thurso
Castletown
Melvich
Armadale
Tongue
Dalhalvaig
Wick
Forsinard
Loch nan Clar
Latheron
Kinbrace
Helmsdale
Loch Shin
Central Route
Brora
Lairg
Golspie
N
W
E
S
1
10
20
Miles
Bonar Bridge
Dornoch
Edderton
Tain
Alness
Elgin
Dingwall
Black Isle
Forres
Nairn
Strathpeffer
INVERNESS

Introduction

There is an entry in the Land's End to John o'Groats record book in the John o'Groats House Hotel which reads: 'I think the satisfaction and pride will develop in the next few days – at present it is just relief.' It was written by David Lindsay from Tasmania, Australia, after walking 920 miles from Land's End in Summer 1993, a journey that took him 45 days. A walk of this magnitude should not be beyond the limits of someone fit and well-prepared, but even the toughest may sit back in the lounge bar with a sigh of relief once it's all over. As far as walking in Britain is concerned, this is the ultimate.

People travel from Land's End to John o'Groats for a variety of reasons and in some startlingly different manners. Many use the venture to raise money for charity, whether they are celebrities, such as Jimmy Saville and Ian Botham, or just incredibly brave young men and women, often battling against their own illness to raise thousands of pounds for specialist medical facilities. Nine-year-old 'Little Joe' Lambert, for instance, walked 875 miles in 40 days in order to raise money for diabetic research, a condition which he suffered from himself. Some people choose to take their pets along, others their families. Britain's most prolific modern walker decided to walk the entire coastline of England, Wales and Scotland in order to join the ends. And perhaps we should not be surprised to learn that two brothers-in-law took turns to push each other in a wheelbarrow the whole length (a feat that they accomplished in only 30 days). Anything seems to go.

Then there are the record-breakers. Although this book is not expressly for those seeking their way into the *Guinness Book of Records*, it is true that the End to End Route has become synonymous with the race against the clock. Linking the two ends of Britain on foot – and on purpose – can be traced back as far as 1863, when the American Elihu Burritt walked from London to John o'Groats, then from London to Land's End, but it was not until a century later that popular interest in the End to End idea took off. In 1960, the Russian-born Dr Barbara Moore battled her way single-handed through severe weather conditions, and on a spartan vegetarian diet too, completing the full End to End in a remarkable 22 days.

Such was the publicity surrounding her adventure that within a few months Billy Butlin announced an End to End challenge walk open to all, which generated enormous public interest. However, out of the 715 that set off from John o'Groats only 138 made it to the tip of Cornwall, many being hopelessly ill-prepared. The first to arrive at Land's End took just under 16 days. Since then the End to End Walk has inevitably become associated with factors of distance and time. It continues to be a source of endless fascination to learn that the End to End challenge – albeit using the shortest possible tarmac route (which has gradually become shorter as new roads and bridges are built) – has been walked in 12 days, 3 hours, 45 minutes, by Malcolm Barnish of the 19th Regiment, Royal Artillery, in June 1986. The women's record is held by Ann Sayer, Chairperson of the Long Distance Walkers' Association, who did it in 13 days, 17 hours, 42 minutes in October 1980. (And while on the subject of End to End foot records, perhaps the most bizarre is held by Arvind Pandya of India, who in May 1990 took 26 days and 7 hours to join one end of Britain to the other – by running backwards!)

Most of the dozen or so End to Enders staggering through the doors of the John o'Groats House Hotel every day are actually cyclists. The record book is full of entries such as 'Never again? Not on a push-bike, anyway', and another that starts with a quote from *King Lear*, 'Man must endure.' The End to End cycling record is currently held by Andy Wilkinson, who made the journey in October 1990 in an incredible time of 1 day, 21 hours, 2 minutes and 19 seconds. But there are plenty of others who nurse vintage cars and motorbikes the distance. Recently a mother and son even completed the journey in a pony and trap; and in May 1984, twenty-year-old Steve Fagan took 9 days, 10 hours and 25 minutes to roller skate from End to End.

But this book is for the walker. It is for those who want to link the ends of the British mainland by foot, and foot only, whether for the good of others or themselves. And although the following routes can be used equally well by those intent on walking 30 miles a day and not 20, and finishing in five weeks and not eight, I would encourage walkers to approach the End to End Walk with enjoyment rather than endurance in mind.

Practical points

When reading the following pages there are two very important points to bear in mind: first, the three routes described are, of course, my own suggestions for tackling Britain's premier walking journey, but I have identified numerous places where they can be varied and adapted to suit personal taste and inclination – do not feel confined to just one specified route; and second, if you think that you can walk the length of Britain using just this book then you are mistaken. It is surprisingly easy to get lost, even on a waymarked trail, so take notice of the further reading list. See this work, instead, as a basis for planning the big adventure, or as a memory of a happy trek completed.

I have deliberately plotted three routes in order to allow the walker to choose from most of the outstanding long-distance paths in the country. In Britain we are blessed with a tremendous range of terrain and scenery within a relatively small area, or within reasonable walking distance, at least. In order to reflect this I have offered the alternative of coast or moorland; a view of the sea or of fields and woodland; plunging cliffs or sedate country lanes. While my routes follow fairly logical, linear patterns, it may be worth considering combining sections of two or even all three routes – depending on which regions you want to visit (or avoid); whether you have walked, say, the Pennine Way or Cotswold Way already; or whether your timetable allows a gentle wander or a hasty routemarch.

It is important to keep your options open and choose your route carefully. All three End to End routes have alternatives and openings for the curious and adventurous – *and where they occur they are described in italicised text*. It may be a diversion of only a few miles, or it may open a door to an entirely new and exciting long-distance path (the Shropshire Way, Dales Way or the Link Through the Tabular Hills) that connects with one of the other End to End routes.

Of course, there is no hard and fast rule that you must stick to official or documented long-distance footpaths, except for the fact that by and large they traverse the best scenery, are frequently waymarked, and the major ones have often spawned a useful local 'service industry' of B&Bs, campsites and cafés. However, walking purists might ask why the long-distance walker should be shackled by defined trails when there are 140,000 miles of rights of way in England and Wales alone? If this is your thinking, then delve eclectically into each chapter, or devise your own route. But there again, should you be reading a walking guidebook at all?

It should be emphasised, if it is not already obvious, that the routes featured are primarily footpaths, not bridleways or roads, and so are expressly for walkers. I have made a point of avoiding surfaced roads whenever possible, and avoiding busy A-roads at virtually all costs, although naturally some have to be crossed, with extreme care. But there are inevitably some sections of the three routes that involve a very small amount of road-walking, usually where public footpaths simply do not exist in a cohesive or plentiful number. Ironically, the only tarmac sections of any length occur at the very beginning and end: mid-Cornwall and mid-Devon (Central Route), and in the final stages through pathless Caithness. But it needs pointing out that by and large these country lanes are usually quiet and uncluttered, providing a clear and firm passage to specific places (and often without the need to constantly refer to map and compass). All this said, stick to the paths!

About the routes themselves, a glance at the map will show that although three stride out from Land's End, only one plods into John o'Groats. This is not meant to reflect the toll of walking casualties or the probable retirement rate of End to End walkers (I suspect that the Pennine Way alone claims far more 'retired hurts' than the End to End route). The reason for the convergence is purely one of physical geography. England's shape and relatively hospitable terrain, plus the profusion of long-distance paths, allows for three independent and very different routes. The South-West Coast Path, whether north or south coast, is a spectacular if tough way to begin any walk, then there is a choice of low downlands eastwards, the peaceful Cotswolds through the centre, or the rigours of Offa's Dyke along the Welsh border. The traditional route after the Dyke has been completed is across Cheshire and on to the Pennine Way at Edale, but I have suggested a quicker and easier route through Lancashire to the Lake District. Meanwhile the Central Route twists its surprisingly green way through the Midlands, and after

Cannock Chase and rural Staffordshire it joins the Pennine Way for the grand march north. Over in the east, I urge you to look at some of the less well-known paths that deserve more admirers: the Hereward Way, Viking Way and Wolds Way. After the Cleveland Hills there are some relatively unknown 'railway paths' that take you comfortably through County Durham, followed by the delightful Northumberland coast.

All through England the three routes mostly follow clear natural or man-made features: the Pennine chain, Offa's Dyke, canals and coastal paths, etc. However, once across the Scottish border the west and then east coast becomes either inaccessible or geographically inconvenient. Ahead there are few set trails; instead, a barrier of rather serious mountains. Although there are conceivably any number of routes for the experienced hillwalker, it seemed natural to adopt a two-pronged approach, one route following the West Highland Way to Fort William and Ben Nevis, and the East Route using former drove roads, military roads and well-used public rights of way into the Grampians and through the heart of Britain's highest mountain range, the Cairngorms. The Great Glen is the obvious and relatively easy link for the former to join the latter, so that all that is left until John o'Groats is the north-east coastal lowlands and the remote hills of Caithness. Some strong or ambitious walkers will no doubt want to tackle the North-West Highlands, but it is a mountain adventure outside the scope of this guide, and if you are keen you should give both route and equipment careful consideration and respect the hills.

The second, basic point about this book is that it does not – in fact, cannot – pretend to be a step-by-step guide to three routes with a total cumulative mileage in excess of 3,500 miles. I have endeavoured to make the text as detailed and helpful as possible, and have highlighted the salient points about the route in each area, especially where specific parts excited or challenged me. There is also a wealth of guidebooks to most of the long-distance paths described, and I have listed appropriate titles. For other routes I have devoted more space where the relevant path is either less easy to follow or more interesting – and less space where, for instance, the route takes the form of a coastal path, with a clear and unmistakable direction.

Along the way

The appendix on Equipment and Preparation gives plenty of detail on aspects to consider before the Walk, but once under way there are some general points that should be borne in mind.

Remember the countryside is a dynamic place! Footpaths are diverted, new roads are built, landslips sweep away whole sections of trails – as in the case of the Cleveland Way National Trail at Scarborough when the Holbeck Hall Hotel slid into the North Sea one night. Even the Pennine Way has been subject to route alteration due to mounting erosion. While I have taken every effort to ensure that the information given in the following pages is accurate, it is wise to do your own homework as well. For instance, if you are heading for a remote youth hostel make sure that it is still open; or call ahead to an estate to ensure that grouse shooting has not closed a moorland path in mid-August; and so on. When walking, it is wise to expect the unexpected.

One particular subject area that lends itself to change and sometimes dispute is rights of way. While major trails can be subject to occasional, mostly minor re-routing, diversions of local footpaths are happening all the time. The subject of rights of way is complex, but it is sensible to have at least a basic knowledge of how the law works and what your rights are. For a general introduction for England and Wales read the Countryside Commission's booklet *Out in the Country: where you can go and what you can do*; or for more in-depth information consult *Rights of Way: a guide to law and practice* (see the further reading list). The whole situation is of course different in Scotland, particularly as regards the law of trespass and I recommend prospective End to Enders read *Rights of Way: a guide to the law in Scotland* by the Scottish Rights of Way Society.

Walking from one end of the country to the other is an experience of a lifetime, almost certainly the single most supreme walking journey that you will ever make within Great Britain. Since it is unlikely that you will repeat it, make sure that you enjoy the Walk! Of course be prepared and properly equipped, but also know where you are going and what you want to see, for so much more besides will be revealed. And yet it is obvious that at the end of the day you will be following a narrow, linear route, so that once you have linked the choppy waters near the Scilly Isles with the swirling pools of the Pentland Firth it is time to let your gaze widen. Seek out some of the lesser-known local trails, perhaps a few seldom-trodden footpaths from the OS map; or instead roam the hills and moors of a quiet and hidden corner of the land hitherto unexplored. You will find that walking from Land's End to John o'Groats is just the beginning of the adventure . . .

THE CENTRAL ROUTE

1 THE DESERTED LANES
Land's End – Taunton
by local paths and lanes
175 miles

2 COTSWOLD BEAUTY
Taunton – Chipping Campden
by the Cotswold Way
152 miles

3 GREEN ROUTE THROUGH THE MIDLANDS
Chipping Campden – Crowden
by the Heart of England Way, the Staffordshire Way and the Gritstone Trail
166 miles

4 THE TOUGHEST TRAIL
Crowden – Kirk Yetholm
by the Pennine Way
243 miles

5 THROUGH SCOTLAND'S HEART
Kirk Yetholm – Aberfeldy
by the Southern Upland Way and Fife Coast Path
164.5 miles

6 THE WILDERNESS MILES
Aberfeldy – Inverness
by local paths
91 miles

7 THE LAST LAP
Inverness – John o'Groats
by local paths and lanes
147 miles

1

THE DESERTED LANES

Land's End – Taunton

At the beginning of any long walk there is such a confusion of emotions that by and large it is best simply to start walking. What time of the day you set off will depend on where you choose to stay the night before. An early start will probably be best, since there will be less likelihood of a ready-made audience of the curious and the ridiculous serenading your first few steps. There is accommodation in Sennen and in various farms and B&Bs along the A30, or you can stay at the State House Hotel – which is part of the Land's End development and is open all year (but it is not cheap). Also, there is Land's End Youth Hostel, but this is five miles away by either coastal path or road, in the Cot Valley. Or alternatively you can camp, but you may feel that a warm and comfy bed is essential prior to the big day. If you are not camping, make sure you book accommodation in advance, since Land's End attracts visitors all the year round.

You will have to take a photograph or two before you depart Land's End, and unless you leave at dawn there will always be someone about to assist. The mini theme park that has been built on the edge of the cliff (which includes the hotel) is perhaps a little preposterous, but inside there are application forms for membership of the Land's End–John o'Groats Association, and outside there is the famous signpost. If you think that the arm pointing to John o'Groats seems daunting (they estimate it at 874 miles), then consider that New York is 3,147 miles away.

So wander towards the rocks below the First and Last House and make sure you are the first and last person in the land, then turn north-eastwards and head for John o'Groats. The adventure has begun.

LAND'S END – TRURO (43 miles)

There is a rather serious problem for the long-distance walker who wants to cross Cornwall and Devon by non-coastal paths. Basically, there aren't any. No, this is a gross exaggeration. What I mean is that there are no west-east long-distance trails to follow, and what local public footpaths and bridleways that do exist are limited in number, and often of variable quality and clarity. A signpost is all very well, but if the path through the field or copse is overgrown or obstructed it makes progress slow and frustrating. That is why much of the Central Route between Land's End and Taunton follows country lanes. Of these there are simply hundreds and hundreds, mostly quiet and very scenic, and some commendably direct. Of course, as a whole they are woven into a delightful patchwork quilt of connecting thoroughfares, and close attention to map or signpost is sometimes necessary to avoid an unintentional circular ramble, but overall progress eastwards can be swift, and at the same time passing countless villages and hamlets off the beaten path. When Newquay or Torbay are heaving with trippers, or when you stare ahead in a mixture of dread and despair at another towering cliff ascent, the rolling lanes of mid-Devon will offer tranquillity and gentleness. There is the occasional hazard of vehicles, obviously, and cafés and campsites are not as prevalent as on the coast, but the out-of-the-wayness of it all compensates; and, with a sensibly restrained early mileage, it should be easier on your limbs.

I have used public footpaths and bridleways wherever possible, and despite their predominantly north-south direction small stages of the Camel Trail, Tarka Trail, and the Two Moors Way have been incorporated. It is regrettable that access to Bodmin Moor is limited; that northern Dartmoor is out of bounds due to its continuing abuse by the military; and that Exmoor is too far to the north of the peninsula to include in a direct, central route. However, it hardly needs to be said that the Central Route before you is open to any amount of adaptation. There are so many possible points of departure for either coast that describing them is futile. If, standing on the edge of Bodmin Moor, the lure of the sparkling sea is too much, then change course and take the Camel Trail to Padstow or lanes across country to Boscastle. Or if you have never walked on Dartmoor you may consider making for Tavistock rather than Launceston and forging a route over the central/southern moors (and see the East Coast alternative route over Dartmoor). But, as many long-distance walkers will testify, the first few days of a marathon walk such as this will see you eager to eat up the early miles, and to get into and ahead with the Walk. In this case perhaps the lanes of the South-West will be the best way forwards rather than the tough coastal switchback.

Mention must also be made of a possible new inland walking route – the Land's End Trail. At the time of writing it has not proceeded beyond a draft proposal, but local RA groups are considering the possibilities of a route from Land's End to Horsebridge, on the River Tamar, via Bodmin Moor. This, of course, would be the ideal End to End Central Route beginning.

The most distinctive feature of Land's End is, naturally enough, the sea. To stand on the most westerly point of mainland England, below the First and Last House, and watch the Atlantic crashing over the jumble of eroded rocks is captivating. It is fitting, therefore, that even the Central Route's first few miles should be alongside the sea.

The tracks are wide, numerous, and in places eroded, but for the first mile north-eastwards to Sennen Cove you will not want to be distracted by intricate routefinding. Settle down, develop a rhythm, and after taking a photo of the lovely sweep of Whitesand Bay, with Cape Cornwall jutting out beyond, consider where exactly to strike inland. I suggest either branching off at Sennen Cove itself, or continuing around the bay until a track climbs the grassy cliffs near Aire Point. Either way, wave goodbye to the sea. If you are faithful to the Central Route, the next time you will meet coastal waters will be in Scotland!

'Avoid the A30' is my advice for End to End walkers in Cornwall. Although you will cross this highway during the days ahead, it is fast and furious, and even End to End cyclists and pram-pushers who use this route must be a little potty, in my opinion. Instead, keep to the north and (if time permits) make a short detour over the rounded, heather top of Carn Brea, a superb early viewpoint. The track from its low summit emerges at a National Trust car park on the B330/Crows-an-wra road, opposite which a bridleway to Carn Euny is signposted. This part of Cornwall is rich in tumuli and cairns, and the remains of previous inhabitation. There are signs of early occupation at Carn Brea; and at the Iron Age settlement of Carn Euny, where considerable excavation has taken place, it is possible to clamber into the fogou, a 65-feet-long underground stone chamber that was possibly used as a storehouse.

Continue via Sancreed, which has two tall, elaborately carved granite crosses common to Cornwall, and around the north of Drift Reservoir by lanes. From the edge of Sancreed Beacon, in particular, there are tremendous views over Penzance and Mount's Bay, with St Michael's Mount prominent. At Tremethick Cross take the road opposite, which although not too busy is nonetheless pavemented, and at the fork left to Madron you can visit the National Trust's Trengwainton Gardens (Wednesday–Saturday only). Madron has some B&Bs and a pub, and from there follow a metalled lane past new houses towards New Mill that soon turns into a rough track. Penzance is only a couple of miles down the road from Madron, and Penzance Youth Hostel even nearer.

Climb out of the small valley and make for Chysauster. This is an excavated prehistoric village that contains a number of small houses built and inhabited between 100 BC and AD 300. It is reckoned to have the oldest identifiable street in England. (English Heritage make a small charge for admission.) Then take a waymarked footpath from Carnaquidden Farm across fields and downland to the quiet hamlet of Nancledra; the views across Mount's Bay get better and better. To the east of Nancledra the map shows a clear bridleway to Canonstown, and although it is signposted on the ground the reality is that this sunken track between hedges is badly overgrown and muddy. Persevere with it if you wish, otherwise take the lane via Trencrom hillfort and Lelant Downs to St Erth, crossing the A30 by the railway station.

From St Erth, a little village with shops and the Star Inn, there are intermittent paths either side of the River Hayle southwards. These are of varying quality, and it is up to you how far you take them before swinging east and making for Townshend. The wide, wriggling lane from here to Godolphin Cross passes the entrance to Godolphin House, which was an important bastion for the Royalist cause in the Civil War. It is believed that the Prince of Wales, later to become Charles II, stayed here during his escape to the Scilly Isles. The House can be visited at certain times. What is also noticeable is that in a county not rich in tree-cover it is unusual to walk through such a dense patch of natural woodland. From the

Godolphin Arms (food) there is a direct lane via Nancegollan to Porkellis, where there is another public house called 'The Star', plus farmhouse accommodation.

On balance it is better to skirt Stithians Reservoir by the road to the north, since you cross a bridge by the Golden Lion that allows views of waders and wildfowl one side, and on the other the many and varied activities of the Peninsula Watersports Centre. Stithians itself is rather unpretty. From here to Truro, about seven miles, there are numerous lanes and minor roads that ensure a quiet passage, possibly via Frogpool and Helston Water.

Truro is a smart and bustling place, the centre of the county's administrative and commercial activity. It is properly a city, being dominated by the first Anglican cathedral to be built since St Paul's. This, and the museum, are worth a careful inspection, although on a more practical level there is also a huge and well-stocked camping/outdoors shop by the quay should any of your gear have already failed you, or if there is the odd item that has been left at home.

TRURO–LAUNCESTON (55 miles)

Leave Truro by quiet lanes in a dead northerly direction, beyond the imposing viaduct, and head up the River Allen to the hamlet of Idless. Enter St Clement Woods (which also seems to be called Idless Wood), where signs, and possibly frantic young people tearing around with maps, indicate that this is the venue for a wayfaring and permanent orienteering course. The plantation is owned and managed by the Forestry Commission, and yellow discs announce the cordial message 'walkers welcome here'. So with confidence make your way along tracks by the stream and after two miles emerge in a shaded, deserted hollow at Lanner Barton. Join a narrow lane that twists and turns its way up to St Erme. Ignore rows of ugly modern houses and concentrate on the lovely parish church instead; such a shame how the two contrast so vividly.

As you walk steadily eastwards the huge china clay quarries of the St Austell district become ever more apparent. The high, bumpy mounds of discarded clay and waste quartz sand have earned the place the nickname 'the Cornish Alps', but this artificial lunar landscape is not one that any walker would be keen to explore. Unfortunately, much of the problem stems from the fact that for every ton of usable fine clay produced, about nine tons of waste is dumped. But with the demise of Cornwall's copper and tin industry, china clay production is vital, and since the St Austell deposits are among the best in the world the 'sky dumps' would seem to be permanent.

After St Erme veer north along lanes to Mitchell or Summercourt, two places now bypassed by the A30 dual carriageway (there are bridges over the racetrack at both). At Mitchell, in particular, there are good views of a nearby windfarm, one of several large developments in the South-West that has generated almost as much controversy as it has electricity.

St Columb Major and St Columb Road sound interesting places, but in fact they are not. Granite-grey, dour, and full of traffic. Stick to the lane from White Cross to Black Cross that runs between the two Columbs, then take the wide but occasionally busy road to the foot of Castle Downs, where there is a footpath up to its conical summit. The hill is crowned by a sizeable fort known as Castle-an-Dinas, and from its wide ramparts, now clothed in bracken, consider the local chief gazing from this outstanding strategic position, probably around 200 BC. The views stretch for miles across central Cornwall, with the bulk of Bodmin Moor particularly close (the china clay hills that dominate the landscape today were of course at that time completely absent). A few steps down the road a public footpath signpost points you across farmland to Tregonetha, then another to St Wenn. By now the grotesque china clay mines and the fumes of the A30 are forgotten, for now you wander down into the beautiful valley of the River Camel, one of Cornwall's finest.

At the small village of Withiel you will notice a stark black cross inscribed on both a public footpath and bridleway sign. This is the Cornish cross, and it is used to denote the Saints' Way, a 30-mile trail from Padstow to Fowey that passes through here after a scenic meander over St Breock Downs to the north. Your route follows the course of a tributary that soon connects with the River Camel. The valleys are deep, partly clothed in natural broadleaved woodland, and mostly devoid of traffic and people. If only more miles were like this!

On meeting the Camel join the Camel Trail, which for 16 miles follows the trackbed of the former Bodmin and Wadebridge Railway between Padstow and Poley's Bridge, north of Bodmin. It is designed for both walkers and cyclists, although the latter seem to predominate. If you keep to the level, winding track all the way from near Ruthernbridge to Poley's Bridge, the distance is about 9 miles. And it is worth sticking with. Forget about routefinding for a minute, and enjoy the crunch of gravel rather than the plod of tarmac underfoot. The heavily wooded valley bottom makes a refreshing change from so many miles of open fields and pasture, and at Dunmere (campsite) you can either enter Bodmin for supplies or simply steam by, oblivious to the town.

The railway along the Camel valley was opened in 1834, and although day trips to Padstow were a usual outing, excursions to Bodmin Gaol to watch the public hangings were also popular. The Gaol, where the Crown Jewels and Domesday Book were stored during World War I, is now open to the public, and not far from the Camel Trail. Also, the Bodmin and Wenford Steam Railway has reintroduced life to the tracks south of the town, and an extension to Boscarne Junction (on the Trail) is under construction.

Leave the Camel Trail at Merry Meeting or Poley's Bridge, and climb steeply out of the valley to St Breward, the highest village in Cornwall. Cows standing in the road nibbling at the grass verges, odd lumps of rock and boulders, and a keen wind will all indicate that you are now on the edge of Bodmin Moor. Make your way up through the straggly village (some B&Bs, shops and a café) and at the top the gorse and rough moorland extend for many miles east. This is now a totally different Cornwall. The views back across the county are no less impressive, with the north coast about six miles away as the crow flies, but significantly longer by path or road. Continue to Treswallock Downs; but if you turn right and take either the public footpath or unfenced road (signposted 'Candra Hill') among the grazing sheep on to the moor there are impressive views of Brown Willy (Cornwall's highest point) and Rough Tor. Unfortunately Bodmin Moor does not enjoy national park status, and 'there are few rights of way and permitted paths, with general access remaining limited. This is regrettable, although in bad weather the bleak and exposed moorland is definitely unwelcoming, and the patchy marsh and bogland can be awkward. Instead, follow a number of high, open lanes around the moor's northern fringe to Crowdy Reservoir. At Davidstow Woods the road crosses a disused airfield; indeed it taxis down one of the runways, strangely enough. A few hang-gliders, the odd military vehicle, and a herd of wild ponies make up the spectacle. Plus there are commanding views of Rough Tor and the surrounding moorland. A stern notice by a cattle grid reads: 'Agricultural common – private land. No camping, fires, motorbikes, racing, testing, flytipping, trading, dogs', which appears to cover most things. Luckily, for the walker, there is an official Camping and Caravanning Club site at a farmhouse close by.

It is about 12 uncomplicated miles into Launceston, mostly by lane. From the disused airfield descend to quiet valleys once more (first the River Inny), then via St Clether and Laneast, across the A395, and down the River Kensey into Launceston. This often tree-lined approach to the former capital of the Duchy of Cornwall is along a direct lane at the foot of steep hillsides, and is a perfect way to round off a day's walking.

Launceston, they will tell you, is the only walled town in Cornwall, and is dominated by the remains of the castle, first constructed within twenty years of the Norman Conquest. It is where the Prince of Wales, also Duke of Cornwall, comes once in his lifetime to collect the feudal dues which are his right within the Duchy. You will come for rather different reasons; probably for food, to use the launderette, and to buy a new toothbrush or some plasters.

LAUNCESTON – TAUNTON (77 miles)

If you have stayed true to the Central Route you will be approaching the 100-mile mark. (It is a sobering thought that you are not even one tenth of the way to John o'Groats yet.) The four, five or possibly six days that it has taken you to reach Launceston will have shaken off the early nerves and allowed any immediate worries or irritations to be dispelled. But if you already crave a little variety then consider veering north towards the coast (maybe via Bideford or Barnstaple). Perhaps a few days of coastal path walking would make a pleasant change from inland tarmac, and allow you to see the South-West in all its guises.

If, however, you are still eager to burn off the miles and make quick headway then press on with the Central Route. Ahead are the rolling hills of Devon, and a succession of lanes and tracks that allow rapid progress into Somerset, and so the gradual swing northwards.

Cross the River Kensey by a minor road and leave the town in a northerly direction. Footpaths lead to Dutson, after which there is a regrettable few minutes' worth of the A388 until branching off for the peace and quiet of a country lane near Nether Bridge. The lane follows the river, a different river, in an unswerving direction upstream until Crossgate. But this is not any other river. It is the Tamar, which rises four miles from the north coast near Kilkhampton, and flows all the way south to Plymouth, providing the most natural county border possible. Cross it by Druxton Bridge, a small but pleasing stone construction among a shaded hollow, and enter Devon. So far already, but only the second county! And this feeling will persist through Devon. As keen as you may be to gobble up the early miles of the Walk, End to Enders frequently admit to being dismayed at how long it takes to get through the South-West. Regardless of blisters and all the other creaks and aches common in the early period of a major walk, it will still need a minimum of a week's hard walking before you are well and truly into Somerset.

So best foot forwards! There now follow many miles of quiet, pleasant country lanes, where you might meet occasional motorists and farm vehicles, see plenty of wildlife in the hedgerows and fields (a rabbit or pheasant here, a buzzard there), and pass through several attractive villages that are unknown to most tourists. There are not many B&Bs or organised campsites, but most pubs provide bar food. The metalled lanes make for easy and fast walking; but as you travel further into Devon the valleys become deeper, and you will find yourself puffing at some of the steep ascents.

From the Tamar climb up via Druxton to St Giles on the Heath. Druxton comprises a couple of buildings, and St Giles a larger assembly of bungalows and a post office. Do not expect these sort of places to have much in the way of facilities. A pub and post office stores are often all that exist, and one of the two will invariably be closed, so make sure that you have enough provisions to keep going.

From St Giles cross the River Cary to Tower Hill, and either take lanes via Broadwoodwidger around the south of Roadford Reservoir (this route allows you to cross the dam near the visitors' centre), or north via Westweekmoor, where a path to Westweek Barton leads above the shore to Germansweek. Roadford Reservoir, the authorities announce, is the largest in the South-West, and when full holds 36,910 megalitres (8,120 million gallons). And Southweek Viaduct, near Germansweek, has the honour of receiving a special mention in the 1988 Concrete Society Awards. From Germansweek continue past the Zion Bible Christian Chapel to Eworthy, then across Broadbury and the A3079 to Northlew. The twisting lanes are narrow and often involve considerable ups and downs. Northlew's village green is not made out of grass, but tarmac. However, the Green Dragon provides refreshment, and there is even a B&B sign in the village.

Now the dark, hulking outline of Dartmoor rises nearer. Unfortunately the northernmost moors that you can see are almost all out of bounds due to military training, but they stay in sight for many miles as you cross the River Lew and wander into Hatherleigh. With shops, pubs and accommodation Hatherleigh is an ideal place to stop. The George Hotel (too pricey, it must be said, for most walkers) dates from around 1450, and has the following inscription on its outside wall:

> Trav'ler, this inn which some call mean
> Approach with awe here lies a Queen
> Nay! Start at not so strange a thing
> For truly she's a female King.
> So rich her hashes, sauces, minces
> My boys! You here may live like Princes.

The wide lane from Hatherleigh to Monkokehampton permits an even better perspective of Dartmoor, then it narrows to single-track and high hedges deny continuous views. Ye Olde Swan, a seventeenth-century coaching inn at Monkokehampton, offers bar meals, and other outdoor types taking refreshment may include cyclists, since your course is also shared by the West Devon Sticklepath Cycleroute. The peaceful road continues in an agreeably direct fashion to Bondleigh and Zeal Monachorum, then past Down St Mary Vineyard (wine tasting and sales) and into the village.

At both Bondleigh and Down St Mary you have the chance to sample a few miles of two other long-distance footpaths, the Tarka Trail and the Two Moors Way, although I prefer the latter. At Bondleigh the Tarka Trail may be followed north to Taw Bridge, and then to Chenson or Eggesford if you wish. It forms a huge 180-mile figure of eight, centred on Barnstaple, and this section is part of the loop south to Dartmoor. The trail is based on Henry Williamson's Tarka the Otter *story, and the waymark is an otter's pawprint.*

However, at Down St Mary the Two Moors Way appears, which is a route of 100 miles linking Dartmoor to the north coast of Exmoor. It, too, is waymarked ('MW'), and presuming that you have not gone off in search of otters, follow the Two Moors Way to Morchard Bishop or Black Dog.

The direction that you should be heading is due east, keeping north of Crediton and south of Tiverton (although both are useful diversions if necessary). Follow the narrow and rolling lanes through either Poughill or Cheriton Fitzpaine, and then drop steeply into the lovely Exe valley at Bickleigh. Although this tiny place rather suffers from a constant stream of visitors to the 'Devonshire Centre' by the river, the valley is particularly handsome, with patches of dense natural woodland. There are a number of B&Bs, and a signpost indicates that the Exe Valley Way, not unnaturally, passes through here – it runs for 21 miles from Stoke Canon, north of Exeter, to Exebridge on the Devon/Somerset border. Bickleigh Castle is also worth a visit, despite extensive rebuilding after a drubbing at the hands of Fairfax and the anti-Royalists during the Civil War. There is a *Mary Rose* exhibition, since Vice Admiral Sir George Carew, whose family owned the castle, was in command when the ship sank at Spithead in 1545.

There are more, steep lanes before reaching Cullompton. The extremely high hedges are frustrating; views of East Devon's deep, pastoral valleys come in glimpses at every field entrance. Cullompton's early rise as a market town was due to the wool trade, and this financed much of the finely decorated Church of St Andrew. The M5 has taken most of the cars and caravans off the main street, and it is this formidable motorway that you walk above in order to follow the river Culm upstream via Bradfield to Uffculme. Despite the Working Wool Museum, Uffculme is an ugly little place that is best left behind. But afterwards the scenery and walking is once again splendid. Follow riverbank paths to Culmstock, emerging opposite the Culm Valley Inn (B&B) whose sign is testimony to the fact that you have just walked along some of the former GWR branch line from Tiverton to Hemyock. An old photo on the wall in the pub shows the building next to a busy level-crossing. Now there is a car park.

Culmstock is a long, drawn-out kind of village, with the languid River Culm drifting through the middle. Above is the western end of the Blackdown Hills, an area of outstanding natural beauty, which you should approach by footpath from the road to Woodgate. There are wide views from the slopes of Culmstock Beacon, despite its modest height, and then head over Black Down Common along a track into woodland, before joining a long and level road that runs across the top of nearly the whole of the Blackdown Hills. It is frustrating that there are so few public footpaths, and that much of the view from the wide lane is obscured by trees and hedges. However, the National Trust make amends by allowing access to the open hilltop site at Wellington Monument. This lofty tower was constructed in 1892 in memory of the Duke, who took his title from the nearby town, and it marks the highest point on the Blackdowns. A key (and torch) is available from a local farm at a small charge. On a clear day there are wide views, and for the End to End walker exciting new views across the Vale of Taunton to the Bristol Channel. You have just stepped into Somerset, and England is opening up.

From the monument there is a path down through a reserve managed by the Somerset Trust for Nature to Wellington, or various hamlets at the foot of the hills. It might be better to stay on the hilltop lane for a little longer, if only to benefit from a sandwich and a pint of Badgers Beer at the Harriers, opposite the Forestry Commission's Buckland Wood by Forches Corner. Then, unless you want to stay at the campsite along the lane to the right, turn left and drop down a steep and wooded lane via Staplehay and Trull to Taunton.

2

COTSWOLD BEAUTY

Taunton – Chipping Campden

TAUNTON – BATH (52 miles)
Taunton is rather a nice county town. There is a very helpful and well-stocked information centre in the library, a busy livestock market, a modern shopping centre; and the County Museum in the castle is also worth a visit. It was here, in 1685, that the 'Bloody Assizes' took place, after the Duke of Monmouth's Pitchfork Rebellion had been unceremoniously defeated on the nearby fields of Sedgemoor. One of the victorious royalists dubbed Taunton 'the sink of all rebellion in the west', and of the 514 Taunton men who appeared before Judge Jeffreys, 146 were condemned to be hanged, and a further 284 were transported.

Leave Taunton for the Somerset Levels and Moors by the Bridgwater and Taunton Canal towpath. Opened in 1827, the canal was designed to be part of a chain in a projected link between the Bristol Channel and the English Channel. But only the Grand Western Canal (Tiverton–Taunton) and the Bridgwater and Taunton Canal were completed.

At Creech St Michael take the lane past the church and follow a public footpath across the railway to the sleepy village of Ham. From here follow the River Tone's east bank all the way to New Bridge, near North Curry (shops and pub). This route is part of the Curry Moor Trail, and information boards help explain the origins and wildlife of the county and its Levels ('somer saeta' means the land of the summer people). The Somerset Levels, 250 miles of flat, damp land, have undergone considerable change in the last couple of centuries, but through the efforts of conservationists, and latterly with the assistance of local farmers, the important wetland habitat is being maintained and in places even enhanced. The plains provide fertile pasture in the summer, but since winter flooding makes widespread access impossible (hence the county's 'land of summer' tag), there have been more and more new rhynes and straightened river channels introduced, with tidal sluices and pumps, in an effort to hold the water at bay. Conservationists, and in particular ornithologists, have however campaigned against altering the flow and draining the land; and a government scheme now encourages local farmers to work the land in a traditional manner, in return for cash grants. Many are doing just this, and with the RSPB purchase of much of West Sedgemoor, waders and waterfowl are returning in greater number each year. It is also benefiting the otter, which has one of its few English pawholds in this part of Somerset. And, according to what time of the year it is, you are likely to wander in the company of dragonflies and lapwings, with marsh marigolds, lady's smock and ragged robin providing a colourful passage. A typical field may have as many as forty to fifty plant species. It makes for gentle and relaxed walking.

The path along the embankment of the river can be followed until Curload, where the English Basket Centre is situated. Reeds are stacked high in bundles outside. There are a couple of B&Bs at Stoke St Gregory, and along the quiet road from Stoke to Stathe a number of farms also offer accommodation. At the junction at the end of this lane carry straight on along a dirt track to Aller. The Old Pound Inn has hotel accommodation, and there is the equivalent for campers behind the trimmed hedges and flags at Bowdens. From Aller Hill there are great views over the Levels, and a chance to take in this peculiar landscape. It is hardly remote, for many of the villages seem to be home to executives from Bath and Bristol, and the M5 is not too far away. Yet there is a tranquillity and out-of-the-way feeling that is most welcome. Partly for this reason it is an attractive stretch for the End to End walker; but also because the gentle, undemanding miles of the Levels allow you to either give your legs a rest and take things easy, or else make quick progress and eat up the pre-Cotswolds miles.

To reach Glastonbury drop down from High Ham to Pitney Steart Bridge, over the River Carey, and follow a dead straight track across Somerton Moor to Walton Hill (aim for the converted windmill) where for a few miles West and Central Routes unite as far as Glastonbury. Then wander along easy hilltop paths to Street Youth Hostel, from where Glastonbury will be in sight. The approach to the town by the lane across South Moor is quieter than plodding the pavements of Street, and the A39 gauntlet.

Whether curious or committed, Glastonbury is worth nosing around in for a few hours. The Tor and the Abbey are inevitably popular, but still very interesting, and there are countless knick-knack shops and cafés to while away a wet afternoon. If you are in need of a spot of spiritual enlightenment then pay a visit to the University of Avalon. Since the Central and West Routes rub noses at this point, there are further comments on this location to be found elsewhere.

Grit your teeth for five minutes and follow the A39 out of Glastonbury towards Wells, then immediately after crossing Hartlake Bridge take the first lane to the right. What peace and quiet! This serene, narrow track takes an unswerving course and over your right shoulder Glastonbury Tor rises dramatically. At North Wootton the Crossways provides good food, but the size of the car park is testimony to the fact that this is not a walkers' pub. Far more interesting is a visit to the nearby Wootton Vineyard, at North Town, where Major Gillespie allows visitors to wander freely among the vines. (The Wootton Seyval 1988 was found to be most agreeable.) Closed all day Sunday.

Take high-hedged lanes across tight rolling hills to Croscombe, west of Shepton Mallet, and then steeply up Thrupe Lane to the prehistoric hillfort of Maesbury Castle. Avoid walking the A37 by crossing it at Gurney Slade, and use lanes and footpaths over Blackers Hill to reach Chilcompton. Midsomer Norton and Radstock are only a couple of miles away, and the museum at the latter has an interesting exhibition on the little-known North Somerset Coalfield. Remember, though, that there are more shoppers and bustle ahead at Bath, so it may be advisable to continue along the undulating minor roads north towards Paulton, and then at Camerton pick up a pleasant footpath along Cam Brook. Follow this delightful gurgle of water as it winds its way through the deep and unspoilt valley to Combe Hay, from where the outskirts of Bath are just over the hill.

There is a youth hostel near the city centre, but if you seek B&B there are plenty along the Wells Road as you drop down into the heart of this attractive Regency city, now a World Heritage City. The underground spa waters have attracted visitors since Roman times, and still today the architecture, museums and all-round physical setting of Bath make it an agreeable place to spend a night.

BATH – CHIPPING CAMPDEN (100 miles)

The next stage of the Central Route is without doubt one of the most beautiful of the entire Walk. The Cotswold Way extends for 100 miles, north-eastwards from Bath to Chipping Campden, and for nearly all of that distance sticks to the prominent scarp of Avon and Gloucestershire's rolling limestone hills.

The Cotswold Way long-distance path was first suggested by the Ramblers' Association in 1953, but was not officially opened until 1970. At the time of writing, the Cotswold Way has not yet been designated a national trail, but that title looks likely to be bestowed upon it within the next few years after appropriate consultation has taken place. It is certainly one of the best managed and waymarked non-national trails in the country. The Cotswold Warden Service, a large group of volunteers under the auspices of Gloucestershire County Council, ensure that the path is kept clear, and that small, white waymarking dots appear regularly on conventional yellow (footpath) and blue (bridleway) signs. Accommodation on the Way is not particularly plentiful, although there are a number of sizeable places within walking distance (Stroud, Gloucester, Cheltenham). Organised campsites are also few, and there is only one youth hostel on the route after Bath. Since the Cotswolds are popular not just with walkers, it is worth planning carefully if you do not have the flexibility that carrying a tent brings.

The Cotswold Way leaves Bath in a north-westerly direction, via the residential outpost of Weston, to make the first of what will be many short, sharp ascents. Pen Hill and Kelston Round Hill offer good views over the city, and down to the Avon. The riverside track that you may have already seen indicated on the map is the Avon Walkway, a 30-mile route linking Bath with Bristol, which is useful should you decide to switch to the West Route and tackle Offa's Dyke instead of the Cotswolds. But presuming that you have not, continue along the top to Prospect Stile, past Bath Racecourse, and along the scarp edge to Little Down hillfort. Walk alongside a golf course, with woodland on your left, and make for the Granville Monument, commemorating a Civil War battle that took place on nearby Landsdown Hill in 1643. A little beyond the monument officially enter the Cotswold Area of Outstanding Natural Beauty for the first time.

By now you will have already noticed the white marker dots of the Cotswold Way. They may not be particularly ingenious or handsome, but they are unobtrusive and allow you to relax, savour the views and develop a walking rhythm, rather than pause at every turn to marry route description with Ordnance Survey map.

Proceed via Hill Farm and Greenway Lane to Cold Ashton. Two main roads have to be crossed, and after a hamlet called Pennsylvania make for Dyrham Wood and then across fields to the village of Dyrham. Nearby is the National Trust's Dyrham House and Park, which has an ancient herd of fallow deer. The Way follows the wall of the park before branching off in the direction of Tormarton, which is reached after an unpleasant scuttle across the A46 as it bridges the M4. Refreshments and some accommodation may be had in the village, before you once more cross the A46 (you will meet it on several more occasions) and follow a path through Dodington Park, landscaped by Capability Brown, to Old Sodbury, where the Dog Inn (residential) has a reputation for excellent food. For a full list of where to stay (plus details of campsites) consult the *Cotswold Way Handbook*, published annually by the Ramblers' Association Gloucestershire Area.

Old Sodbury is the 'original' – Little Sodbury and Chipping Sodbury are newer – and beyond the route goes through the middle of Sodbury hillfort, eleven acres of Iron Age defences that were also used by Romans and Saxons. There is another, smaller fort at Horton, a mile further on, after which the Way turns right just before Horton Court (a splendid medieval hall) and follows a lane into Hawkesbury Upton. Dunkirk and Petty France, two hamlets to the south, owe their origin and place-name to skilled Flemish weavers lured to the Cotswolds in the Middle Ages, for although the area's wool was of good quality, lack of knowledge meant that most of it was exported raw. Rest by the village pond and consider whether you want to climb the 144 steps of the Somerset Monument, dedicated to a General who served under Wellington at Waterloo; it is situated on the path as you leave the village (although the monument is not always open to the public).

Leave the road below the monument for Frith Wood, then descend to Lower Kilcott. Follow a quiet lane down the valley, turning off before Hillesley to reach Alderley, and then Wortley. The Way now climbs wooded hillside and enters Wotton from the east, but if your legs are tiring and the sun is waning you may wish to omit this minor diversion and take the lane straight from Wortley into Wotton-under-Edge.

There are several places to stay, and a number of welcome tea rooms at Wotton. This former wool town also has three sets of almshouses, still administered by local charities. The official route out is along Gloucester Street, but I found that a far more pleasant walk is to be had along Tabernacle Road past the church, then up a steep, tunnelled path which joins a surfaced lane by a surprise viewpoint. A couple of hundred yards up the lane turn left at the signpost to Wotton Hill, where the official route is rejoined on open meadows by Jubilee Plantation. This small, fenced-off clump of pines were originally planted to celebrate the victory at Waterloo, but then were ingloriously chopped down for the purposes of a bonfire. Now replanted and regrown, use them as a windbreak as you sit on the high hillside and gaze at the tremendous view: Somerset Monument is visible as the hills recede southwards; across the plain eastwards is the River Severn, with the outskirts of Bristol and the towers of the bridge often visible.

After a waymarked path along field edges, enter the pleasant glades of Westridge Wood to reach Brackenbury Ditches, another hillfort, and on to the delightfully named Nibley Knoll. The panoramic views from this open meadowland top are as good as those from Wotton Hill, except here they are literally overshadowed by the imposing monument erected in 1866 to William Tyndale, famous for translating the Bible into English and being executed for it in 1536. In North Nibley the Black Horse Inn offers B&B, morning coffees, food, etc. Nearby Nibley Green is the site of the last battle fought by private armies in England, when Lord Berkeley and Viscount De Lisle, plus about 2,000 retainers, skirmished in 1470.

Across fields to Stinchcombe Hill, where there are further views of the Tyndale Monument, River Severn and M5, three features that have stayed in sight for many miles. At Drakestone Point a viewing board estimates that Land's End is 180 miles away, although not having the aerial benefit of a crow you will of course have had to tread a rather longer mileage. The scenic detour around the golf course adds some extra distance, so some walkers may consider cutting out this loop and dropping down the steep wooded hillside

Land's End: enjoy being first and last in the country, while the Atlantic crashes into the fearsome rocks (*below*).

Glastonbury Tor from the south, near Street Youth Hostel (*above*); and the clipped yews in the churchyard at Painswick, near Stroud (*below*).

Cleeve Hill (*above*) is the highest and probably the windiest point on the Cotswold Way, a route efficiently waymarked and signposted, (*below left*), near Fish Hill, and (*below right*), at its northern terminus in Chipping Campden.

The Heart of England Way provides a gentle and scenic ramble through Arden country (*above*); but further north the Gritstone Trail at Tegg's Nose is a sterner prospect (*below*).

Pennine Way miles: north-south walkers ascending Bleaklow from Longdendale (*above*); High Force, Teesdale (*below left*); and approaching Windy Gyle along the Border fence in the lonely Cheviot Hills (*below right*).

The Tweed is met for the first time at Kelso (*above*), but it is not until Maxton a few miles upstream that a bankside path can be followed. (*Below*), the Pentland Hills from Arthur's Seat, Edinburgh.

The Lairig Ghru (*above*) cuts a swathe through the Cairngorms, and the view from its northern end (*below*) towards Aviemore and Loch Morlich is extensive.

There are many exposed miles through the Flow Country of Sutherland and Caithness (*above*) before the north coast is reached. (*Below*), the journey's end, and a celebratory drink overlooking the Pentland Firth and the Orkneys.

into Dursley. Once an important clothing town, Dursley has lost most of its charm to modern buildings and industry, like the engineering works you pass as you leave the town for Cam Peak and Cam Long Down, also known as Tableland, due to its flat top. These are two splendidly lumpy but grassy hills, but their steep slopes are likely to leave you puffing.

The path enters Coaley Wood, allowing visits to Uley Bury hillfort and Hetty Pegler's Tump, a Neolithic long barrow. At Coaley Peak Country Park, on Frocester Hill, ice-cream vans supply Sunday afternoon family outings with gooey fare, and there is often an array of model aircraft on show, while real gliders may be taking off from the gliding club over the road. Press on through the wooded edge of the escarpment (Stanley Wood is in the capable hands of the Woodland Trust) then down to Middleyard and King's Stanley. Ebley Mill, at Stonehouse, was once the largest cloth mill in the valley, but now houses the offices of Stroud District Council. A full range of shops, banks, etc are available in the town, a couple of miles along the valley of the River Frome, although the industry and built-upness of it all may jar after so many unspoilt rural miles. Far better to cross the A419 and continue up and around Doverow Hill towards Randwick and Standish Wood. Follow the waymarks closely through this long woodland section, since the path curves around the steep hillside until it is heading east for the lofty summit of Haresfield Beacon. The panorama is superb, with views across the Severn to the Forest of Dean.

The Way now winds around the wooded scarp to Scottsquar Hill, and to Edgemoor Inn, on the Stroud–Gloucester road. Continue opposite through farmland and descend to Painswick, 'the Queen of the Cotswolds'. The Queen would perhaps sleep sounder if the A46 did not run through the middle of her residence, but nevertheless this is an extremely attractive and well looked-after place. The Parish Church of St Mary has a fascinating churchyard containing ninety-nine immaculately clipped yews, each about 200 years old, and many seventeenth- and eighteenth-century table tombs inscribed to local clothiers and their families. For refreshment and merriment look no further than the Royal Oak, with a sheltered courtyard out the back smothered in flowers and fussed-over by white doves.

Walk up Gloucester Street out of Painswick, and turn right down the lane rather worringly signposted 'cemetery'. But the path soon departs for the partly wooded slopes of Painswick Hill, passing a golf course and Catbrain Quarry in the process. Rest for a moment at the top, from where there are the first close-up views of Gloucester, then enjoy more shaded walking through Pope's Wood. At Cranham Corner cross the road junction and enter Buckholt Wood, an important ancient beechwood that forms part of the Cotswold Commons and Beechwoods National Nature Reserve. Follow the signs carefully to Cooper's Hill. Here, every Spring Bank Holiday Monday, a number of people race down the steep grass slope in pursuit of a 7lb Double Gloucester cheese, which is rather a peculiar thing to do, it must be said. Minor injuries and concussion are frequent. It is thought that the custom may have evolved as a means of reinforcing commoners' rights to graze sheep on the hillside. Continue into Witcombe Wood, and after several miles of quiet and relaxing shaded walking emerge below Birdlip.

At a viewpoint known as the Peak an indicator board translates what you can see (or think you can see) into names and distances: Hereford 22 miles, Worcester 25 miles, Birmingham 45 miles. The bumps of the Malverns are obvious, plus the protruberance of Bredon Hill quite close by; and 44 miles to the west is the distinctive slope of Hay Bluff, at the end of the Black Mountains, where the End to End West Route descends wearily into Hay-on-Wye.

The route ahead is evident, around the jutting head of Crickley Hill, but to get there you must first descend to the noisy road junction by the Air Balloon, an all-day pub. Crickley Hill Country Park has an interesting information and exhibition centre, where you are told that the hill is formed of oolitic limestone and is geologically famous for its outcrop of pea grit. The site is also noteworthy for detailed excavation of Neolithic and post-Roman settlements, although they could do with a twentieth-century tea room.

After darting out to Shurdington Hill and back again, the Way takes farm tracks to Leckhampton Hill, where it joins popular paths across scrub and rough turf to the remains of limestone quarries high above Cheltenham. There are 'beware of adders' signs at the foot of the hill, but these are not visible to Cotswold Way walkers. Leckhampton Hill is famous for the Devil's Chimney, an isolated column of rock that is a result of intensive quarrying. Although climbing the eroded pinnacle is now prohibited, once upon a time thirteen people all managed to squeeze on to its tiny summit at once.

The whole of Cheltenham is spread out at your feet. Particularly noticeable is the huge, anonymous block of GCHQ, complete with massive aerial dishes on its roof. Follow the upper slopes of Charlton Kings Common around to Seven Springs (a suggested source of the River Thames). Now you can either take a longish diversion through quiet fields and woods or else brave a mile's walk along the A436. There is a verge, of sorts, to begin with, but then an uphill stretch that is narrow and hemmed-in.

The alternative section is fully waymarked, and both rejoin to reach Dowdeswell Reservoir via Lineover Woods. It is a rare spectacle to see a fairly large patch of (inland) water in these parts, especially flanked by a thick stand of conifers. Climbing steadily, the Way follows a lane for a short while before branching off and making its way among the hawthorn and rough grassland of Cleeve Common. This is a Site of Special Scientific Interest (SSSI), and supports many butterflies and varieties of orchids. At the end of the plateau is Cleeve Hill, the highest point of not just the Cotswold Way but also of Gloucestershire, at 317m. The views are tremendous, but it is bare and windy. Underneath the hill is Rock House, once a Victorian golf-clubhouse and now the only youth hostel on the Cotswold Way.

Follow Costwold Way marker posts around and over the golf course, leaving the semi-moorland after a large loop for a track to the now uninhabited Wontley Farm, then by the edge of a field to Belas Knap. This is a long barrow, constructed around 3000 BC, and when it was first explored in 1863 it revealed the bones of thirty-eight human skeletons, plus items of flint and pottery. It has several chambers, including two shallow ones which you can crawl inside (their stone walls have been strengthened). It must be said that they would provide excellent protection if, for instance, it began pouring with rain. But the thought of spending some time inside a gloomy burial chamber may not be to everyone's taste.

From Belas Knap head down through steep pasture and woodland to a lane, off which a farm track, and then waymarked field paths, takes you to the entrance drive of Sudeley Castle, by Winchcombe. The castle dates from the 1400s, but after damage during the Civil War it is mostly Elizabethan buildings that survive, plus some modern 'theme' developments. Winchcombe is a busy and popular Cotswold town, and accordingly has plenty of pubs and B&Bs (some of the tea rooms even have 'walkers welcome' signs!). In the Dark Ages it was the royal seat of Mercia. You will see signs for the Wardens' Way, a local trail established by the Cotswold Warden

Service; and also for the Wychavon Way, a 42-mile route that begins on the River Severn north of Worcester and finishes at Winchcombe.

From Winchcombe to Hailes Abbey, a gentle couple of miles, you will be treading the path used by pilgrims of many centuries, although today there are just a few remains left of the thirteenth-century Cistercian abbey. Continue along the foot of the scarp on paths to Stanway, notable for its Jacobean manor house and attractive if rather odd thatched cricket pavilion, which is raised from the ground by staddle stones. Follow a waymarked course across the parkland of Stanway House to reach Stanton, the archetypal picture-postcard Cotswolds village, with carefully manicured limestone buildings, each with neat beds of colourful flowers.

The route has for some miles been keeping to the low ground below the escarpment, but leaving Stanton it climbs back up the hillside, and at the top of what is a fairly steep pull it turns left at Shenberrow Hill and wanders along the hilltop to Buckland Wood. Height gained is ultimately height lost. Descend to Broadway and into Worcestershire via Buckland Coppice and West End, entering the village of Broadway by the modern parish church. The wide main street appears at first glance to consist entirely of antique shops and guest houses, but is worth a closer inspection. The Lygon Arms, built in 1620 and visited by Cromwell, was a famous coaching inn, although rather different coaches are pulling in today. For its unusual name look no further than General Lygon, a local eccentric, who planted his estate with trees and bushes in the precise formation that the armies at Waterloo took, so that he could regularly re-enact the battle.

If the prospect of the steep climb up to Broadway Tower depresses you, take heart from the fact that this is the last major ascent of the Cotswold Way, and that ahead lies low and gentle Warwickshire. Broadway Tower is actually in the corner of Broadway Country Park, family-oriented and devoted to mock farmyards and semi-rare breeds of animals. It charges admission, but Cotswold Way walkers are quite properly allowed to enter for free on a public right of way. They say you can see twelve counties from the tower, and there are impressive views over Bredon Hill and the Vale of Evesham.

Leave the base of the tower through rough pasture north-westwards, and cross the A44 with much caution near the former Fish Inn. Traffic approaches this spot at speed whether coming up or down the hill. Then follow the grassy Mile Drive to Dover's Hill, scene of the Robert Dover games each Spring Bank Holiday (an amateur and rather odd event, begun in 1612 as the 'Olympick Games' by Captain Robert Dover). Chipping Campden sits quietly below. Enter this charming Cotswold town via Hoo Lane, which leads into the High Street, and to the beginning of the Heart of England Way – your next trail – by the arched market hall in the main street.

Chipping Campden is a former wool town that has retained its elegance and character. There are many fine old buildings, plenty of pubs and cafés for refreshment, and the fourteenth-century Woolstaplers' Hall houses both the museum and tourist information centre. Altogether, it is an agreeable place at which to end your Cotswold journey.

3

GREEN ROUTE THROUGH THE MIDLANDS

Chipping Campden – Crowden

CHIPPING CAMPDEN – MILFORD (80 miles)
The Heart of England Way provides the 80-mile link between the Cotswolds and Cannock Chase. It was first planned in 1978, when a number of local walking groups came together to form the Heart of England Way Association. The result is a gentle, undemanding trail that follows a pleasant and surprisingly rural route around and between some of the most densely populated areas in the country, with Coventry to the east and Birmingham westwards. Although the official guidebook approaches the route from north to south, directions are also given for the northbound traveller, and at times these may be needed. The distinctive Heart of England Way logo (a clump of green trees on a white background) is prevalent, along with standard public footpath signs, but overgrown hedges and ploughed-up fields can cause some routefinding problems. It is best to keep the OS map handy, and even if you do lose the Way momentarily there are plenty of quiet roads and linking footpaths that will help you maintain the correct direction of travel.

Leave Chipping Campden by St James's Church, then fields and lanes via Mickleton Hills Farm lead to the village of Mickleton. There is more easy field-hopping around the western edge of Meon Hill, an Iron Age fort traditionally associated with witchcraft, and soon you arrive at Lower Quinton, followed by Long Marston. After the rolling Cotswolds the land is now gentle and undemanding, with most given over to market gardening and intensive agriculture. Join the course of Noleham Brook to Dorsington, after which there is a short stretch of tarmac and more field paths until Barton, where the Cottage of Content provides welcome refreshment. Now follow river meadows until finally meeting the River Avon at Bidford on Avon, where there are plenty of cafés and pubs.

The Way crosses the Avon by Bidford's fifteenth-century bridge, and heads north for Alcester via Wixford along quiet paths and gentle riverside tracks among willows. Alcester (pronounced 'Ulster') has a rich architectural store: half-timbered Tudor buildings in the High Street, Georgian houses in Henley Street; and yet it is certainly modern enough to deal with the regular flood of visitors it receives, with cafés and a choice of accommodation.

From the B4089 take footpaths via New End and the Alne Hills towards Greenhill Farm. Round Hill, just off the path, is a super vantage point, and worth the modest climb for a lunch overlooking the green patchwork of fields and woodland known as 'Arden'. There are more field boundaries and thickets to be negotiated, then the route skirts Banhams Wood and on to Henley. Of course there is plenty of opportunity to deviate from the set route and see more of the area (villages such as Great Alne and Wootton Wawen), particularly if – like me – you lose your way and end up taking one of the quiet and rolling lanes instead.

Henley-in-Arden is an attractive old market town that gets clogged up with traffic coming to see an attractive old market town. It used to be an important staging post in the days of coaching, as the high street inns bear testimony. There are several B&Bs, and if the weather is anything other than cold you must sample the delicious home-made Henley Ice Cream.

The Way leaves via the earth ramparts of a motte and bailey castle built by the de Montfords in Norman times. There are wide views from this relatively low position; the spread of red-brick and tiled roofs below indicates that much of greater Henley is in fact quite modern. This next passage should be uncomplicated, crossing the Stratford-upon-Avon Canal at Lowsonford and the Grand Union Canal at Rowington. The path wanders through the churchyard of St Michael's, where several of the Ferrers family are buried. For 500 years the Ferrers owned the adjoining Baddesley Clinton, a fine late medieval manor house, which is now in National Trust hands and open to the public. Then once over the A41 a series of fields lead to Balsall Common, a quiet and leafy if rather dull sprawl of mostly modern houses, followed by another busy road crossing. However, peace returns via the charming village of Berkswell. Depending on your persuasion, you can either pause at the twelfth-century Church of St John the Baptist, or at the sixteenth-century Bear Inn, which has outside a gun captured from the Russians in the Crimea in 1855.

Meriden is two miles on, and again the Way enters through a quiet and picturesque churchyard. There is a B&B near the open-all-day Queen's Head, and further still is the village green, where the 500-year-old cross is said to represent the true centre of England. The nearby Happy Shopper confirms this fact in three-foot-high lettering.

Continue over bumpy, green farmland (and the M6) to Shustoke Reservoir, an uninspiring private boating lake, and then on to Kingsbury. Despite some pleasant leafy walking around Dumble Wood, industry and urbanisation are never far away. Daw Hill colliery is near, and Hams Hall power station is an uncomfortable neighbour for several miles. The slight elevation also offers glimpses of the urban fringes of Birmingham and the vast West Midlands conurbation.

Despite an attractive church and old mill, the large village of Kingsbury is an ugly mish-mash of modern architecture, and it is worth continuing across the River Tame and seeking refreshment in the far more relaxed surroundings of Kingsbury Water Park. This former gravel quarry has been transformed into thirty carefully managed pools and lakes that provide leisure and recreation for walkers, cyclists, anglers and yachtsmen. At the same time it is also a valuable refuge for many forms of wildlife. When I visited in May '93 the wardens had sighted lesser whitethroats, gannets, Temmincks stints and terns (five Black and one Arctic) – in just one month. There is also an official campsite, as well as the Country Café, a great place for fresh, home-made food (try 'Joan's scones'). Kingsbury Water Park is also the start for the 100-mile Centenary Way, which passes through Nuneaton and Warwick to end near Stratford.

The towpath of the Birmingham and Fazeley Canal takes you north for two miles, to where a wonderful swivel bridge and turreted footbridge provides an exit to the village of Drayton Bassett. The queues of cars are likely to be for the nextdoor Drayton Manor Zoo and Country Park, a popular regional attraction.

As you leave the flat valley of the Tame the ground gradually rises, and there are thicker, wilder plantations. Cross the A5 near Weeford and follow paths into the quiet semis of Lichfield, via the Horse and Jockey (Ansells) on the A51. Pause awhile in Lichfield, and sample what Dr Johnson called 'genuinely civilised life in an English provincial town'. Mind you, he was rather biased, since he was born here. But it is must be said that the Samuel Johnson Birthplace Museum in the town centre by the market place is actually very interesting and well-maintained, and the three-spired cathedral that rises above the Minster Pool is impressive. For good quality food try the Pig and Truffle.

The official Heart of England Way guidebook can explain the intricate twists and turns involved in reaching Cannock Chase from Lichfield, although I found quiet surfaced lanes as pleasant as anything. Ascending Gentleshaw and Cannock Woods, take a look back at Lichfield and the shimmering Midlands for almost the last time. Now the countryside will change, and you can look forward to a more diverse and dynamic landscape.

Cannock Chase covers 26 square miles, and is the smallest area of outstanding natural beauty in the country. It was originally part of the much larger Cannock Forest, and was granted to the Bishop of Coventry and Lichfield by Richard I in return for donations to a Crusade. Since then its low gravelly hills and woodland have variously accommodated royal hunting, a charcoal industry, German World War I POWs and, currently, timber production; the Forestry Commission has sizeable pine and spruce plantations. Of course the Chase also offers a crucial site for recreation. Nearly 4 million people live within 20 miles of its leafy boundaries, and walking, horseriding and off-road cycling are all popular.

Enter the Chase by Castle Ring, opposite the Park Gate Inn, an Iron Age construction that comprises nine acres of grassy ramparts and swampy ditches, plus the remnants of a much later building thought to be a medieval hunting lodge for the Royal Forest. From the lofty edge of the castle the Chase lies outstretched. There are a couple of crude man-made landmarks visible: a high concrete radio transmission tower, and ahead squat the unsightly but irresistible monster cooling towers of Rugeley power station. Both can be used as markers for navigational purposes should you go astray in the next few miles. Immediately below, the mix of thick forest and scrubby heath extends for several undulating miles, and the broad, sandy track to Wandon (a mile away) is evident. This first, dramatic view of Cannock Chase is quite exhilarating. It is wide, although clearly not endless, but above all the feeling of natural ruggedness is invigorating after so many miles of soft and pastoral, but ultimately tame, landscape.

Leave the Scots pines for the track to Wandon. A few yards south of here the Camping and Caravanning Club have their official Cannock site. Cross the road and follow Marquis Drive west; notices warn of subsidence, and the importance of keeping to the proper path, but in dry weather this is usually a firm if unmade stony surface. There are still Heart of England Way signs, and the Way is irregularly featured on newer OS Landranger maps, but due to the proliferation of tracks it is wise to keep guidebook and map handy. There are also numerous signs that read: 'Mountain bikers: all riders MUST keep to bridleways, and give way to walkers.'

At the visitor centre, off the Drive, there is more information on the Chase, its management and its wildlife. Deer are especially important, for over 100 were killed by vehicles in 1992–93 alone. After crossing a couple of roads, and beyond White House, the Way bounces over a much more open patch of heath. Beyond the Katyn Memorial, erected by the Anglo-Polish Society to honour 14,000 Polish officers massacred in Katyn Forest in 1940, is Anson's Bank, where picnics and kites usually abound, and from where there are views north over rural Staffordshire.

The Heart of England Way continues past a large glacial boulder believed to have originated in Scotland, and along the distinctive trackbed of the so-called Tackeroo Railway, built to serve the World War I army camps on the Chase. The official end of the Way is at Milford, where you can enjoy an ice cream or a drink on the popular green. But for those eager for a new chapter, a new long-distance footpath, and the lure of northern England, watch out for signs for the Staffordshire Way near the boulderstone, and bid farewell to the Heart of England.

MILFORD – RUSHTON (48 miles)

The Staffordshire Way connects Kinver Edge (west of Stourbridge) with Mow Cop Castle (on Congleton Edge), and runs for a total distance of 92 miles. The End to End route follows just under 50 of the most scenic and interesting of those miles, from the woods and heaths of Cannock Chase via Uttoxeter and the beautiful Churnet valley, finally leaving the Way at Rushton where you immediately pick up the Gritstone Trail. Ahead lies high Pennine country.

The Staffordshire Way is a regional route, completed in 1983, and created by the county council who are responsible for maintaining access and providing waymarks. The standard symbol accompanying public footpath and bridleway signs is what is known as the Staffordshire Knot. It has to be said that at times the waymarks are used rather sparingly – compared, say, to the Cotswold Way or even the Heart of England Way – but there again the End to End walker will not need the kid glove treatment by now. Map and compass work should be second nature, making enjoyable or time-saving detours possible, or in some cases even preferable.

If you have followed the Heart of England Way to its conclusion at Milford, then either take the towpath of the Staffordshire and Worcestershire Canal directly to Great Haywood, or else keep to the south of the water and arrive via Shugborough Park and Essex Bridge, the longest packhorse bridge in England. If you have joined the Staffs Way actually on Cannock Chase, then follow the signs north along a clear, sandy track to the Punchbowl car park on the A513, and enter Shugborough Park from the roadside. The mansion and grounds are impressive; the county council even has its own museum housed in the old servants' quarters. The 5th Earl of Lichfield (the photographer, Patrick Lichfield) still lives at Shugborough, which must get a bit hectic for him when 1,000 members of the public turn up every Sunday.

Once over Essex Bridge join the bank of the Trent and Mersey Canal and continue east via Colwich until the outskirts of unlovely Rugeley get dangerously close, when you should bear left and skirt the village of Colton to reach Blithfield Reservoir across farmland.

Although there are pleasant views over the reservoir, access to the shore is restricted. This is the largest expanse of water in the county, supplying a daily average of 75 million gallons to a population of 1.25 million covering 600 square miles. After skirting the dam the route makes for the village of Abbots Bromley, where there is a blend of listed buildings in various styles, including five pubs. Every September the village hosts what is known as the Horn Dance, when sensible and serious local people adorn themselves with reindeer horns and dance around the locality for a whole day.

Leaving the friendly if odd folk of Abbots Bromley behind, proceed across fields into Bagot's Park. The woods are all that remain of the thirteenth-century royal Needwood Forest. Follow the line of pylons between a gap in the trees over the low hilltop, then via a series of farms to Uttoxeter, close to the National Hunt racecourse on the town's eastern edge. This old market town has some fascinating local history: The Old Talbot public house is dated around 1650 and a few yards away there is a curious monument, now with a modern newsstand built inside it, which marks the spot where the schoolboy Dr Johnson was forced to stand in the rain as punishment for refusing to help on his father's bookstall.

The next section of the walk presents an altogether different picture, for the valley of the River Dove is wide and gentle. After negotiating the A50, cross the lovely six-arch, fourteenth-century stone Dove Bridge. Now wander through the farmland of Derbyshire for a while, with the river meandering lazily below. Ahead, the prominent Weaver Hills are punctured by a gaping quarry. Finally cross the Dove to enter Rocester (it rhymes with 'toaster'), a place notable for Richard Arkwright's cotton spinning mill, and the massive and rather incongruous JCB factory.

One of the obvious pleasures of walking from one end of the country to the other is the constantly changing scenery. Some long-distance paths incorporate only one broad type of landscape within their boundaries, but others offer a delightful variety within an often short distance. The northern section of the Staffordshire Way is one such, for after the heaths of Cannock Chase and the open pastures of the Dove valley, the Way leaves Rocester and plunges into the steep, mixed woodland of the Churnet valley. From the viewpoint on Toothill Rock, by Alton, you may understand why some have dubbed this area 'Staffordshire's Rhineland', since apart from the physical geography there is also the arresting spectacle of a gothic castle rising above the woods on the other side of the valley. It is part of the monster theme park of Alton Towers which, although usually audible, is mostly out of sight to the Staffs Way walker. However, should Thunder Valley, Fantasy World or Land of The Make Believe intrigue you, then this could be one of the more curious of your stops along the way.

Beyond Alton, where there is a profusion of B&B and pub accommodation (the Bulls Head is a particularly handsome place), the valley narrows and the woodland thickens. At Dimmings Dale, Forest Enterprise has created an attractive series of woodland walks around a restored smelting mill and reservoir, where holly, birch, rowan and bilberry are all being encouraged to grow following the clearance of rhododendron. Refreshments are provided at the Ramblers' Retreat café, and on a clearing at the head of the valley above the pines and larches there is a beautifully situated youth hostel.

The trail continues through Hawksmoor Nature Reserve, and down to the River Churnet just south of Kingsley Holt. After descending steeply to the Caldon Canal, recently restored, follow the quiet towpath for six miles to Wall Grange. The walking is undemanding and highly enjoyable, since the secluded, mixed woodland that overhangs the canal is a haven for wildlife, especially birds. Consall Nature Park and the RSPB's Booth Wood both play host to the likes of redstarts, pied flycatchers and woodpeckers. Relics of former local industry are also evident. Consall Forge once dealt with iron from nearby foundries, but the only activity in this quiet clearing today is either the repainting of canal boats, or queuing for opening time at the happily isolated Black Lion pub. At Cheddleton, further along this once important commercial thoroughfare, the Flint Mill is now a museum of industrial archaeology, and during the summer the preserved Churnet Valley Railway is often in steam.

The Way crosses both the canal and railway at Wall Grange, near the entrance to Deep Hayes Country Park, and then keeps to the west of Leek alongside what are occasionally wet meadows by the canal feeder and heads for Rudyard. From the brow of the hill near the small country park at Ladderedge (the A53 has pavements) there are good views over Leek and beyond, to the Roaches and the western edge of the Peak District. Leek is the largest place encountered for some time, and offers a good range of shops and eating places, although accommodation is rather limited. Full details from the helpful tourist information centre.

Rudyard Reservoir, beyond the village, was originally built to supply the Caldon Canal, and its scenic location inspired the parents of Rudyard Kipling when choosing a name for their new son. It is a long and attractive lake, deservedly popular, and its sloping, wooded southern shores bear a resemblance to the more famous Windermere. There is a choice of a disused railway-walk along the eastern shore or the official route, which is much more interesting, among the woods and then scrubland to the west. A mile on from Rudyard Reservoir is Rushton where the End to End walker quits the Staffordshire Way for the high gritstone moors of Cheshire.

RUSHTON – CROWDEN (38 miles)

The Gritstone Trail extends north for 18.5 miles from Rushton to Lyme Park. Hidden and sometimes steep valleys link the bare, high hills, which offer panoramic views of the plains of Cheshire on one side and the rising Pennine moors of Derbyshire on the other. The trail is well-waymarked, with yellow bootprint signs and the letter 'G' on a black background, as well as the more conventional finger posts. Your strong End to End legs should be able to complete the trail in one day.

At Rushton, where the Knot Inn is perhaps the best of the three hostelries on offer, signposts indicate the Mow Cop Trail (west) and the Gritstone Trail (east, initially). It should be pointed out that the Mow Cop Trail in fact represents the final nine miles of the Staffordshire Way, over the Cloud to Mow Cop Castle and Congleton Edge. Confusingly these same nine Mow Cop miles are sometimes included in the Gritstone Trail's length. (The Staffs County Council's official guide to the Staffs Way does this.) But your involvement with Staffordshire is at an end; the county border with Cheshire is at hand, and so leave the verdant Dane valley on this new trail, and climb steadily on to the grassy slopes of the Minns. As you close the gate behind you at Hawkslee Farm and stride up to the quite low but exposed ridge, there is an immediate sense of elevation and airiness. Looking behind, the Cloud and Mow Cop loom darkly, with the Roaches further east; below is the flat plain of Cheshire, with the 250-feet-diameter Lovell radio telescope at Jodrell Bank evident in the middle distance. What a glorious panorama!

The notices that request closing gates due to stock grazing indicate that you have entered the Peak National Park. Cross the road at the end of the ridge in order to ascend Croker Hill. Near here the route is briefly joined by the Cestrian Link Walk, a 112-mile unofficial route that links the end of the Offa's Dyke Path with the beginning of the Pennine Way. From the Gritstone Trail the Cestrian Link heads east over Wildboarclough and Combs Fell to Errwood Reservoir, then via Dove Holes and Peak Forest to Edale. This is no doubt fine for those desperate to start the Pennine Way, but before you start locating Edale on the map, why not read on a little further, and learn more about the End to End Central Route – and why it avoids the opening miles of the Pennine Way.

Ahead the green waves of Macclesfield Forest sweep down towards the abrupt, rocky protuberance of Tegg's Nose, which is where you should be aiming. So descend the moorland from Croker Hill to Lowerhouses, and once around a couple of small reservoirs by Langley there is a long and steep plod up to Tegg's Nose Country Park, where there is an information/refreshment centre by the car park. Tegg's Nose was a busy quarry until 1955, and some mining relics remain; and it was here that the Gritstone Trail was formally opened in 1978.

Resume across fields opposite the visitor centre. From these high pastures there are extensive views of Macclesfield and Manchester, with an unbroken Pennine backdrop. Closer at hand there are more quarries, and Kerridge Hill, the next destination, is unmistakable with the distinctive White Nancy folly on top. The route avoids Bollington, then climbs out of the clough and passes Berristall Hall for fields to just beyond Brink Farm. There is a clear track over the open moorland of Sponds Hill, the last proper Gritstone Trail viewpoint. Now down to the Bow Stones (shafts of Anglo-Saxon crosses) and through woodland into Lyme Country Park. This is a 1,300-acre deer park with open, rolling grounds and a fine Hall made out of local stone. It has a café, information centre, gift shop, and so on.

From Lyme Country Park there is a choice of two routes up on to the backbone of England in order to join the Pennine Way. I will describe both, since they are equally attractive, but the second route joins the national trail further north than the first, and to that extent my preference is for the second.

If you are adamant about walking every foot of the Pennine Way then you will have left the Gritstone Trail earlier, perhaps near Macclesfield for the Cestrian Link Walk to Edale. But there is much to be said for a few miles' worth of patience and prudence. As long-distance walking has rocketed in popularity over the last fifteen years, so the pressure on the major trails has grown, and many have been steadily worn down. Sadly but perhaps inevitably the most famous of them all, Tom Stephenson's Pennine Way, has suffered the most. On a sunny summer's day there can be literally dozens of cheerful if sometimes ill-equipped walkers setting off from the Old Nag's Head in Edale for the long trek north. Unfortunately many give up after only a day or so, following a tortuous struggle with the mire and bog of Kinder Scout and Bleaklow. It is these desperately eroded miles that I would urge End to End walkers to avoid. There is nothing defeatist or dishonourable in skipping miles of gooey peat groughs, especially if your own boots will exacerbate the problem. Besides, you've already had a fair stroll to reach the Pennines!

The first route leaves by a clear track across Lyme grounds to East Lodge. The curious building isolated on the hill to the left is known as the Cage, an Elizabethan hunting lodge. Follow short footpaths above Higher Disley and Lane Ends, then drop to Newtown and cross the A6 into New Mills, where signs point to the pleasant Sett Valley Trail. This runs for 2 ½ miles along the course of the former Manchester–Hayfield railway, and is easy and direct. At Hayfield there are a few shops and pubs, with friendly lodgings at the George. You are now on the edge of the Pennines and in popular walking country, which explains the handy outdoor equipment shop at the top of the main street. This is the place to buy spare laces and extra tent pegs, since before the morning is out you will be puffing on top of the Pennine Way, so make sure you are fully prepared.

Take the minor road out of the village to Kinder Reservoir. At a small, disused quarry on the left, just past the Sportsman pub, there is a plaque on the rockface dedicated to the 'Kinder Scout Mass Trespassers' who met here on 24th April 1932. Scores of young men and women from industrial Manchester braved violent gamekeepers to demonstrate for fair access to the moorlands of Derbyshire. In the ensuing protest several ramblers were arrested, and subsequently jailed; others were injured. But through their defiant actions the southern Pennines were gradually opened up, and walkers' rights nationally were given a crucial platform. Be grateful.

After Kinder Reservoir there is a steep and rather rough track up William Clough to join the Pennine Way just south of Mill Hill. Kinder Downfall is a little further back down the national trail, and is best viewed from the reservoir below. In wet and stormy weather this miniature waterfall can explode into life; the spray is often borne high into the air by swirling winds. At Mill Hill the path turns abruptly north-eastwards, but progress across Featherbed Moss to the Snake Pass is painfully slow and awkward due to the interminable peat groughs. The bare moors continue across the road, towards the Wain Stones on Bleaklow Head. It is imperative that you consult map and compass and keep to the correct course, since the bare and featureless waste continues to confound many hapless walkers. It is also worth noting that some guidebooks may be at variance with the actual course of the path on the ground at several points. In an effort to lead walkers away from some of the most eroded patches the authorities have introduced short diversions to the waymarked route, such as on the approach to Bleaklow Head. The bottom line is: if in doubt obey official signposts, and avoid what you think are short cuts and profitable detours, since they are probably not, and it is likely that you will be making the erosion still worse.

It will also be apparent that path-improvement measures have been carried out on this stretch. The long chains of stone slabs across the ground (and more may follow) are a result of helicopters flying in 140 tons of gritstone paving from disused Lancashire cotton mills in order to lay a firm and identifiable path. Drops were also made near Blackstone Edge and on the Border ridge in the Cheviot Hills, and it is one of a series of counter-erosion projects along the Pennine Way that have at various times included floating matting, the laying of duckboards, and the painstaking process of stone pitching (a centuries-old technique of constructing intricate stone pathways). Then, after all the mud and fuss, it is time to lose height and drop into Longdendale. The way down by Torside Clough is long and steep, and after crossing the dam between the reservoirs head up the valley towards Crowden Youth Hostel.

The second route from Lyme Country Park avoids the morass described above, and in that respect is eminently more attractive, although Black Hill is still to come. Leave the grounds by a public right of way westwards that passes through Haresteads Farm, after which there is a choice of either the Macclesfield Canal or Middlewood Way north to Marple. The former is part of the Cheshire Ring Canal, which links six historic canals together to form a circular route of 97 miles around the county, and holds the enticing record of having more pubs per mile than any other UK long-distance footpath. The latter is a former railway line that has been converted into a dual walkway and bridleway that stretches 11 miles from Macclesfield to Marple. Take your pick, since they both provide excellent walking. However, the canal provides the best pedestrian link to the Etherow valley. At Marple join another local trail, the Goyt Way, as it leaves the waterway to the north through Brabyns Park, near where there are two impressive flights of locks, followed by the famous Marple Aqueduct. Follow the Goyt Way over the road and into Etherow, another country park, at Compstall. The lakes that were created for local cloth and gunpowder works now serve wintering ducks and geese, as well as canoeists, yachtsmen and anglers, and there is a small visitor centre and café nearby. Follow another waymarked trail, the Etherow–Goyt Valley Way, upstream through meadow and grassland, where some important semi-natural deciduous woodland (beech, oak, ash and sycamore) can be found. The clean, fast-flowing stream once spawned a vigorous textile industry, although only Lymefield cotton mill is still working. From Idle Hill there are views over the eastern suburbs of Manchester, but I suspect that most End to End walkers will not linger. Ahead the Pennine massif looms ever larger, and the real challenge is approaching.

The Etherow–Goyt Valley Way ends at Tintwistle, by Bottoms Reservoir, but a short diversion into Hadfield may be wise to stock up with provisions, since there are no superstores until Edinburgh. Now you once more enter the Peak National Park, and keeping the reservoirs on your left follow the Longdendale Trail (a component part of the Southport–Hull Trans Pennine Trail, a new walking/cycling route still under construction) for 7 fast and direct miles up the valley, and join the Pennine Way as it crosses the Torside Reservoir dam.

4

THE TOUGHEST TRAIL

Crowden – Kirk Yetholm

CROWDEN – HAWES (86 miles)

There is no denying that the Pennine Way provides the most satisfying, continuous means of walking through northern England into Scotland. For roughly 256 miles (or, if you have joined at Crowden, for about 243 miles) the route strides over high, bleak moors and fellsides, via unspoilt dales and by crashing waterfalls, and through scenery that is amongst the wildest that you will find in England. It hardly needs to be said that this is a trail for experienced walkers.

There are waymarks, for sure, but it would be misleading to say that they are regular, since it is neither practical nor aesthetically desirable to litter open moors and rough hills with signs, and since much of the route is across high and open ground it is essential that map and compass skills are up to scratch. However, on some sections – such as the boggy miles of Black Hill approaching – the direction of the route is all too clear, thanks to the constant tramping of boots. And this, of course, is the negative side of walking the country's oldest, most famous and most popular long-distance path. It is unlikely that you will be without company for more than a few hours; despite campsites and youth hostels, private accommodation is limited, and in the summer months may be difficult to find. Severe erosion is occurring in a number of places where the fragile landscape has been unable to deal with both the overgrazing of sheep and the constant attention of visitors, and you should always observe notices where path restoration work and counter-erosion measures are taking place.

In summary: you may be fit and confident in your walking ability by now, but remember that the Pennine Way remains the most challenging trail of them all. It is nevertheless a route to enjoy and to savour, and the next couple of weeks' walking will be through a much more wild and untamed England than you have previously experienced.

Leave Longdendale half a mile south-west of Crowden Youth Hostel by a steady track up by Crowden Brook to Oaken Clough. Gradually swing round north-eastwards on to the slopes of Black Hill, a massive and inhospitable expanse of bog that has few admirers. Wainwright called Black Hill 'a desolate and hopeless quagmire'. If your gaiters have already been muddied by Bleaklow (and maybe by Kinder Scout as well), Black Hill will repeat the discomfort. For those End to Enders who have joined at Crowden via Etherow Country Park, this will be your Pennine Way baptism – by mud.

At the 582m summit pass from gooey Derbyshire into sticky Yorkshire. The original route strikes out north-west over Dean Hill, but problems with erosion have led to a new, recommended route via Dean Clough and Wessenden Head, and this remains the better option. Cross the Holmfirth road and follow a track over the hillside past a succession of reservoirs. At Standedge, cross the A62, and after several more miles of bleak moorland come to a major trans-Pennine crossing, the M62. To your left, Greater Manchester stretches in a grey haze for many miles; and the conurbations of West Yorkshire are not too far away in the other direction.

Cross the motorway by a high and airy footbridge, and immediately the traffic is left behind as the Way strides over Blackstone Edge. The dark, flagged surface is possibly of Roman origin, and from the 472m top there are more high views over the sprawl of Manchester's northern outposts. Then the trail passes a series of gloomy and featureless reservoirs, and beyond Coldwell Hill, at Withens Gate, it is crossed by the Calderdale Way, a 50-mile circular route around the District. If you turn left, towards Todmorden, Mankinholes Youth Hostel is less than a mile away.

From Stoodley Pike Monument, a massive millstone construction built to commemorate the defeat of Napoleon in 1814, descend to the Calder valley and a complete change of scene. The old mill town of Hebden Bridge straddles the hillside a mile to the east, where there are shops and beds. Now cross road, railway and canal in order to ascend fields and regain height. Green pasture makes a pleasant change from dark peat and sombre gritstone. Follow a clear track for a couple of miles over hillside to the narrow defile of Graining Water, afterwards turning right to reach Walshaw Dean reservoirs. Leave the middle of the three reservoirs for a path over the dull, peat slopes to Withins (also known as Top Withens), a lonely and ruined farmhouse high on the moor that is believed to have been the model for Emily Brontë's *Wuthering Heights*. Notices now warn against entry to the crumbling shell for reasons of safety. Despite this, some foolish romantic has etched on the wall a love heart between the names 'Kathy' and 'Heathcliff'. Haworth Moor is naturally popular with all manner of visitors, and from Withins a line of stone flags leads down the hillside, directed by wooden signposts that also point to the Brontë Falls and the Brontë Way. The signs are in both English and Japanese.

The Pennine Way veers left, down to the shore of Ponden Reservoir, or if you continue straight onwards the touristy town of Haworth is less than three miles away. Here the massed tea rooms on the steep, cobbled main street offer such naughty delights as Yorkshire Parkin, Yorkshire curd Tarts, and the appropriately named Fat Rascal (a kind of flat, fruit scone – hefty fuel for hungry walkers!).

Back on the Pennine Way, leave the western end of Ponden Reservoir and climb back up to the bare heather tops via Crag Bottom. On Ickornshaw Moor conditions can get very boggy, and the exposed terrain can be most unwelcoming in adverse conditions. Until the Pennines you may have encountered periods of bad weather, but unless you have set off very early (or late) in the year it is unlikely that you will have reached for the protective clothing too often. However, from the Pennines onwards the walking becomes higher and tougher, and whether you are on the Pennines, Southern Uplands or Pentlands – let alone the sterner stuff further north – make sure that you are adequately equipped.

The Black Bull on the A6068 offers welcome refreshment (a variety of bar food is served), then after a couple of miles of rolling farmland reach the small settlement of Lothersdale, followed by a short climb to the 388m viewpoint of Pinhaw Beacon. The land is still empty and remote, but there are surfaced lanes that the path both crosses and for a short distance joins, should bad weather or fatigue drive you off. Before long, the Way reaches Thornton-in-Craven, a small village with a few amenities. If you are planning to stay in places such as Thornton it is best to purchase a copy of the Pennine Way Association's *Accommodation and Camping Guide*, an invaluable pocket-size directory. And since there are 18 youth hostels along the course of the Pennine Way, it may also be worth contacting the Youth Hostels Association for details of their *Pennine Way Bureau*, a booking service for YHA members.

The next 10 miles are relatively straightforward and easy, and after the bogs and moorland of previous days this may be welcome. From Thornton follow a clear track to near East Marton and join the towpath of the Leeds and Liverpool Canal for a short while. Forty miles to the south-west, End to End West Route walkers will also be treading its well-used towpath miles, but in the rather more built-up environs of Wigan.

The southern Yorkshire Dales slowly begin to fill the horizon, and the busy village of Gargrave on the river Aire marks their approach. Continue up Airedale, a friendly and attractive walking route, with easy terrain and an abundance of wildlife. On Eshton Moor cross the boundary of the Yorkshire Dales National Park; then afterwards the path sticks close to the gurgling river, and gambols north via Airton to Malham.

There is a purpose-built youth hostel in the centre of this popular village, where all-day breakfast is served at the Malham Café. Of particular note is the Buck Inn, where I entreat you to sample the delicious 'Malham and Masham Pie', made with a not ungenerous dash of Theakstons beer.

At popular times Malham simply swarms, since it enjoys a situation among some of the most stunning limestone scenery in the country. A mile to the east is the huge rocky gorge of Gordale Scar, and although it is possible to clamber up between the towering cliffs and continue to Malham Tarn, it is probably unwise with a full pack on your back. Better instead to visit the spectacle on an evening stroll after supper.

The Pennine Way officially continues north from the village along a signposted track to Malham Cove, a massive limestone amphitheatre whose 80m-high cliffs are quite daunting from below. And only then do you notice people climbing and abseiling the face. However, your route is up a carefully reconstructed footpath around the side, leading to an amazing stretch of pavement above the Cove, where you bound from one huge block of limestone to the next. With expansive views of Malham and Airedale (and even of Pendle Hill on a clear day), this is the perfect place for morning coffee.

The Malham Tarn Estate has recently permitted far greater access to the land south of the Tarn, defined on public notices dotted about the area, so it is possible to make your own way north, perhaps via the dry valley known as Watlowes, and some remarkable sink holes – where gurgling streams simply disappear into the ground through the porous carboniferous limestone. Then follow the clear track around the eastern shore of the lake, a large and unexpected patch of water popular with waterfowl, and through woods past Malham Tarn House, now a field centre for outdoor study. Turn north through pasture and into a far more desolate land. Here, even the tough, curly-horned Swaledale sheep look cold. The destination is the bare top of Fountains Fell, and the approach via Tennant Gill can be muddy and unclear, particularly in misty conditions.

From the top of Fountains Fell the splendid shape of Pen-y-Ghent presents itself, to many the only real 'mountain' of the Pennine Way. Whether you imagine it an upturned boat or a crouching lion, its steep and shapely form is your next destination, so descend to an unfenced road and follow this south-west for a short distance to an area of shake holes. The path to Pen-y-Ghent is unmistakable, since the hill is popular with both casual and serious walkers, the latter including those masochistic individuals who take part in the Three Peaks Challenge, a day-long, 24-mile 'walk' linking Pen-y-Ghent with Whernside and Ingleborough. Sadly this has resulted in serious erosion around the flanks, and elevated duck boards and reconstructed paths have had to be introduced in order to span the mud. Despite this, the short, sharp push to the summit (694m) is entirely worthwhile, for there are fine views in every direction, and from here there is a long descent into Ribblesdale via a moorland track and green road.

Horton in Ribblesdale has a few amenities, in particular the famous Pen-y-Ghent Café that provides hungry walkers with hot meals up to 6 p.m. most evenings; and Stainforth Youth Hostel is four miles down the road. It may be as well to stock up at the village, for the next 14-mile stretch to Hawes has virtually nothing to offer the walker – except miles and miles of lovely open, unspoilt hills. From the Crown Inn take a quiet green road north out of Ribblesdale, through a landscape dotted with shake holes and pot holes, most notably Sell Gill Holes. From Horton to this point the Pennine Way has been sharing company with the Ribble Way, a 72-mile trail from the River Ribble's mouth, near Preston, to its source nearby on Gayle Moor. Some End to End walkers may have used the Ribble Way as a means to reach the high Pennines from the Lancashire Plain, so joining the West and Central Routes. *However, as the Pennine Way makes for Çam Fell, and the Ribble Way wanders off to find its birthplace, so to speak, another long-distance footpath enters the scene. The Dales Way, a justly popular 81-mile route from Ilkley to Bowness-on-Windermere, joins the Pennine Way at Cam End, and End to Enders who are keen to see the Lake District should now veer west on the Dales Way via Dentdale and Sedbergh to Windermere.*

If the clouds are low or the wind is biting, the lonely and exposed moors of Cam Fell and Dodd Fell can be a cold and hostile place. Mind you, if it is sunny and mild this is then a relatively easy and very enjoyable jaunt. The path is direct and generally straightforward, especially between Cam Fell and Dodd Fell where it follows an elevated Roman road that packhorse trains named Cam High Road. Unfortunately, as the limestone country is left behind, so the bog and surface water increases, particularly on Ten End. With Wensleydale approaching, eventually join Gaudy Lane and enter the village of Gayle, then along Gayle Beck and into Hawes.

HAWES – ALSTON (80 miles)

Hawes is an agreeable place, a small but active market town, with a youth hostel and nearby campsites as well as private accommodation. From the choice of shops you will be able to purchase some white and flaky Wensleydale cheese, still made locally.

Leave via the Dales Countryside Museum, which now boasts new exhibitions and galleries, for lanes and paths north; then over meadows to the village of Hardraw. The famous waterfall is upstream from the Green Dragon Inn, and will prove even more of a spectacle if you have had some typically damp Pennine weather in the past few days. The Way climbs quite steeply up bare slopes to Hearne Top, and continues along the broad shoulder of Great Shunner Fell to the 716m summit. There are wide views from this exposed position; and in bad weather make sure that you are confident of your direction of travel.

The track off the hillside leads to the village of Thwaite, and from there around the slopes of Kisdon Hill to Keld. The views over Swaledale are superb, or if you prefer you can detour via Muker and join easier tracks by the youthful River Swale, which bounds its way noisily down between the hills. At Keld, another tiny settlement bearing firm Norse roots, amenities pretty much begin and end with the youth hostel. Tucked away in the narrow dale, there is a distinct feeling of isolation and seclusion. The nearest pub is the Farmers Arms at Muker, 3 miles back, and it is not unusual for several hostellers to chip in and hire a taxi for the journey. Around here you are likely to meet walkers on Wainwright's Coast to Coast route, which is heading either east down Swaledale to Richmond or west to Kirkby Stephen.

Cross the Swale by a footbridge in order to ascend the hillside opposite on a walled track. Head north above Startindale Gill to Stonesdale Moor, then across ground that bears the scattered remains of old mineworkings to Tan Hill Inn. At 528m it is the highest pub in England, and was built originally to serve the men who worked the meagre coal seams nearby. When the clouds are racing and the wind is biting it feels like the most remote and loneliest place on earth, and you may be reluctant to forsake the warmth of the fire or the Theakstons for the 8-mile hike to Bowes. If this is the case then the pub permits camping around the back, and also provides bed and breakfast – but don't count on there being rooms available.

To reach the Stainmore Gap, a major Pennine divide, either take the path across Sleightholme Moor, which can be a boggy and treacherous affair in wet weather; or for an easier and safer passage follow the Brough–Reeth road for 2 miles, branching off for a track known as the Sleightholme Moor Road – which the Tan Hill path meets near Sleightholme Beck. Cross the Beck at Intake Bridge and continue downstream. Near Trough Heads the Pennine Way divides into two, with one arm continuing down the valley to Bowes and the other heading directly across the fellside to Blackton Reservoir. The first option, known as the Bowes loop, is preferable if you are seeking refreshment and accommodation, and is only 3 miles longer than the main route. (On leaving the village cross old MOD land and the bare Cotherstone Moor to rejoin the Way.) If you are sticking with the original course, leave Trough Heads in a north-west direction, and after crossing the River Greta by a natural limestone arch known as God's Bridge negotiate the traffic on the A66 with great care. The vehicles that hurtle along Stainmore Gap are following a trans-Pennine route that was first used as long ago as the Bronze Age, then much later by the Romans, who built a fort at Bowes. Beyond the A66, the Way wanders over Bowes Moor and Cotherstone Moor, largely featureless ground where the odd glance at the compass may be necessary.

Baldersdale Youth Hostel, near Blackton Reservoir, is only a few minutes off the track, and also has camping facilities. From here the route continues north into Lunedale and passes between two further reservoirs, before crossing Harter Fell and into Teesdale. The Pennine Way does not actually cross the river to visit Middleton-in-Teesdale, but if you have a few moments to spare it is worthwhile, for here are shops, pubs and plenty of B&Bs, and even a tiny fish and chip shop, plus a helpful information centre behind the Teesdale Hotel.

Now the route is through attractive meadows and patchy woodland on the south bank of the Tees, and the further you walk upstream the more breathtaking the river scenery becomes. Beyond Wynch Bridge, Low and High Force waterfalls thunder over the Whin Sill, and many reckon the latter to be the finest falls in the country. Not the high, wispy strands of Hardraw Force here, rather a surging crash as the Tees is squeezed between dark dolerite cliffs into a huge pool below. Hardly surprising, then, that it is immensely popular with visitors, and a good idea might be to stay in or around Middleton and so enjoy this stretch of the Tees in the comparative peace of an early morning. And there are more pleasures to come.

Beyond High Force the route continues up the twisting valley of the Tees along sections of restored pathway (another beneficiary of the 1992 Operation Flying Flagstone drop), and to yet another waterfall, Cauldron Snout, below the dam of Cow Green Reservoir. Upper Teesdale, a national nature reserve, is internationally famous for its rich flora. The 'Teesdale Assemblage', a community of wild flowers, is exclusive to this area, and the Alpine mixture includes spring gentian, bird's eye primrose and yellow mountain saxifrage.

Enter Cumbria, and maintain the westwards direction across empty and barren moorland for a number of miles. The track is well-walked, and MOD 'Keep Out' signs to the south provide useful markers. Stone slabs and wooden planks help avoid the boggier parts of the path. When Maize Beck appears join its north bank, and after another mile or so suddenly High Cup appears at your feet. This is one of the highlights of the entire Pennine Way. The massive but narrow U-shaped valley plunges down towards the Eden valley and the Cumbrian fells. For someone who, as an eager teenager trapped in south London, used to stare often and longingly at the cover of J.H.B. Peel's classic *Along the Pennine Way*, this is a special place.

The clear path skirts the western rim of High Cup before descending gradually and approaches Dufton via a pleasant, unsurfaced walled lane. After miles of steep dale slopes and open moors the scenery is gentler and kinder for a moment. Appleby, historic county town of the former Westmorland, is only 3 miles away, and has most facilities, but although Dufton is little more than a large village, it has B&Bs, a youth hostel, and a couple of campsites. This is one of the more positive aspects of the trail's popularity. Recent research concluded that the Pennine Way attracts an estimated 12,000 long-distance walkers, and perhaps as many as 250,000 day walkers every year. This heavy volume of walking traffic inevitably needs refuelling, and the first group (campers excepted) obviously needs somewhere to lay weary limbs for the night. So if you walk the trail today, certainly during the popular months, you will find that a surprising number of farms offer B&B, or perhaps turn an in-field into a rudimentary campsite for a season. Some out-of-the-way cottages and farmsteads provide a welcome pot of tea and snacks, and of course this service industry is as valuable to the local community as it is to thirsty walkers. Indeed, a 1990 survey by the Countryside Commission estimated that altogether the thousands of Pennine Way walkers spend a total of £2 million a year along the route – quite a financial injection for the local economy.

The Way returns to the open hillside for the 20-mile haul to Alston by a sunken track called Hurning Lane. Keeping the summits of Dufton Pike and Brownber Hill at a thankful distance, proceed up to Knock Old Man along a cairned path and then swing north-west to Great Dun Fell. Routefinding is aided by the radio transmitting station, with masts, which sits on its 848m top. Little Dun Fell, a mile further on, is hardly any lower, but ahead the bulk of Cross Fell draws nearer. This is the high-point of the Pennines (893m), and if the wind is keen – and it invariably is – the exposed, grassy top will feel like the Arctic. A stone wind shelter offers some protection. But it is as well to bear in mind that snow patches can last into early summer here, and it is wise to approach the Dufton–Alston section with appropriate care.

If the clouds permit, take a last look at the huge panorama (the hills of the Lake District and southern Scotland are easily visible from here) and scamper down towards Skirwith Fell, northwards, then east on a clear track known as the Corpse Road (once used to transport the dead to a burial-place elsewhere). This firm track continues across the bare moorland, with old mine shafts the only features of any note, and only the plaintive cry of the curlew likely to rise above the sound of the wind. Eventually the path drops down into the village of Garrigill, a relief for all those who have been buffeted and ravaged by the elements on Cross Fell. Although there is some accommodation here, including B&B at the George and Dragon, most will continue for a further four miles along the South Tyne River to Alston.

Alston claims to be the highest market town in England, and owes its origins to lead mining. Although the Romans were probably the first to start digging, it was not until the 1600s that the London Lead Company really began extracting in earnest, and so the North Pennines became the focus for an intensive but short-lived industry. Other settlements on the Pennine Way – such as Middleton-in-Teesdale – also owe their current size and appearance to the rise of the lead-mining industry. Apart from lead, nearby Alston Moor is also important as the place where three of northern England's main rivers rise: the Tees, the Tyne and the Wear.

Relax and enjoy some creature comforts this evening, for as you scrutinise the map it is evident that the high Pennines are almost at an end and Hadrian's Wall and the Cheviots are approaching. The End to End Central Route has almost finished with England, and the enticing prospect of Scotland draws nearer.

ALSTON – KIRK YETHOLM (77 miles)

The section of the Pennine Way between Alston and Greenhead (16 miles) lacks the height and grandeur of the recent high fells, and some may feel it suffers as a result. But at least this will be easier walking, and the likelihood of getting seriously lost is remote.

From Alston, head north on the west bank of the South Tyne. Or in simpler terms, follow the river for eight miles to Lambley. Unfortunately little of this is along the river bank; rather, it uses tracks parallel to the A689 to enter Northumberland and reach Slaggyford, after which you fall into step with the legionnaires along the Maiden Way, a Roman road built around AD 80. An alternative after Burnstones is to follow the course of the former South Tyne railway to Lambley. Both allow swift progress, and although the walking may not be dramatic it is nevertheless pleasant and straightforward.

Head north-west from near the village of Lambley, as the Way switches from moorland to an area of old mineworkings, then across Hartley Burn and through farmland. Over Hartleyburn and Blenkinsopp Commons the unremarkable scenery and the occasional vagueness of the path requires navigational attention; then at Gap Shields Fan follow a track east – either turning north and crossing the busy A69, or else on into Greenhead, where the youth hostel is situated in a 100-year-old former Methodist Chapel.

Now the Walk becomes interesting once more, for Hadrian's Wall is reached. If you did not enter Greenhead then you will join the Vallum, a large ditch that the Romans built behind the Wall and which represented the extent of the military zone. Otherwise follow a burn for a mile north from the village, and to the remains of Thirlwall Castle, which was built around 700 years ago with stones from the Roman Wall. Head east, close to the Wall's original course, and enter Northumberland National Park. Ahead is the first, short stretch of surviving Wall. However, little of the 73-mile construction survives in its original state, and what does or has been restored is generally lower than its original full height of five metres. Nevertheless, as you walk the ramparts it only needs a little imagination to pretend that you are striding along the outermost edge of the Roman Empire, the last line of defence between civilisation and the barbarians. Consider, too, that over a million cubic yards of stone were quarried in order to build not only the Wall but also the forts and many milecastles and turrets, a task that took a total of eight years.

Beyond the grass-covered remains of Great Chesters (the Roman infantry fort of Aesica) is the best-preserved stretch of Hadrian's Wall. The breathtaking roller-coaster that the Wall takes along the next few miles makes for exciting walking, although the exposed, dark grey cliffs of whinstone can leave the walker vulnerable in bad weather. After Winshields Crags, at 345m the highest point of the Whin Sill and from where the Galloway Hills can be visible, the

Pennine Way drops to cross a minor road. A mile to the south is Once Brewed Youth Hostel, next to the National Park's main information centre, where there are exhibitions and audio visual presentations, plus a small snack bar. Also nearby is the Twice Brewed Inn, and legend has it that the pub (originally sited half a mile to the east) acquired its name after a visit by General Wade who complained that the beer was not strong enough, and so made the innkeeper brew it a second time.

The Way now follows the Wall, occasionally along the top of it, but mostly by its side. There are views to the moors and murky forests, and of the picturesque Crag Lough below. If you are lucky enough to walk this section without running into a succession of other visitors it can be an extremely rewarding experience. However, some of the visitors will be other ramblers, since this is popular walking country; and in fact plans for a Hadrian's Wall long-distance footpath are currently under discussion. At the time of writing it is not clear when, if at all, this trail will officially come about. Nevertheless, the Wall continues to attract people keen to follow its coast to coast route, whether for the unspoilt scenery or its outstanding historical and archaeological importance.

The Way leaves the Wall at Rapishaw Gap, before Cuddy's Crags and the well-known Housesteads fort (Vercovicium) which boasts the only example of a Roman hospital in Britain, plus a latrine with flushing tank. Occasionally glancing back towards the Wall, head north across open ground before joining a wide track through Wark Forest, part of the Border Forest Park. Leave the track for a path out of the sitka spruces and on to the moors of Hawk Side. It is a quiet and lonely place here, more so since the route is back into the trees. Over a road, and after more plantations, emerge on Ground Rigg. Beyond Warks Burn is a succession of farmsteads and fields, and a quite gentle, pastoral landscape. Once across Houxty Burn pass the interestingly named Shitlington Hall to reach Bellingham via heather moorland east of Ealingham Rigg.

Bellingham is pronounced 'Bellinjum', and that's almost as lively as things get around here. It is said that the town deliberately made itself look grey and bleak in order to deter sixteenth-century border reivers from raiding the community. Whatever the excuse, there are shops, several pubs, and a nearby youth hostel; but it is not a beautiful place.

However, it is as well to stock up for the last couple of days of the

Pennine Way. The remaining 40 miles to Kirk Yetholm are tough and remote, and apart from a few isolated farms only Byrness Youth Hostel (no meals, no store) and Byrness Hotel offer any facilities.

Depart Bellingham on the road past the youth hostel, leaving it for Blakelaw Farm, and then over rising ground to moorland. Keep heading north, crossing the Bellingham–Otterburn road, and make for the cairned top of Deer Play, and then Whitley Pike. Routefinding is now greatly enhanced by the presence of a fence; follow this around Padon Hill to Brownrigg Head. The large cairned monument on Padon Hill was built in the 1920s to commemorate Alexander Padon, a Scottish Covenanter who held services at this spot. In clear weather the views are dominated by the smooth curves of the Cheviot Hills ahead.

The Pennine Way now dives into the edge of Kielder Forest. This is Britain's largest forest, and is another part of what is collectively known as the Border Forest Park, over 250 square miles of mostly artificially planted conifers. The forest tracks are at least distinct and firm, but many walkers find the overpowering stillness and gloom of the massed ranks of spruces depressing. There are a few birds, a few small creatures, but compare these miles to sunny Airedale, Upper Teesdale, or even Hadrian's Wall, and your heart will yearn for space and life. Still, these afforested miles at least allow you to muse on End to End highlights behind and still to come; and with Scotland fast approaching there will be more tree-lined miles in the next few weeks.

After what seems an age the clearings of Redesdale come into view, and at last something new to look at. Proceed along the valley by the River Rede, which also carries the busy A68 Edinburgh–Newcastle road (take great care when crossing it a little later), and past two farms locked in a battle to outdo each other for the longest place-name: Blackhopeburnhaugh and Cottonshopeburnfoot. Finally trudge into Byrness, a small and unlovely Forestry Commission settlement where most walkers make for the youth hostel. This village was one of several created by the Forestry Commission after the Second World War for forest workers. There is a café and post office, but the chief source of refreshment is provided by the Byrness Hotel, a couple of minutes' walk along the main road, and which provides bar meals. This is the only place on the last 45 miles of the Pennine Way where you can get a drink, so you may wish to enjoy the moment. However, do not enjoy it too much, for there are some tough miles ahead if you are counting on reaching Kirk Yetholm by tomorrow night.

It is 25 miles from Byrness to the end of the Pennine Way, but add on a couple more if you wish to ascend the Cheviot. Since there is little more than an isolated farm or two during this distance most people make an early start and set their sights on Kirk Yetholm, and if the weather is behaving itself the main problem for the fit End to Ender is likely to come from the boggy ground rather than personal stamina. Of course, if you are carrying a tent you don't have to worry so much about covering the full distance in one day.

The Pennine Way begins its last, long heave by heading straight up Byrness Hill. At the top you can look down on Redesdale, confident in the knowledge that there will be no more conifers to walk through until well into Scotland, while ahead there are once more expansive views of wild and open hillcountry – and this is your direction. Continue north to Houx Hill and Ravens Knowe. Notices on the land to the east indicate that it belongs to the MOD, so should conditions be poor and visibility limited rely on compass bearings and not luck. (The sound of roaring tanks and gunfire may also help identify your general location; preferably they should be distant.) The Upper Coquet Valley has been controlled by the military for over fifty years, and disputes over public access continue. The course of the Pennine Way is not in question, but should you want to explore the lovely hills to the east make sure that you check with Otterburn Training Area officials when live firing and manoeuvres are taking place.

Beyond Ogre Hill is the England–Scotland border fence. It is a satisfying moment to think that you have now walked the length of England, linking what are almost the nation's two most extreme points. However, there are still some hard miles until Kirk Yetholm, so save the celebrations for a few hours. Besides, the Way stays with the border fence for only a short distance before turning sharply to drop down by the infant River Coquet. At Chew Green there are the grassy remains of a Roman marching camp, and for a while the course of Dere Street is followed. A path across rough and sometimes boggy ground reunites you with the border fence – a vital routefinding aid – as it rolls high and majestically to the windy summits of Lamb Hill, Beefstand Hill and Mozie Law. From there make the direct but sharp ascent to the 619m top of Windy Gyle, and from this airy position enjoy a wide and uncluttered panorama that on a clear day includes Cross Fell and the Pennines, the Moorfoots and the Lammermuirs.

It may seem odd to wait until nearly the end of the Pennine Way before mentioning Tom Stephenson, the real founder of the trail, but out of all the miles of wild and dramatic upland scenery along the Way, it was the lonely Cheviot Hills that were closest to his heart. This admirable man, long-time secretary of the Ramblers' Association, first floated the idea of 'a long green trail' as far back as 1935, but it was not until thirty years later that the Pennine Way was officially opened at a ceremony on Malham Moor. Stephenson reckoned the 'great heaving swells and deep-set glens' of the Cheviots the finest of all, and as you walk along the Cheviot ridge from Windy Gyle to King's Seat be thankful for the years of dedication that he poured into the 250-mile route.

However, as you follow the border fence north-west towards the huge lump of the Cheviot you may have other thoughts on your mind – or on your feet. Even if the weather is fine, the ground is usually waterlogged, and the rough going across the peat hags is arduous. As you squelch up to Cairn Hill the prospect of an extra couple of miles to take in the summit of the Cheviot may not be too appealing, and much will depend on the weather, hours left in the day, etc, as to whether you choose to visit the 815m top. Ultimately much depends on your whole End to End outlook. If you view the Walk as a chance to scale the heights and explore the hidden corners of the country, then a short detour to the top of the Cheviot is recommended.

To reach Kirk Yetholm from the mess on Cairn Hill, follow the path by the border fence around the head of the College valley to the Schil. There is a mountain refuge hut near Hen Hole, since this high and lonely spot can be dangerous in bad weather. Make sure that you pay the Cheviots the respect that these remote hills deserve.

Descend the Schil, the last major hill on the Way, and cross the border into Scotland for good. There is now a choice of routes for the last few miles. The first is low-level, a useful bad weather alternative, and follows a track by Halter Burn to Burnhead Farm. The other sticks to the border ridge, over Steer Rigg to White Law, from where there are fine views to the Tweed valley and even the North Sea. Descend via a clear track to a quiet, metalled road for the last mile of the Pennine Way.

The meadows and trees around Kirk Yetholm and Bowmont Water appear soft and civilised after so many desolate miles of bare hilltop. Pennine Way walkers will throw off their rucksacks in a mixture of relief and sadness; but with exhaustion above all else. However, for you this is only one chapter of a far greater epic. While your fellow Pennine Way walkers will be looking up the bus timetables to Kelso next morning, you will be lacing up the boots once more. The Pennine Way, and England, is over; now the delights of Scotland are to come.

5

THROUGH SCOTLAND'S HEART

Kirk Yetholm – Aberfeldy

KIRK YETHOLM – SELKIRK (35.5 miles)
After the rigours of the Pennine Way, and especially after the crossing of the Cheviot Hills, it is tempting to stay in Kirk Yetholm, either at the Border Hotel ('The end of the Pennine Way' is helpfully painted in four-foot-high letters on the side of the building) or the youth hostel, depending on your budget. Those successfully completing the Pennine Way are traditionally rewarded with a free half pint of beer at the hotel (it was originally a whole pint, but Wainwright – who first made the offer – found demand too high!). However, since you have walked about 740 continuous miles and not the Pennine Way's derisory 250-odd, a half pint seems scant reward. Kirk Yetholm was once famous for its gypsies, after sixteenth- and seventeenth-century persecution had driven many to the safety of the undisturbed Border hills. Charles Faa Blythe was the last gypsy king to be crowned, in 1898, and the event is reported to have attracted thousands of spectators to the village.

Apart from hotel and YH, there is really nothing else to waylay you. Town Yetholm, just over Bowmont Water, has a little more life, but you may wish to press on to Kelso now that you are exploring Scotland. The town is 8 miles away, but it is best to ignore the B6352, which is rather narrow, in favour of an extra, quieter mile over Venchen Hill to Hoselaw Loch. From this open piece of water there are great views back to the Cheviots. Forwards, follow a succession of deserted minor roads (and first a farm track) and thread your way into Kelso.

Kelso is an attractive and busy Border town, and it may be the case that determined walkers who have camped the previous night will want to omit an overnight stay in Kirk Yetholm and instead enjoy the choice of B&B, pubs and hotels that Kelso offers – for a celebratory first night in Scotland. Just around the corner from the central, cobbled square is Kelso Abbey, founded by King David I in 1128 when he gave revenues and land to Tironensian monks from France. After centuries of Border warring it fell to the Earl of Hertford finally to destroy the Abbey, in 1545, as part of Henry VIII's so-called 'Rough Wooing', when he attempted to force the Scots to accept the marriage of his son Edward to Mary (later Queen of Scots).

Kelso is also the place where introductions to the finest river in southern Scotland are made: the River Tweed. Here the river sweeps wide and majestically, and it will be your intermittent companion until Peebles. The Tweed is 97 miles long, contains sixteen types of fish, and because of its natural importance the whole Tweed basin has been designated an SSSI. Fine views of the river are to be had from the grounds of Floors Castle, on the banks north of Kelso, which is open Easter to September; it makes for a relaxing and scenic afternoon stroll should you have an hour or two to spare.

Leave Kelso by the Selkirk road, and once over the Teviot bridge descend to the riverside path by the remains of Roxburgh Castle. There is little left of this once Royal residence, since constant Scots–English warring led to its virtual demolition and the removal of the whole village to its present site two miles up the River Teviot.

Once at Roxburgh there are several small lanes that can be linked together to prevent contact with the A699 until Maxton, where you cross and enter woodland before emerging on the banks of the Tweed at Benrig. The footpath along the bank to Newton St Boswells and Leaderfoot is attractive but sometimes unclear among the trees, and local people tell me that it can be difficult after heavy rain. Across a footbridge are the ruins of Dryburgh Abbey, where Sir Walter Scott is buried, and on the same bank a little upstream is 'Scott's View' on Bemersyde Hill, from where you too can gaze adoringly at the Eildon Hills.

There are plenty of places to stay as you enter Melrose (look for the distinctive blue B&B signs outside buildings), including a youth hostel, but this charming place is often crowded in high season. One reason is Melrose Abbey, another the Motor Museum, but more than this it is due to the proximity of the Eildon Hills. A jaunt up these bosomy volcanic lumps is highly recommended, although the waymarked 'Eildon Walk' is becoming severely eroded in places, and in these areas you should observe the official notices which read: 'No access please: your feet are killing me.' The hills are best known through the pen of Sir Walter Scott, although it is told that his namesake, Michael Scott, wizard and scholar (1175–1230), was responsible for cutting the Eildon Hills into three parts after a challenge by the devil. The present-day challenge is likely to be from other walkers and tourists jostling for camera angles, or from the army who fire at things on their range to the west of you at weekends.

The Sir Walter connection is everywhere. Head west along lanes from Melrose to Abbotsford, Scott's attractive tree-cushioned house by the Tweed, which is open to the public between March and October. Then take a drovers' road up by Cauldshiels Loch and once more you are alone on the hillside.

Selkirk is the destination, little more than 2 miles away, and is the home of a large and filling sugary cake, the Selkirk Bannock, which is packed with raisins and peel, and is a desirable if weighty addition to any walker's rucksack. Here, too, is the 'Common Riding', an annual event that takes place in the summer with local people parading on horseback to commemorate the return of the sole Selkirk survivor from Flodden Fields.

SELKIRK – EDINBURGH (47 miles)

Leave town steeply down to the rugby pitches by Ettrick Water, and prepare for the hills once more. If the weather is particularly bad one option is to follow the road along Yarrow Water to Yarrowford, near Broadmeadows Youth Hostel, from where the green and broad Minchmoor Road provides an easy climb up to Hare Law. Otherwise follow the rough path up Long Philip Burn and join the Southern Upland Way near the Three Brethren, which are three stone cairns that mark the boundary of Selkirk Burgh, Yair and Philiphaugh. Now that you are once more on an official long-distance footpath, the 212-mile Southern Upland Way, look out for wooden posts bearing white thistle waymarks, should you need guidance. This section is another old drove road, which weaves its way across the grassy tops towards Traquair Forest. Your main company are likely to be pipits, skylarks and sheep – the latter breeds will probably be Border Leicester or Cheviot. There are a few places where the going is a little boggy, but by and large this is fine, airy walking. It is a route that centuries ago Scottish monarchs took on leaving Traquair House for hunting expeditions, and was also used by the Marquis of Montrose in 1645 as he fled from the Royalists after the Battle of Philiphaugh (on Ettrick Water, near Selkirk).

The Minchmoor Road descends across forest tracks to the hamlet of Traquair, where there is a massive World War monument, a phone box, and not much else. Where the Southern Upland Way forks left take the lane straight ahead, past Traquair House. 'See the secret stairs and spooky cellars,' implores the promotional leaflet to what is claimed to be the oldest continuously inhabited house in Scotland. Then continue along the B7062, by the Tweed once more. Just to the north is Innerleithen, with B&Bs and campsite, should you not have the time or energy to make Peebles. Cardrona Forest is accessible, and there are several waymarked routes. However, since they are all circular there is not much point venturing into the conifers, and I suggest that you remain on this relatively quiet road (most of the traffic uses the A72 across the river), which is part of the Tweed Cycleway, for the 7½ miles to Peebles.

Like Kelso, Melrose and Selkirk, Peebles is yet another interesting and agreeable Border town. An evening stroll along the Tweed to Neidpath Castle is highly recommended, as is a pint on your return by the open fire in the Crown, in the High Street.

The Peebles–West Linton section may seem messy and confusing at a glance, but in fact if you pay close attention to the OS map as you walk there should be few problems. Leave Peebles by Young Street, where there is a signpost for Rosetta, and after passing a large caravan and campsite take the public footpath 'Hamilton Hill to the Meldons'. At Upper Kidston Farm join a surfaced track, and follow this across bare and exposed land to the impressive-looking Stewarton farmhouse, from where a track leads up into the trees on the ridge. Descend around Green Knowe and down Fingland Burn to Romannobridge, where the Romanno Inn provides both food and drink. West Linton is only a couple of miles away, but despite shops and three hotels there are few B&Bs and no campsite. But the Lynton Hotel is a cheery place for a meal, even if you can't afford to stay the night there.

Now the only obstacle that remains between you and Edinburgh are the Pentland Hills. There are a number of clear and direct tracks over and through the Regional Park, any one of which will get you nearer to Edinburgh and, mist notwithstanding, will offer good views. Many of these paths have been in use for centuries. For instance, West Linton to Harperrig Reservoir (7 miles) via Cauldstaneslap provides a fine and satisfyingly direct crossing. Or, further to the north-east a public footpath from Nine Mile Burn leads up and on to West Kip, East Kip, Scald Law and Carnethy Hill. These last two summits are the highest on the Pentlands (around 580m), and between them runs an old kirk road, or corpse road, which was used for taking the dead from isolated farms and hamlets to the parish church for burial. However, bear in mind that the tops of the Pentlands are rough and exposed, and it is sensible to stick carefully to rights of way, particularly in late April–May when grouse, partridge, pheasants and merlin are all nesting. From July to September the ling and bell heather provide a wonderful purple and pink carpet, and an extended wander is recommended – but keep a watchful eye out for grouse shooting after 12th August, when access may be restricted, and for some army activity on the northern slopes.

My suggested route makes for the lane off the busy A702 opposite West Linton (signposted 'Baddinsgill'), then turn right where a Scottish Rights of Way Society signpost indicates Carlops. Once there, ignore the metalled track up into the hills and instead take the path a little further on from the bridge at the northern end of the village. North Esk Reservoir should be kept on your right, and after a mile and a half of sometimes rough walking you will reach the rocky outcrop of Bore Stane. The path then drops into the valley of Bavelaw Burn, and at Listonshiels turn right on to a straight drive, eventually turning off for Threipmuir Reservoir, and Red Moss Nature Reserve. A track extends to the tree-lined Harlaw Reservoir, from where there are lanes and paths into Balerno. Here you can join the Water of Leith Walkway (the former Balerno Branch Railway line) for 4 miles to Slateford, and into the heart of Edinburgh.

Your grand route up the centre of England and through the Scottish Borders has finally come to an end. Now you face the supreme challenge: the Highlands and the Far North. Ease your pack off and relax for an evening, for ahead the real hills begin!

EDINBURGH – ABERFELDY (82 miles)
As you leave the Scottish capital and head north there is a tremendous sense of progress, and of entering a new and altogether fresh phase of the Walk. The Tweed at Berwick is a handsome divide between the two countries (even if the border is actually a few miles to the north), but as you walk up the Firth of Forth from Edinburgh and approach the two mighty Forth bridges, it is as if a new kingdom awaits. True, the Highlands do not really start until after Perth, but the sense of adventure is keen, and the impetus to press on is greater than ever.

From the city centre head for the Firth of Forth at Granton Point or Muirhouse. There is an easy, surfaced path along the waterfront, which provides a scenic route to the mouth of the River Almond. Here a brief detour upstream to Cramond Bridge is required if you choose not to take the foot ferry. If this is the case you may have to seek permission to enter the grounds of Dalmeny House in order to return to the shore path, which is open to the public all the year round. Dalmeny House is the home of the Earl and Countess of Roseberry, and can be visited at certain times. Otherwise skirt the handsome, wooded Park and continue to Queensferry.

The Forth Road Bridge has secure, partitioned gangways for cyclists and pedestrians, to whom the crossing is free. Perhaps the best views are from the northern end of the road bridge, looking back towards the railway bridge. This phenomenal structure holds the attention far more than the modern road crossing, and on the north side of the latter there are steps that take you safely under the A90 and down into North Queensferry, allowing a stop for lunch at a firth-side picnic site directly underneath the massive girders of the 104-year-old feat of engineering. North Queensferry has shops and a couple of small hotels, but it is likely that you will want to press on, now that the mountains are approaching, so at the junction of Main Street and Kirk Road take the track underneath the bridge by Waterloo Well. From the hillside there are good views of the Firth of Forth and around the Fife coastline, which is your route for the next few hours. The Fife Coast Path theoretically stretches from nearby Inverkeithing via Leven and St Andrews to Newburgh, on the Firth of Tay, although both waymarking and documentation is sketchy and there is no complete, continuous path. However, for the curious or intrepid there are miles of interesting and sometimes glorious coastline to explore, and although it would naturally add many extra miles you would not end too far away from Perth, where the main Central Route could be resumed.

The Fife Coast Path is particularly notable for its variety, and that is certainly true of the opening section, which is intermittently indicated by brown finger posts. Beyond Port Laing beach you have to walk the pavement around Inner Bay, where there is a fascinating if gruesome marine breaker's yard, with hundreds of rusting hulls and pieces of dead ship. Then before the railway bridge at Inverkeithing turn back towards the water and around a large paper mill. Inverkeithing received its first Royal Charter from William the Lion in 1159, making it one of the oldest in Scotland. Today, the thirteenth-century tower of St Peter's Church, plus the Burgh Museum at the fourteenth-century Friary, are worth pausing over; then follow the road out past the former Prestonhill greenstone quarry to the shore. Ahead is a new development called St David's Harbour Village. At the time of inspection it was little more than a sprawling building site, but it is hoped that the course of the coast path should not be drastically altered.

Continue around Downing Point, and after some more modern houses take the clear track along Dalgety Bay to woodland. Whilst it may not be a dramatic stretch of coast in terms of cliffs or beaches, it is certainly peaceful, and you should be rewarded with views over the Firth of Forth to the distinctive upthrust of Arthur's Seat, above Edinburgh, with the Pentland Hills in the far distance. But it is now necessary to join lanes in order to reach Aberdour, and so avoid the oil terminal at Braefoot Bay. The coastal path is clearly waymarked as it passes a golf course and enters Aberdour, a village in two parts, separated by the Dour Burn. Here there are a few shops and a ruined castle, plus an attractive harbour. But unless you are keen to stay with the Fife coast it is time to head inland, and set your sights on Perth.

From Aberdour take the small Fordell road north-westwards, staying alert to the danger of the occasional heavy lorry emerging from Goat Quarry. There is a track that can be followed along the crest of the wooded Cullaloe Hills, but since this emerges on the narrow and busy A909 near the Fife Ethylene Plant it is not as attractive as it first seems. At Fordell cut across to the B981, and proceed north via Hill of Beath to Kelty. This brief section of roadwalking is not particularly attractive, but at least it is short-lived. Press briskly on, and at Kelty head a short distance east to the B996 and enter the grounds of Lochore Meadows Country Park by a small car park (signposted). This land reclamation project has turned former industrial land into an attractive outdoor park that now hosts pony trekking, golf and orienteering. The loch itself is used by canoeists and windsurfers, as well as trout fishermen, and it is the north shore that you should now follow to the edge of Ballingry. Ahead is the prominent lump of Benarty Hill, which can be reached either by Forestry Commission tracks up the southern slopes, or from the east via Ballingry Farm (seek permission before crossing their land). The summit may only be 356m, but if the weather is good the views are impressive, particularly northwards. At your feet lies Loch Leven, a national nature reserve, and on the far shore is Kinross, your next destination. Edge around to the viewpoint on the northernmost slopes of the hill, for here the RSPB have an instructive viewfinding board (Denmark is apparently 640 miles away!). A clear path leads down to the RSPB's Vane Farm visitor centre on the road beneath, where you can learn about some of the fifty species of birds that breed in the vicinity each year, or the 250 species of plants recorded on the reserve. Geese, and in particular the pink-footed variety, turn up in thousands here every autumn to winter. Now either follow roads around the west of the loch to Kinross, or if you are feeling fit then turn right and take an excursion into the attractive Lomond Hills.

Kinross offers both accommodation and shops, and after Milnathort head directly north on a minor road over the M90 to the hamlet of Middleton. At Newhill fork left, and then at Temple Hill depart the lane for an unsignposted track, leaving this just before Craigfarg for a quiet green lane which emerges on to hillside above Glenfarg Reservoir. The dirt track ahead is obvious, from the dam to Auchengownie, after which it rejoins a small, surfaced lane at woods near Rossie Ochil. (There is also the option of simply staying with the narrow, tarmac lane via Pathstruie.) This is the eastern end of the Ochils, a relatively low but nevertheless scenic band of hills between Stirling and Perth. It provides a welcome return to quieter and less populous surroundings, with rabbits and skylarks more likely to be companions than humans. And should you not want to sample the Fife Coast Path then there is ample opportunity to craft your own route through the heart of the Ochils after crossing the Forth – study the relevant maps.

Two narrow lanes follow the Water of May down to the River

Earn, near Forteviot. Once over the river turn sharp right and head for Perth. The grounds of Dupplin Castle are private, which means a couple of miles' roadwalking to reach Perth; alternatively, take the minor road east at Aberdalgie and head over Kirkton Hill instead.

Perth is the only place of any real size before Inverness, the other side of the Cairngorms, and although there will of course be shops and stores along the way it may be a good idea to buy a few items now. There is a youth hostel, plus an array of charming Georgian terraces and buildings about the town. Perth was once the capital of Scotland, after Kenneth MacAlpin became the first king of a united nation in AD 838, and it was he that made nearby Scone an important royal centre (all forty-two kings of Scotland have been crowned here).

To leave, take the track along the west bank of the Tay northwards. The River Tay is Scotland's longest river, measuring 100 miles from its source in the mountains above Loch Tay to its estuary in the Firth of Tay. Across the open grass of North Inch is Balhousie Castle, where the Black Watch Regimental Museum is situated. Proceed up the wide river; a small detour will be necessary to cross the River Almond, then leave the Tay at Luncarty, and after scampering over and along the A9 for a few yards, turn off by Newmill Farm (B&B) for the peace and quiet of a country lane that heads straight for the hills (signposted Tullybelton). Veer left along another lane for Little Glenshee, which consists of not much more than a farm and outhouses, and where there is a public footpath sign for Strathbraan. Perth is often referred to as the gateway to the Highlands, and with this track through Glen Shee you are finally entering the big stuff.

However, it should be pointed out that Glen Shee is not especially severe, and the track is fairly easy and unmistakable (there are even a few yellow direction arrows). And yet the views are first class, and after miles of farmland and low hills here, finally, is the mountainside and heather moorland that you have been waiting for.

At this juncture it is as well to issue a couple of words of warning re walking in the Scottish hills, however old hat it may be to some. First, do not think that just because you have walked all the way from Cornwall you are tougher than the elements. Even in the height of summer the Scottish hills can prove dangerous – especially in places as remote as the Cairngorms – so make sure you are adequately equipped. In addition, there are of course only limited places to stay for those without a tent, and with sometimes dozens of miles between places to buy food it calls for careful preparation. Second, the date that you walk the hills is all important, since grouse shooting and deer stalking can put some land out of bounds between mid-August and mid-October. There are a number of shooting butts by the Glen Shee track in Strathbraan, for example, so it is wise to contact the appropriate estate should you be in any doubt. A full list of addresses can be found in *Heading for the Scottish Hills*, produced by the Mountaineering Council of Scotland and the Scottish Landowners' Federation.

When you reach the A822 from Glen Shee turn left, and in less than a mile turn right for the pass to Aberfeldy. Amulree, a little further down the road, was where the clans gathered for the 1715 Jacobite Rebellion, and now has a hotel and tea rooms. There are forest tracks up the east of Glen Cochill, if you want to avoid the road, or better still search out General Wade's Military Road. It is rather indistinct early on among the thick heather, but as the ground rises the course becomes apparent, and it can be followed for some considerable way until near Loch na Craige. There, the present A826 takes it over for a little time, and you should follow its direction and descend rapidly into Aberfeldy.

For those wishing a wilder and more desolate course, albeit rather longer, consider Glen Almond. There are a few tracks and useful minor roads along the lower reaches of the River Almond from the Tay, but after Newton Bridge the mountains gather and the tarmac ends, and a lone signpost points to the hills: 'Path to Loch Tay'. Although the track is long the height is modest and the gradient generally gentle, and when you eventually arrive at the loch a minor road leads to Kenmore, and then a hillside track to Aberfeldy.

6

THE WILDERNESS MILES

Aberfeldy – Inverness

ABERFELDY – INVERNESS (91 miles)
Aberfeldy may be small, but it still boasts two supermarkets and, more curiously, a rather grand amusement arcade. From here your route is down the river as far as Strathtay, then over hillside to Pitlochry. Begin by crossing the Tay at Aberfeldy, then it is easiest to walk the minor road along the north bank, through patches of attractive mixed woodland, leaving it at Strathtay where a Scottish Rights of Way Society signpost indicates a public footpath to Pitlochry. Its course is gentle, skirting a golf course, then ambling over rising hillside before entering woodland on the eastern shoulder of Dunfallandy Hill. There are handy signposts here and there, and in a clearing in the trees are a number of standing stones. Leave the woods above Pitlochry and join a metalled lane that enters the town by the Festival Theatre.

At first glance the Victorian holiday resort of Pitlochry appears to be made up solely of hotels and knitwear shops. However, there is a youth hostel, campsite and many B&Bs, and afterwards an excellent route along the River Garry by Loch Faskally to the Pass of Killiecrankie, much of it a pathway through woodland (there are a number of nature and forest trails, as well). At the Killiecrankie Visitor Centre you can learn about the famous battle that was fought here in 1689, when a Jacobite army under 'Bonnie Dundee' routed Government troops from England. Despite river, road and railway squeezing through, the gorge remains impressive.

Blair Atholl is three miles away, reached by a quiet lane along the Garry's east bank (most traffic keeps to the two roads on the other side of the water) which leads to a track and then a footbridge over the river. Blair Atholl is smaller than Pitlochry, but Blair Castle dwarfs any of Pitlochry's stately hotels, in terms of both grandeur and authenticity. It is the home of the Duke of Atholl, and of the Atholl Highlanders, the only private army in Britain.

This is also the place where the End to End Central Route finally summons up courage and heads into the serious hills. While the A9 goes roaring off to Kingussie, you should now head north-west up Glen Tilt into the heart of the Grampian Mountains, making for the famous Lairig Ghru crossing of the Cairngorms. Ahead are many miles of peaceful and unspoilt walking; and although there is ample opportunity to bag a few Munros on the way, or take a 'day off' and visit some new places, the cross-mountain routes described here follow definite tracks and should present no real difficulty if you are adequately equipped and know exactly where you are. Those not carrying a tent would do well to book a bed at Inverey Youth Hostel in advance. It may be fairly strenuous walking at times, but unless the weather deteriorates (in which case turn back or modify your route) the next 30 miles should be among the most scenic and enjoyable of the whole trip.

The route up Glen Tilt is a designated Scottish Right of Way, officially established in 1853 after the 6th Duke of Atholl was taken to court for refusing access to a Professor Balfour and his party of botany students from Edinburgh. For the first few miles you can either take the track from the caravan site near the castle, or from Fenderbridge on the east bank of the Tilt. The two come together at Gilbert's Bridge, and then at Gow's Bridge, by Marble Lodge, after which the main track sticks to the west bank. Continue on the straightforward riverside track, as the steep-sided glen adopts an unerringly direct approach. At the Falls of Tarf the Scottish Rights of Way Society have provided an elegant footbridge over a treacherous ravine. The bridge was constructed in 1886, and was dedicated to the memory of an eighteen-year-old boy who drowned in the river a few years before.

Herds of red deer are common in this area, and you are likely to see more during your passage through the Cairngorms. Make your way along the glen to Bynack Lodge, where Queen Victoria took tea during her journey through the hills in 1861, although today it is a ruin; and it is also an area which can be boggy in wet weather.

This is a wild and desolate place, and apart from the old walls of the lodge there is little cover. However, the Dee is not far ahead, but Geldie Burn – like Bynack Burn before it – may present problems if it is in spate, when it should be treated with great care (wading may be necessary). Once on the other side there is a clear track again. If you follow it west up the Geldie Burn you eventually cross over to Glen Feshie, which can be walked the whole length to Feshiebridge, and then on to Aviemore. This option is rather easier, if longer, than the Lairig Ghru ahead, but at the same time it is less spectacular and involves many miles of exposed and remote moorland scenery. I suggest that you continue for a further mile past plantations to White Bridge, over the River Dee.

Should you need fixed accommodation then carry on along the track by the river to the Linn of Dee. Inverey Youth Hostel is nearby, and Braemar about another five miles after that. This is also the direction in which you should head, at least initially, if you perhaps already know the Lairig Ghru and wish to use the more easterly crossing known as the Lairig an Laoigh (via Linn of Dee, Glen Derry, Fords of Avon, and finally arriving at Loch Morlich from the east).

Sticking with the main route, turn left immediately after White Bridge and begin the approach to one of the most celebrated of Scottish mountain passes, the Lairig Ghru. It was formerly a drove road for cattle, and has been a regular thoroughfare for local people and travellers linking Deeside and Speyside for centuries. The track is well-established, although it is rather rocky and uneven on the descent the other side. But for now it keeps above the infant River Dee, whose tight meanders are dwarfed by the towering summits of Braeriach, Cairn Toul and Ben Macdui (the fourth, third and second highest mountains in the UK respectively). The landscape is simply awesome; and if the weather is unsettled this giant glacial trough can really live up to its Gaelic name of the 'gloomy' or 'forbidding' pass. With so much high ground about (many of the peaks are above 1,200m) it is worth keeping a careful eye on the weather as well as on the mountains themselves, since conditions can change suddenly. In this high, rugged terrain, also stay alert for birds and wildlife that you would not normally expect to see in the lowlands, such as golden eagle, ptarmigan and snow bunting.

The path plods and sometimes squelches up to the Pools of Dee, underneath steep, smooth slopes on one side and high, wild corries on the other. It is from around here that the royal river begins its long descent to Aberdeen. It is worth pointing out that the summit of the Lairig Ghru is itself 835m high, so not surprisingly it is a windy and exposed place. There is next to no shelter; even the Sinclair Hut on the northern side has been removed due to persistent misuse. The descent northwards is long and bumpy, even though path restoration work has been carried out in some places. The Cairngorms is a popular walking venue, and you are likely to meet more walkers and backpackers here than you have done for some time.

As the view over the coniferous plantations around Aviemore widen, you should decide which direction to take out of the Lairig Ghru. The main track leads through lovely pines and heather to Coylumbridge, a mile from Aviemore, but if possible I would forego the dubious charms of the 'all-the-year-round resort' and instead take the right fork through the rocky Chalamain Gap to the Cairngorm road and Loch Morlich. Even though it involves some more ascent it is shorter than carrying on to Coylumbridge. There is also a turning a mile or so later signposted 'Rothiemurchus Lodge', but this route can be very boggy and is in fact not a proper right of way.

Loch Morlich is almost entirely surrounded by thick woodland, but attracts outdoor enthusiasts of every description, and at its eastern end there is a large campsite with showers and shop, Loch Morlich Youth Hostel, and Glenmore Lodge visitor centre. Nearby you can observe Britain's only free-ranging reindeer herd, and if you fancy a day's diversion you could even wander up to the restaurant on the slopes of the Cairngorm (there is a chairlift for the weary).

To continue to Inverness, join the beginning of a track from the road at the western end of Loch Morlich, signposted 'Public footpath to Milton of Kincardine'. It is long and direct and, since it runs almost entirely over forest land, appropriate care must be exercised if felling is in progress. The track finally emerges on the B970, where you should turn right and walk along the road past Highland Drovers, an off-road driving centre (where jeeps and not cows are driven), and into Boat of Garten. 'The osprey village', as it calls itself, has B&Bs and shops, and is the northern terminus for the Strathspey Steam Railway. Two miles away, and in far quieter surroundings, ospreys may be seen at the RSPB's reserve on Loch Garten.

Leave Boat of Garten by the road westwards (pavement) and

cross under the railway on a gated lane that leads off at the junction of the A95 and B9153. Take the utmost care when crossing the A9, and then enter the drive of Kinveachy Lodge. Almost immediately turn right on to a rough track, and follow it past some cottages to a junction of tracks where you must bear left. This is another of General Wade's Military Roads, a peaceful thoroughfare that is still used by walkers and cyclists, and which remains a public right of way. It runs over the forested hillside to Sluggan, then around Inverlaidnan Hill to Ishnarn and Slochd Mor. General Wade was appointed Commander-in-Chief of North Britain in 1725, and his intensive programme of road-building was intended to aid the speedy movement of government troops around the Highlands in order to counter any further Jacobite unrest. By 1765, Wade, and his Inspector of Roads, William Caulfeild (a name often misspelt), had overseen the construction of over 1,000 miles of carefully engineered roads, and such was the craftsmanship that much still remains today. The End to End West Route borrows some along the West Highland Way (most notably the Devil's Staircase near Glencoe), and you should have already walked some of Wade's handiwork between Strathbraan and Aberfeldy.

At Slochd summit the modern A9 closes in, but there is a safe track off the road for all but a few yards, and then you should take the minor road that branches off to Findhorn Bridge. Wade's route takes to the hillside opposite, but from this point on it only survives in small bursts. Instead, I suggest that after the rather unlovely concrete arches of Findhorn Bridge (built in 1926 to replace Telford's 1833 original) you turn left and follow the single-track lane up Strathdearn to Garbole. It is a gentle and serene place, bypassed by all but the most curious traveller. At Garbole there is a gated track over high, heather moors towards Inverness. It is unlikely that you will meet anyone at all on this rough, unfenced road, and the sense of wilderness returns quite strongly, reinforced by a distant vista of mountains to the north. Then from Strathnairn there are several combinations of minor roads that will take you the last few miles into Inverness.

[illegible] and then along the line of Kirkcudbright [illegible]

[illegible] Devil's Bridge [illegible]

[illegible]

7

THE LAST LAP

Inverness – John o'Groats

INVERNESS – BRORA (69 miles)

Inverness, 'the Capital of the Highlands', has all that you may expect of such a place: burger bars, Marks & Spencer, a large industrial estate, and so on. To be fair, there is also a highland music centre and pleasant walks along the River Ness underneath the nineteenth-century castle, the earlier version having been blown up in the Jacobite Rebellion of 1745. But after sitting impatiently at the launderette for an hour you may simply want to resume walking once more. Ahead is the last leg, the final push, and this is brought home as you approach Kessock Bridge, an impressive modern structure that carries the A9 over the narrow gap between the Beauly and Moray Firths to the Black Isle (there is a safe pedestrian walkway). A roadsign says: John o'Groats 120 miles. It seems that you are almost there!

The views from the bridge across the Beauly Firth to both the town and the mountains westwards are superb, but the din of the traffic will soon be insufferable, so unless you want to visit the tourist information centre a little further along the road take a lane immediately left which drops down to the shore at North Kessock. This former fishing community once enjoyed a local importance for its small, sweet herrings, but today it is a quiet and rather forgotten place. Leave North Kessock by a lovely lane that snakes along the shoreline westwards, and if you are alert you may see seals, porpoises and dolphins. A few miles to the east, in the Moray Firth, killer whales and minke are occasional visitors.

Unless you want to go to Muir of Ord (in which case take roads west) cross the A832 at Milton for a green lane to Drynie Park and Bishop Kinkell, then to Conon Bridge.

Dingwall is only another couple of miles further on, but if you want to avoid the main road altogether then consider meeting the alternative West Route at Strathpeffer – there are forest tracks south of Loch Ussie, or better still a path along the north bank of the River Conon to Moy Island.

Strathpeffer's early popularity was due to its spa waters, and you can still try the local sulphur waters of the Morrison Wells in the sampling pavilion in the square. An official sign reads: 'Visitors are welcome to sample the spa waters if they wish. Please note, however, that the water comes direct from underground wells and has not been treated in any way. It should not, therefore, be regarded as regular drinking water and should only be consumed in small quantities.' Not surprisingly it tastes revolting, and the smell is even worse. But apart from its water Strathpeffer is an agreeable place, with many grand old hotels, a large number of B&Bs and a youth hostel, all dotted around a narrow, leafy valley.

Leave Strathpeffer for the Forestry Commission's plantation on the slopes of Cnoc Mor, either by the lane next to the youth hostel or the turning before the visitor centre. There are various waymarked trails, plus a newly built and very curious cross between a maze and a stone circle. Take either of two tracks out of the woodland and on to Knock Farril, a small but elevated grassy ridge that is the domain of rabbits and buzzards. It also has one of the best examples of a vitrified fort in northern Scotland. Built around 700–500 BC, the fort's stone walls fused together after the intense burning of its wooden casing caused a dramatic combustion. From the ramparts there are good views back over Strathpeffer, looking almost Alpine from above, and in the other direction to the Cromarty Firth and Dingwall. Approach the latter down the lane below the hill. Despite its modest size, Dingwall has been an important administrative centre since Viking times, and its name derives from the Norse word 'Thingvolls', meaning parliament or place of justice. Today it is the county town of Ross-shire, and has the full range of services.

With under a week's walking left, how are you going to reach John o'Groats? As the end approaches, paths and tracks become increasingly scarce, and there are even fewer and fewer roads. The obvious route to John o'Groats is along the narrow coastal strip towards Wick, but this is occupied by the A9, a fast and busy highway that I do not recommend walkers to use for any more than the shortest of distances. From Helmsdale to Lybster the A9 is the *only* feasible route (path or road) along the coast, unless you want to battle over rough, heather-topped cliffs and through deep ravines. There is no continuous coast path, and few inland tracks. This is why I recommend following the north-east coast for as far as realistically possible. There is some shore walking at Dornoch and from Golspie to just after Brora, then from near here is a rarely used lane off the A9 that climbs into the hills. After a while this joins the quiet, single-track A897 all the way to the north coast at Melvich. *An alternative route is to head for Bonar Bridge and Lairg, then paths over the hills to Loch Choire and Loch Badanloch; or further north via Loch Nave to Bettyhill.* It is as well to remember that apart from places such as Lairg and the coastal villages there are few shops and even fewer places to stay. If you walk into the hills you will have to be self-sufficient and fully prepared, and while there is plenty of scope to devise your own route over the moors and high ground, bear in mind that hunting, fishing and so on is taken seriously by the estates in this remote area, and unauthorised visitors can be unwelcome.

The easiest way to reach Tain from Dingwall is to follow minor roads that shadow the A9, through Evanton, Alness and an extensive area of forest. A more interesting way is to work a passage along hill and woodland tracks from the Strathpeffer valley to Glen Glass, then over the Fyrish Monument on Cnoc Fyrish. The Fyrish Monument, a curious local landmark, is a replica of the gateway to Negapatam, an Indian town sacked by General Sir Hector Munro of Novar in 1871, and was built simply to provide work for local people. Plunging back into the conifers, head up Strath Rusdale for a track towards Bonar Bridge, should that be your direction, otherwise make for the Morangie Forest (from the burns of which the famous Glen Morangie whisky draws its water), possibly via Strath Rory and the Iron Age fort at Cnoc an Duin.

Tain and Dornoch are two pleasant towns that sit either side of the Dornoch Firth. Both offer modern amenities, including accommodation, but both are rich in heritage. Tain is a Royal Burgh that was granted its first Charter over 900 years ago, and of particular interest is St Duthac Memorial Church (St Duthac was born in Tain about the year 1000, and his relics were returned here from Ireland 250 years later), and the medieval-looking Tolbooth in the centre of the town. To cross the Firth, popular with sunbathing seals, pass the distillery and take the new, wide road bridge. Once on the other side turn right for the 'Cuthill' lane to Dornoch, or else walk the edge of the sands (the firmest section is from the Point into the town). Some visitors come here just to play the world-famous golf course, but I suggest that you spend a few minutes in the thirteenth-century cathedral. Dornoch was also the site of the last witch-burning in Scotland, in 1722, after a woman purportedly turned her daughter into a pony.

There is a track by the golf course north via Embo to Skelbo, on the shore of Loch Fleet. Skelbo Castle was built originally of wood, in 1259, and although now in ruins is still picturesque. It is necessary to walk the A9 around the head of Loch Fleet, a nature reserve managed by the Scottish Wildlife Trust where cormorant, shelduck, eider and wigeon all visit. Then leave the road and cut through to the long, sandy beach by the links and enter Golspie.

Golspie is not overly large, but is the administrative centre for Sutherland. By the Sutherland Estate offices, as you exit the town on the A9, take a short lane (Duke Street) to a footbridge. Follow orange signs across the coastal fields of Dairy Park, part of a local network of waymarked trails, and past Dunrobin Castle. The beautiful, turreted castle is the ancestral home of the Earls of Sutherland, and is open at certain times; but the gardens are open all year round and entry to them is free. Dunrobin claims to be one of Britain's oldest continuously inhabited houses (parts dating from the 1300s), and boasts 189 rooms. From the castle it is possible to walk all the way to Brora along a coastal track, passing Carn Liath, a well-preserved 2,000-year-old broch, and several banks and rough beaches that are popular with common seals.

BRORA – JOHN O'GROATS (78 miles)

There is a lovely sandy beach north of Brora that at low tide can be walked for nearly two miles, otherwise follow the edge of the links. Negotiate the railway at one of several pedestrian crossings, then walk along the main road to the hamlet of Lothbeg. It is the last time you will see the A9 until John o'Groats, so bear with it. The stone in the lay-by near Lothbeg marks the place where the last wolf in Sutherland was killed, in 1700. The turning for the tiny lane to Kildonan is easily missed (it has a sign warning that the road is liable to snow blockage). In the absence of any decent tracks or footpaths along the coast, this empty, single-track lane is an ideal walking route. It follows the river up the narrow glen until a bridge, near the remains of several standing stones. But the best part is further on, after the road has crept around the flanks of Beinn Dhorain and Ben Varie (a good-weather if strenuous alternative would be to go over and not around them!). From here there are superb views over the Strath of Kildonan to many of Sutherland's finest mountains: Ben Armine, Foinaven, Ben More, Quinag and Ben Loyal. Follow the road above large plantations down to the River Helmsdale by Kildonan railway station, which is basically just a platform. The road widens, and joins the single-track A897 northwards.

Should anyone not want to take this inland route then continue along the A9 to Helmsdale, where there is a youth hostel and a few shops, after which you enter Caithness and the cliffs steepen and the narrow coastal plain disappears. There is some relief from the main road at Badbea, a bleak and isolated collection of ruined buildings where crofters evicted by the Highland Clearances tried to make a living (many emigrated to New Zealand in the end). There are a few tracks, including one up the beautiful Berriedale Water, allowing a return to the coast via Dunbeath Strath, scene of Neil Gunn's classic book Highland River. *Unless you want to visit Wick the best route to John o'Groats is north along a minor road to Watten that begins just after Lybster. This quiet, almost dead straight lane passes the Grey Cairns of Camster, chambered burial cairns dating from around 2000 BC, and affords good views over the flat and empty miles of Caithness. The hills are now behind, but this can still be a bleak and desolate place in rough weather. From the Brown Trout Hotel at Watten crossroads it is merely a question of threading your way through minor roads to Lyth, then a long and empty lane across moorland to Upper Gils and to the finish.*

Returning to the main route, the small area around Kildonan, in particular at Baile an Or and Carn nam Bath, was where a Gold Rush took place in 1868–70 when thousands flocked to the Helmsdale River. Ultimately the landowner, the Duke of Sutherland, made more money than most of the prospectors by granting expensive licences for tiny plots of land. Then when his salmon fishing began to be disturbed he called a halt to the digging and everyone had to pack up and leave. Especially if the weather is poor, you may wander along the strath and be forgiven for wondering whether anyone lives here at all nowadays. Not many, is the answer, which is why those who are tentless must plan very carefully. At Kinbrace, 7½ miles from Kildonan Station, there is a shop and a solitary B&B (Tigh-Achen-Echan), plus what must be one of the most remote primary schools in the whole of Britain. The desolate moorland, peat bog and open mountainside stretches in every direction. Snow posts line the road, and the feeling is of utter isolation and exposure. Patchy conifer woods offer some protection from the wind that howls down from the twin giants of Ben Griam Mor and Ben Griam Beg. These crude commercial plantations that sprang up a decade ago on the open moorland were the source of bitter controversy between tree-farmers and conservationists (planting has now ceased). However, vehicles are few and, the wind notwithstanding, you should be able to make good time along the firm surface – it is roughly 21 miles from Kinbrace to Melvich, on the coast.

The lonely hotel at Forsinard offers welcome if expensive comfort. There is a short track eastwards to Sletill Hill from around here, should you want to leave the tarmac, and I have also heard of people following the course of the railway line north-eastwards. The platform building at Forsinard is worth visiting, for it has been turned into the Flow Country Visitor Centre. The 'Flow Country' is the peatland area of Caithness and Sutherland – the wilderness that you are currently walking through – and 'flow' is a northern term used to describe any flat or deep wet peat bog. Over 50% of Caithness and Sutherland is covered by blanket bog, the largest expanse anywhere in Europe. It acts as a sponge that releases water into the surrounding river systems and lakes, providing plentiful trout and salmon for anglers, but also a habitat for birds such as the greenshank, greylag goose and common scoter.

Near Trantlemore you can leave the A897 by crossing the Halladale River and following a deserted lane north via a string of lonely farms and cottages. After Upper Bighouse the tarmac gives way to a rough but walkable track that leads all the way to Melvich. This is not a large place, but there are several B&Bs, a campsite by the Croft Inn and a post office stores.

As the sea comes into sight, and the realisation that this is not the east or west coast but the north, the feeling really is one of entering the last lap. Now head east and set your sights on John o'Groats.

For the first few miles follow the A836 across moorland (or walk the rough coastline if you prefer). As you approach Reay there are expansive views out to the Orkney Islands across the choppy Pentland Firth, although closer at hand the futuristic shapes of the Dounreay Nuclear Power Development Establishment are more likely to hold your attention. There is an exhibition centre for the curious, in which case continue along the main road for another couple of miles. Otherwise visit the lovely bay at Sandside for a spot of lunch, or the Reay Stone in the west wall of the chapel at the old burial ground (a Dark Age cross-slab, possibly tenth century), then leave the main road for an inland lane via Shebster and Westfield to Thurso. After miles of mountain scenery this landscape is gentler but no less desolate. Caithness is sometimes referred to as 'the Lowlands beyond the Highlands'. There are scattered farms, but little amenities for the walker until Thurso.

Thurso is the most northerly town on the Scottish mainland (720 miles from London), and was an important staging post for the Vikings. Ferries to the Orkneys and not longships now leave the harbour at nearby Scrabster, but there are still plenty of shops and beds to satisfy the needs of the long-distance traveller. From Thurso it is only 20 miles to John o'Groats. It is feasible to walk the actual coast, which apart from Dunnet Head is mostly low, rough cliff. There is no real path for most of the way, but the dunes and golden sands at Dunnet Bay are particularly handsome.

However, at this stage it is likely that you will want to maintain momentum, eat up the remaining miles and power to the finish; in which case it is probably easier to take a string of long and quiet lanes that afford superb views of both the moors to the south and the Orkneys across the firth to your left.

Leave Thurso on the A836, but before the houses end turn right up Mount Pleasant Road and quickly out into bare, open land once more. At Mayfield, turn left for Castletown, which earlier last century used to be an important centre for the production of flagstones, exported via the purpose-built harbour to many parts of the world. Then take further quiet lanes past Loch Heilen to Instack. The road ahead is direct and uncompromising; there are a few cottages, several young conifer plantations and miles of exposed, rough pasture. The cliffs of Dunnet Head and the distant mountains of Hoy and the other Orkney islands hold the attention for a while, but it is likely that you will be lost in your own thoughts. Even the Queen Mother's official Caithness residence at Castle Mey will be of negligible interest. As all long-distance walkers will know, the last few miles of a marathon walk are spent in a mood of reflection. Perhaps there will be impatience to wrap up the last few, routine miles, and relief that the finishing line is almost in sight. Certainly there is likely to be a little sadness. Euphoria and self-satisfaction at the achievement will come later.

As the lane rounds the gentle flanks of the Hill of Rigifa the turreted top of the John o'Groats House Hotel comes into view. Beyond is the distinctive white lighthouse building on Duncansby Head. Press on, past the youth hostel at Canisbay, and along the main road for the last few steps.

John o'Groats derives its name from Jan de Groot, one of three Dutch brothers who arrived in 1496 at the request of King James IV to run a ferry from the mainland to the Orkneys. Only a few years before the islands had been part of the combined kingdom of Denmark and Norway, and James was anxious that they should now remain firmly under his control. A ferry still operates from the small harbour below the hotel (the day-excursion is highly recommended as a well-earned relaxation for successful End to Enders). There are also a few houses, several B&Bs, and a modest collection of gift shops. Otherwise the scene is dominated by the elegant John o'Groats House Hotel, outside the main door of which is a start/finish line for End to Enders to pose by. Inside the hotel you may wish to sign the record book and complete the application form to join the Land's End – John o'Groats Association. Outside, on a grassy bank, the man with the camera by the famous signpost looks strangely familiar.

Of course, the place has always attracted tourists, and coaches frequently pull into the car park. But the remote location of John o'Groats has, up until now, saved it from the kind of commercial development that has, for some, spoilt Land's End. However, there are as yet unspecified plans for a new tourism complex to be built at John o'Groats.

Late afternoon or early evening is probably the best time to arrive on foot. But this is not quite the end. Leave your rucksack at the hotel and walk the final two miles to Duncansby Head, preferably along the deserted beach and rising clifftop rather than the tarmac lane. Out to sea are the Orkneys, and in the gathering dusk the lighthouses blink. Duncansby Head represents the finality, perhaps the real end of the land, although the most northerly point of the

British mainland is not here but actually along the coast at Dunnet Head. Despite this, Duncansby Head really feels like the outermost corner of the land. The cliffs are high and sheer, home to auks, fulmars and shags, and a little to the south the famous stacks rise like huge sharks' teeth from the surf. In many ways the resemblance to Land's End is uncanny: rugged cliffs, treacherous rocks, outlying islands, and of course the feeling that here terra firma ends. There is simply no more land to walk on. It is the end of a magnificent journey. Well done.

THE WEST ROUTE

8 HIGH CLIFFTOP MILES
Land's End – Barnstaple
by the South-West Coast Path
186 miles

9 INTO THE WEST COUNTRY
Barnstaple – Chepstow
by the South-West Coast Path, the Tarka Trail
and the West Mendip Way
166 miles

10 KINGLY FOOTSTEPS
Chepstow – Chirk
by the Offa's Dyke Path and the Wye Valley Walk
131 miles

11 NORTH-WEST PASSAGE
Chirk – Arnside
by the Maelor Way, the Sandstone Trail
and the Douglas Valley Way
171 miles

12 ENGLAND'S FINEST MOUNTAINS
Arnside – Carlisle
by the Furness Way and the Cumbria Way
111 miles

13 THE BARE HILLS
Carlisle – Strathblane
by the Southern Upland Way
137.5 miles

14 HIGHLAND GRANDEUR
Strathblane – Inverness
by the West Highland Way
and the Great Glen Route
159 miles

8

HIGH CLIFFTOP MILES

Land's End – Barnstaple

LAND'S END – PADSTOW (96 miles)
Most people who walk from Land's End to John o'Groats using long-distance footpaths adopt what is in effect a combination of my West and Central routes. The major trails that they use tend to include the South-West Coast Path (north coast), Offa's Dyke Path, Pennine Way and West Highland Way. Three of the four are incorporated in the End to End West Route, and the other – the Pennine Way – is close enough to be included by the ambitious and the enterprising.

For much of the way the West Route takes the most uncomplicated and direct course possible, and since this includes three prominent trails there are long sections where waymarks and guidebooks make routefinding relatively easy. The downside, however, is that despite stunning scenery all three paths are physically challenging, involving much ascent and descent, and crossing high and exposed ground. The opening 250 miles (no mean distance on its own) is along the South-West Coast Path, which comprises part of the Cornwall Coast Path and the Somerset and North Devon Coast Path. This may turn out to be one of the toughest parts of all, since the frequently rough terrain and constant ups and downs are likely to tax untrained legs and unhardened feet to the full. Take it gently!

For an easier beginning you may like to consider taking the inland paths and country lanes of the Central Route, and so join the West Route a little further along the coast (perhaps after crossing the

River Camel near Bodmin Moor). But for many people Cornwall's north coast is, quite rightly, one of the highlights of the whole trip, and taken steadily and sensibly you can balance the spectacular views and uplifting walking with gradually attaining a suitable level of strength and fitness. Ahead are some of the finest hills of Wales, England and Scotland, so it is best to start as you mean to go on.

It is a good idea to start early and quickly on the first day of the Walk from Land's End. Wherever you choose to stay the night before – hotel, B&B, youth hostel or tent – get the photographs and handshakes over and done with and set off.

The first clifftop mile will allow you to warm your limbs, stop and adjust your pack, and generally calm yourself down after the early morning butterflies. Mats of sea campion and stonecrop dot the clifftop, but the paths are wide and well-trodden, and routefinding should not be a problem. At Sennen Cove it may be wise to ignore the café and press on, since it is always a good idea to establish a rhythm for the day ahead and get a few quick miles under the belt. So continue above the glorious sweep of Whitesand Bay, popular with surfers and sunbathers, to Cape Cornwall, which curiously enough is the only 'cape' in England and Wales. In medieval times it was referred to as 'Cauda Maudi', or 'tail of the world'. Land's End Youth Hostel is one mile south of the Cape, along the Cot Valley. There is a campsite at Botallack, and the seventeenth-century Manor Farm nearby is where the TV series *Poldark* was filmed. It now provides B&B, and apparently hosts annual meets of the Poldark Appreciation Society. Over the next ten miles or so the visual history lesson is quite absorbing: from the Bronze Age Kendijack Castle to the remains of Cornwall's recent mining industry. Disused tin works will already be apparent, and while they are certainly fascinating, and lend a strange, sad air to the coast, the half-hidden mine shafts and crumbling buildings can be dangerous if you stray too far from public footpaths. At Pendeen, five minutes off the coast path and where accommodation may be found, Geevor Tin Mine and museum are open from Easter onwards, and give the best account of Cornwall's once flourishing but always gruelling efforts at mineral extraction. Mining ceased at Geevor as late as February 1990, after the collapse of the tin market in 1985.

On the coastal path itself, Pendeen Lighthouse is definitely worth a visit. It was built in 1900 in an effort to reduce the appalling number of wrecks on this perilous coast. The £260 light bulb can be seen 27 miles away, and from the lantern you can see the half-submerged ledges and jagged rocks extending out into the ocean.

Thoughts remain with the sea and with shipwrecks, for at Portheras Cove metal fragments from the *Alacrity*, which went down in 1963, still pose a danger to bare feet. Now the coast is more indented, with hidden coves and powerful cliffs. Some of the latter provide excellent rock-climbing, particularly the granite face of Bosigran Cliff, but you would be advised to watch where you are putting your own two feet; the faces are sheer and are best left to the nutters with the ropes (Bosigran Cliff was where World War II commandos trained).

The Tinner's Arms in Zennor (just off the path) serves St Austell Ale and home-made food. D.H. Lawrence stayed in Zennor when writing some of *Women in Love*. Unfortunately it did not impress the locals, who accused him and his German-born wife of being spies and hounded them out of the area. Whether aspiring writer or walker, there is very little accommodation to be found around here; indeed, very little altogether on this first section to St Ives, so plan carefully if you are not carrying a tent.

The 6½ miles to St Ives is over rough and sometimes boggy ground. It is surprisingly remote; there are no crowded bays or lanes with ice-cream vans at every turn. In fact it is worth emphasising that away from the well-known honeypots the Cornish coast is still wild and mostly empty, and should not be underestimated. Inland the hills are dotted with standing stones and burial mounds. If the weather is fine this will be an enjoyable stage, as long as you do not overreach yourself. Remember, these are early days, and there is more challenging stuff ahead.

St Ives is the first settlement of any real size so far on the Walk. Here the walker will be well provided for in terms of food and accommodation. In addition, the splendid Tate Gallery St Ives has recently opened above the north beach, showing paintings and sculptures from the St Ives School. On the main quayside you will observe that there are nowadays few working fishing boats in the harbour, but in 1896 St Ives ranked fourth in the country for the amount of fish caught and landed. At that time the busy folk of St Ives fished mackerel in February, followed by crabs, lobster and crayfish in the summer. In autumn the all-important pilchard season began, and the year closed with the search for herring.

After negotiating the bungalows and the begonias, the coastal path follows the curving railway line around Carbis Bay, then through dunes between the golf course and Porth Kidney Sands (an important site for terns) and along the main street of Lelant. At Griggs Quay, the Old Quay House offers good bar food but expensive beds. The road-walking into Hayle really isn't very nice; but then Hayle isn't particularly nice, either. There is a path around the Lagoon (also called Carnsew Pool) should you want to leave the road and observe the local birdlife. Hayle Youth Hostel, marked on some maps, has been closed.

If the tide is out and you find the plethora of tracks among the dunes from the River Hayle's mouth confusing, the vast sandy beach is a far better option. The RSPB purchased 300 acres of intertidal mud, sand and saltmarsh here in 1993 – for the princely sum of £1! Like their reserve at Marazion Marsh, it is an important site for waders, as well as rare North American vagrants blown off course during migration. At Gwithian you can lunch with the surfers, and there are a couple of campsites. From the low cliffs of Godrevy Point you can see the lonely lighthouse on Godrevy Island, which was the inspiration for Virginia Woolf's *To the Lighthouse*. Here, and off Navax Point, grey seals are often to be observed. Or rather, they will be observing you. Grey seals have a curious habit (known as 'bottling') of sitting in the water with their heads and necks thrust up and placidly staring back at their human onlookers.

The six miles to Portreath provides a further stretch of invigorating and sometimes strenuous clifftop walking, and is part of the 200 miles of Devon and Cornwall coastline that is owned and protected by the National Trust (more than one third of the coast of the two counties combined). Launched in 1965, the Trust's Enterprise Neptune aims to safeguard as much of the coast as possible, and walkers should be grateful for the active conservation work that is being carried out, as well as largely unrestricted public access.

At Portreath you may wish to call a halt to the day and put your feet up in a café or the pub. It is quite likely that your feet will be hurting and your legs aching. This is to be expected in the first few days of any long-distance walk, no matter how hard you trained beforehand. However, the rigours of the South-West Coast Path are likely to exacerbate the strains, such is the up-and-down nature of a rugged coast path. It is worth bearing in mind that the South-West Coast Path ascends an average of 148 feet per mile, which easily outstrips the Pennine Way's 127 feet. The Offa's Dyke Path climbs a dismaying 153 feet every mile – and that is still to come! But do not let any of this deter you. See it on the one hand as the ideal physical 'hardening process' for the weeks and months ahead, so that you'll be proud of your physique and stamina by the time you stride over the Devil's Staircase above Glencoe; and on the other as providing the mental adjustment necessary for such a unique and challenging enterprise.

Care must be exercised on any clifftop with erosion and crumbling rock, but around Porthtowan beware in particular of disused mine shafts. This section of coast abounds in old workings. At Chapel Porth you can refresh yourself with a 'hedgehog'. Served at the beach café, it is essentially Cornish ice cream smothered in clotted cream and sprinkled with honey-roasted nuts. Some people's idea of heaven, no doubt.

St Agnes Head sports a large kittiwake colony beneath the gorse and heather top, and St Agnes a smaller human community (but with the necessary amenities for the rucksacked variety). Three miles further on is Perranporth, where there is a handily placed youth hostel. Perranporth is named after St Piran, Patron Saint of tinners. Legend has it that he floated to Cornwall after being chained to a millstone and thrown into the sea by the kings of Ireland. Today, most people visit Perranporth to sunbathe or surf, or a combination of the two. The proficiency of the surfers varies dramatically, and like other beaches along this north coast the sight of lifeguards cruising around in Land-Rovers barking orders from megaphones is common. The walk from this relatively small but popular centre along the sands of Perran Beach is delightful, although it is easier on the ankles to walk the sand near the water's edge rather than the steep but soft dunes. At high tide you may be forced up on to the path along the low cliff edge. Take care not to stray into Penhale Sands. This is a military training area, and although the path is direct and waymarked (seaward of a line of white posts) flags and sentries are usually posted along its 2-mile perimeter when things are likely to start blowing up.

Undeterred, if wary, press on to Holywell, where the Treguth, a thirteenth-century thatched public house which serves twentieth-century food, is worth a brief inspection, then via messy duneland and Kelsey Head into Newquay. To actually enter Newquay you have to cross a small river, the Gannel, which means either taking a ferry to Pentire, a tidal ferry or tidal footbridge at the foot of

Trethellan Hill (this is usually dependent on the café being open). Otherwise walk a little further upstream and cross by the A3075 roadbridge near Trevemper, although this adds several miles. It is also possible to wade the Gannel at one point, but with a full pack, tired legs, and the vagaries of the tide to contend with I would choose one of the other options. Either way, welcome to Newquay: everything from Burger King to bowling alleys (and much more besides). It is north Cornwall's premier resort, and at the height of the season it simply heaves. Inland alternatives are possible, but there again these large family seaside resorts are part and parcel of Cornwall – ever since the railway brought them in reach of the urban masses. And if the noise and clutter appals, at least you will appreciate the rest of the coast even more.

It is about 23 miles from Newquay to Padstow, the next main centre en route. The path sticks on or close to the coastline all the way, and for the most part the gradient is moderate and the route clear. The wide sands of Watergate Bay look tempting to walk along, but – as with all beaches and bays – take the utmost care. Official advice is against walking on a rising tide, certainly never into a restricted bay or cove by cliffs. Tide charts and tables are widely available at newsagents, tourist information centres, post offices, etc, and it is sensible to make a note.

There are cafés, small hotels and much colourful surfing activity at Mawgan Porth. The path weaves in and out of the fragmented, eroded coastline; and the granite stacks and islands of Bedruthan Steps were apparently used by a giant as stepping stones. Here there is a National Trust shop and café (open April–September), and further on a post office and campsite at Porthcothan. Pause for a moment at Griffin's Point, which has an Iron Age promontory fort, and which is purported to be the last place the Cornish chough was recorded as nesting in Cornwall. This red-billed and red-footed member of the crow family is now confined to just a handful of remote British sea cliffs, but is still regarded by many as the Cornish national emblem. A happier ornithological note is struck by the return of nesting peregrine falcons to the Cornish coastline. Trevose Head has a lighthouse that can be visited at certain times; the headland provides a fabulous viewing station, as the north Cornish coast unravels itself at your feet, particularly to the south. There is a youth hostel and campsite at Treyarnon Bay.

The Doom Bar, at the River Camel's estuary mouth, is not a

depressing public house but a notorious shell sandbar which wrecked over 300 ships in the 150 years up to this century. Legend has it that it was formed when a curse was placed on the town by a dying mermaid after being shot by a local.

Around the corner is Padstow, a popular holiday resort with all the usual amenities, but a bit more charm than most. The ferry across the Camel Estuary to Rock is continuous in the summer daytime, but a little more restricted out of season. For those End to Enders who have decided to spurn all mechanical assistance until John o'Groats, I'm afraid you have a long walk upstream. However, the first section is really quite pleasant. From Padstow harbour, follow the quayside past the boatyard and sea cadet hall and join the Camel Trail, a well-surfaced cycleway which avoids the busy A389 and extends all the way to Wadebridge (ignore the roar of the new A39 bridge – it is unsuitable for pedestrians). Padstow is also the northern terminus for the Saints' Way, a 30-mile route from the north coast across the peninsula to Fowey on the south.

The return to Rock along roads is about 3 to 4 miles; or alternatively you can cut out the Pentire Point peninsula by taking minor roads to Port Isaac (roughly 6 miles).

PADSTOW – BARNSTAPLE (90 miles)

From Rock, follow the estuary path to Polzeath and on to Pentire Head. You may like to make a short detour near Daymer Bay to St Enodoc's Church, where John Betjeman is buried – he describes the place in his poem 'Sunday Afternoon Service at St Enodoc'. Pentire Head, or 'head of the land', is generally regarded as one of the outstanding viewpoints of the entire South-West Coast Path, and so resist any temptation to cut off the headland at New Polzeath. Port Isaac, which provides food and accommodation, has a fifteenth-century quay (although the usual catch here was herring and not the more popular pilchard), plus some incredibly steep and narrow alleys, known locally as 'drangs'. One such, Temple Bar, is only 18 inches wide.

The coastal path now hugs the cliff edge for over 8 miles to Tintagel. There are some general facilities at Trebarwith Strand, otherwise the cliffline is bare and exposed. The drops are severe in places and the surface can be rough, so due care must be taken. Even experienced walkers have come a cropper on slippery rock, or been caught unawares by a sudden gust of wind. And while issuing the warnings, remember that strong tidal currents can make swimming hazardous in some of the coves and bays – watch out for notices and flags if you're thinking of braving the Atlantic waters.

Even if you are unfamiliar with the north Cornwall coast, the likelihood is that you will still have heard of Tintagel and the Arthurian legend. It is one of those Land's End-type places: undeniably beautiful, even spiritually uplifting, but would be ten times better without anyone else around. The remains of the castle are probably Norman, but there are also traces of a monastery, quite probably England's first, built by Celtic missionaries from Wales around the fifth century AD. Either way, the spectacle of the broken walls clinging to the tiny island far above the crashing waves is dramatic. If you have the energy, the steep stairway to the top will reward you with spectacular views. However, walkers should continue to pay attention to the state of the path: there are very steep drops, and in places the path is eroded and can be slippery. For provisions or refreshment, the village of Tintagel is half a mile away, but it can get nightmarishly busy in the summer months when all the King Arthur tosh can be too much. There is also a youth hostel, housed in converted slate quarry offices.

The coast remains wild and rocky for some miles. Fulmars and auks ride the strong winds above the cliffs, and you may see puffin colonies on Long and Short Islands.

The narrow, snaking harbour at Boscastle is formed out of a superb natural haven between the cliffs, and at high tide the waves almost lap the walls of the youth hostel. Beyond is a waterfall at Pentargon, followed by High Cliff, which at 223m is appropriately the highest cliff in Cornwall. On a clear day Lundy Island is visible. The drop may not be sheer, as it is at Henna to come, but the approach and ascent have been made trickier by erosion, and you should beware taking misleading tracks. The next couple of miles to Crackington require further care with unstable scree and slippery loose rock and slate. Watch where you put your feet, and don't get too close to the edge. If you inadvertently end up on a track at the cliff edge or the foot of some scree, retrace your steps and join the main path.

Between Crackington Haven and Widemouth Bay (7 miles) there are no facilities, but gradually the walking becomes easier and at Dizzard Point there is an unspoilt stretch of scrub oak forest, the most westerly in England, where the coastal path has to move inland to avoid landslips. At Millook Haven take a look at the famous zig-zag cliff face, where the sedimentary rocks have been folded in a bizarre fashion.

At the risk of putting personal prejudice before objective reporting, all I will say of Bude is that it has its admirers, but I am not among them. If you choose to linger, the Falcon Hotel's bar meals are highly recommended (surprisingly cheap and wholesome). The hotel is south of Bude Canal, as you walk into town. Certainly you will need all the sustenance and energy that can be mustered; the next 14 miles to Hartland Point are perhaps the toughest of the whole of the north Cornwall and Devon coast, with a succession of steep drops and tricky climbs. The coastal scenery is particularly notable for its broken and eroded appearance, since the soft shales and mudstones that make up the cliffs are easily worn down by the sea, leaving the tougher sandstone below. There are few points of refreshment along this stretch, and most of them are seasonal, such as the National Trust café at Sandy Mouth, and near the churchyard inland at Morwenstow. But impressive natural features continue to hold the attention: Henna Cliff is second only to Beachy Head as the highest sheer cliff in England, and Speke's Mill Mouth boasts a dramatic waterfall (cascading 20m). Before that, at Marsland Mouth, Cornwall gives way to Devon. The county border is provided by the River Tamar, which rises only four miles away from here, then flows all the way to the south coast at Plymouth. But you may find yourself looking forward to a bed and a hot meal at Elmscott Youth Hostel far more than county counting.

At Hartland Point there is a striking change of direction from roughly north to east, not that you notice it on the ground (but it looks impressive on the map). The rocky headland is as savage as they come, and many vessels along with their crews have been lost. Accordingly, the lighthouse, built in 1874, has one of the most powerful beams to be found anywhere on the British coastline.

Between Barley Bay and Shipload Bay the path passes safely seawards of Hartland RAF station. Now the walking is generally much more straightforward and easier, and there is even a fairly extensive patch of woodland and gorse-covered scrub. The path passes above the picturesque village of Clovelly, which is worth visiting if you have a few moments to spare. Local people use home-made sleds to transport goods down the steep sloping cobbles. Clovelly is best seen at the very beginning or end of the day, when the noisy hordes are once more back in their coaches and cars.

From Clovelly follow a winding but easy track around woodland. It is known as the Hobby Drive, and was dug in order to provide winter work for hard-up fishermen and to keep French POWs from the Napoleonic Wars occupied. After Babbacombe Cliff the coast evens out and once through Bideford Bay Holiday Village you enter Westward Ho! The resort, named after a novel by Charles Kingsley, is a little disappointing. You would think that any place with an exclamation mark at the end of it must be a little bit special, but Westward Ho! is basically a characterless collection of shabby cafés and prefab bungalows. Even the 500-feet-long pier built here at the end of last century was washed away by the sea without much resistance.

A pebble ridge skirts the dunes and saltmarshes of Northam Burrows Country Park, but it makes for awkward walking at times and can become a little tiresome. Eventually it brings you to Appledore, where there is a small shipyard and a seasonal ferry to Instow. Otherwise follow the banks of the River Torridge, go underneath the crude and unsightly A39 bridge, and cross the river in the town centre using Bideford Long Bridge, a medieval construction with twenty-four arches, each a different size. Bideford has a long history; it is in fact one of only four Devon boroughs mentioned in the Domesday Book. (Alternatively, you may wish to omit the Northam Burrows chunk by following roads the short distance from Westward Ho! to Bideford.)

Once over the Torridge, follow the course of a former railway line via Instow into Barnstaple. This handy track has been developed by the local authority for both walkers and cyclists, and provides a level and firm surface all the way into the town.

9

INTO THE WEST COUNTRY

Barnstaple – Chepstow

BARNSTAPLE – MINEHEAD (68 miles)

Barnstaple is a large, bustling kind of place. You may want to hang about for a while, or else get clear of it as soon as possible. However, first of all consult your OS map and decide on your route. The coastal path now juts out west to Croyde and Woolacombe, before swinging back and along to Ilfracombe (29 miles from Barnstaple town centre). There are some tremendous sandy bays and low cliff walking. However, others may find this peninsula unnecessary and exasperating, and of course there is no reason why you have to stick rigidly to every foot of the official coast path.

So at Barnstaple you could head up the northern bank of the Yeo valley along footpaths to near Chelfham, then north-east from Loxhore Bridge to woods below Bratton Fleming. There are further footpaths, and lanes, to Wistlandpound Reservoir, popular with fly fishermen. Then take a long track towards Parracombe, and pick up the infant River Heddon nearby and follow it north through the trees to Hunter's Inn, or else further east to Woody Bay, and so rejoin the coast path.

Another inland option is to follow the waymarked Tarka Trail. It is based on Henry Williamson's book, Tarka the Otter, *and you will have already walked a small section as you approached Barnstaple from Instow. The Trail stretches for 180 miles in a rough figure of eight, with Barnstaple in the middle. One part of the top loop follows the coastal path around to Lynton, and the other – the option here – tracks the River Taw upstream until Bishop's Tawton, then east to*

Landkey, and via a steep wooded valley to West Buckland. At the River Bray the Trail then veers north on to exposed moorland at the heart of Exmoor National Park, where it joins the Two Moors Way and where careful navigation is necessary, before returning to the sea and to the West Route at Lynmouth. This Barnstaple–Lynmouth Tarka Trail alternative totals 32 miles, and is an appealing detour for those wanting to vary the coastal route and explore a little more of Devon. Look out for the otter pawprint waymarks.

If you have decided to stick with the coast path follow the cycleway from Barnstaple to Braunton, then down to the mouth of the River Taw and along by Braunton Burrows National Nature Reserve, one of the largest areas of sand dunes in the country. Beyond Staunton Down is Croyde Bay, where you are likely to see more surfers in action. It might look like fun, but I can vouch for the fact that it involves a lot of hard work for very little reward – and even in a wetsuit the water is bloody freezing!

The high cliffs of Baggy Point are popular with seabirds, such as fulmars, shags and cormorants, as well as with rock climbers. Then descend to the glorious sweep of Woolacombe Sands, which provides excellent low-tide beach walking. It is worth bearing in mind that the Bristol Channel has the second highest tidal range in the world – sometimes over thirty feet – and although wide open beaches such as at Woolacombe are relatively safe, other coves and bays can trap the unwary. Woolacombe itself is small and unlovely, offering the usual ices and sunhats; there is accommodation here and at Mortehoe, including campsites. If you are lucky with the weather, the Welsh coast will come into view at Morte Point, and it will be a thrilling sight for the End to End walker. You will feel that you really have made some significant distance, and that the Welsh hills are not too far off. Unfortunately they *are*; the Bristol Channel is long, Chepstow remains over the horizon, and the north Devon cliffs are still to come. But don't be deterred! If you are already fretting about Wales at this stage, then you will have some serious worry lines by the time Inverness heaves into view.

Continue along the coast to the small settlement of Lee, where the fourteenth-century Grampus Inn allows you to rest and reflect on life, and Wales. At Ilfracombe, an attractive resort popular since Victorian times, accommodation includes a youth hostel. The harbour is one of the few safe havens for small boats on the north

Devon coast, a fact confirmed by the existence of a lighthouse on the harbour headland since 1522.

Leaving Ilfracombe, the coastal path flirts with the A399 in places, but there is no longer any prolonged roadwalking since new sections of path were opened in the last few years. At Combe Martin they mined silver in the thirteenth century, then minted coins for the Royalists during the Civil War. Today it is rather residential and dull, but at least you now enter Exmoor National Park. From here to Lynmouth the walking becomes loftier and much more strenuous, and there are few places for those without tents to stop overnight. Plod up the hillside around the conical lump of Little Hangman, crossing more heather, western gorse and bracken to scale its bigger and meaner brother, Great Hangman. At 318m, this is the highest point on the entire South-West Coast Path, and there should be good views over the moors; but in rough weather it can be hard going, especially difficult in high winds.

There is a steep descent to the wooded Heddon valley. Half a mile upstream Hunter's Inn serves hot and cold food, has hotel accommodation, plus a number of free-running peacocks (though they do not appear to be on the menu). This quiet area, including Woody Bay, which you will come to shortly, is a site of special scientific interest. It has 'hanging' sessile oaks (with lobed leaves and stalkless acorns), which support wood warblers, redstarts and pied flycatchers. This section of cliff may be more varied, but it is still rugged, and so do not underestimate your arrival time if a bed in Lynton Youth Hostel is waiting to be claimed.

Lynton is reached via a minor road that takes you past Lee Abbey, a Christian retreat, and through the Valley of Rocks, an unusual dry valley crowned with eerie, jagged tors. It runs parallel with the sea and, more bizarrely still, houses both Lynton Cricket Club and a herd of wild Cheviot goats. Then call a halt and explore Lynton, and the tiny seafront below at Lynmouth, where there are cafés and pubs, Exmoor National Park Centre, and a unique cliff railway (the upward car is powered by the weight of water in the tank of the one travelling downwards).

Ascend the cliffs once again and pass from Devon into Somerset. Overall it is a pleasant and largely unchallenging walk of eleven miles to Culbone. Landslips have made a few diversions necessary, and more may occur, so follow official signs. Culbone Church is the smallest complete parish church in England, over 800 years old.

There is some fairly dense woodland to negotiate, but it is short-lived as the path emerges on to the shingly beach at Porlock Weir.

The miles of rollercoaster cliff walking are almost at an end. From Porlock Weir, where the pink-painted Anchor Inn provides refreshment, a pebble ridge leads to Bossington, and then via an open bridleway inland across Selworthy Beacon to Minehead. This is where the South-West Coast Path officially begins – or, in your case, ends. It is quite an agreeable place, with banks, bakers and B&Bs in good supply. You should treat yourself to a little luxury tonight, since the coastal miles are almost at an end; and those gruelling clifftop ups and downs are nearly over. Soon the Walk switches inland and new horizons loom. Press on!

MINEHEAD – GLASTONBURY (43 miles)

I have dim childhood memories of a fun-filled day spent galloping around the Butlins holiday camp on the Minehead seafront, and I am happy to report that this garish and gaudy spectacle still survives. It has been joined by something equally monstrous called Somerwest World, and you may regard both in joy and horror as you leave the seaside town by The Strand. Soon the coastal path begins, and this sticks rigidly to the shore via Dunster Beach to Blue Anchor. The mud and shingle beach is not particularly scenic and there is little of interest, except when a steam train from the West Somerset Railway is passing through. Continue to Watchet, a small resort with working docks. There is a campsite, plus the familiar fish and chip shops and postcard vendors. It was while staying here in 1797 (scoffing chips and scribbling rude postcards, no doubt) that Coleridge drew inspiration for *The Ancient Mariner*.

This is the last time that you will walk the actual coast, apart from a little of the Severn Estuary, until north Lancashire. Now the route veers inland, and initially it follows a minor road through Doniford and up past a particularly grim caravan park to West Quantoxhead. Take care crossing the A39 (but it is not the first time that you have encountered this beast) and follow the track up and on to the delightful Quantock Hills.

The range itself is only about 12 miles long, but the gentle and open moorland provides a miniature paradise for walkers and wildlife. Sheep and ponies graze side by side; adders slither among the bracken, and overhead falcons and jackdaws patrol the skies. Wordsworth and Coleridge lived here for a time, rambling and composing. Follow what is known as the Pack Way or spine road, wide and direct, which runs from above West Quantoxhead all the way to beyond the summit of Will's Neck. It has doubtless been trod by the feet of many ages, and its airy miles provide glorious views over the Bristol Channel (to the Welsh coast if it is clear) and the lush Somerset countryside, including the ugly Hinkley Point power station. There are youth hostels either side of the hills, at Holford and Crowcombe.

Leave the rutted track just before Will's Neck, which at 384m is the highest spot on the Quantocks and is worth a small diversion for the views, and keeping the conifer plantation on your left follow the clear track down towards Hawkridge Reservoir. Here you may be forgiven for thinking that the trout fishermen outnumber the trout. Take the lane to the right and head for Bridgwater (approximately 5 miles away). There are a few footpaths but, as Hamish Brown discovered, they are not well-kept, and I can report that little has changed. Best stick with minor roads through Four Forks or Enmore.

Bridgwater is functional, if not beautiful. There are some B&Bs on the Minehead road (A39) as you enter the town centre from the west. On departure take the A372 past the railway station, then once over the M5 leave the traffic by turning left for the village of Chedzoy. You are now on the Somerset Levels, flat and eerily empty plains that were slowly built up from clay deposited by the sea. It provides rich pasture, as well as an important wetland habitat for birds such as snipe, redshanks and curlews, and whimbrels on passage. At other times Bewick's swans and plovers winter.

From Chedzoy follow the south bank of King's Sedgemoor Drain for several miles. In the fields outside Westonzoyland there is a simple fenced-off monument commemorating the Battle of Sedgemoor, where in 1685 Royalist troops defeated a ragged army of West Country men. The so-called Pitchfork Rebellion came to a bloody and inglorious end in these peaceful fields (try to ignore the pylons), and retribution at the 'Bloody Assizes' in Taunton was brutal.

By turning left at Greylake Bridge you can visit the Greylake Inn (B&B) or the transport café; otherwise continue along the Drain in the company of reed buntings and herons until Cradle Bridge, and then head for Walton Hill. This ridge of Jurassic strata above the Levels provides for open and airy walking, and the views –

particularly of Glastonbury Tor – are superb. On Ivythorn Hill (like Walton Hill this is National Trust land and there are clear footpaths) you will see oak and ash, but particularly hazel, which is being grown once more for coppicing. After passing Street Youth Hostel either descend directly to the houses and shops, or else bypass Street altogether by taking lanes via Butleigh Wootton and enter Glastonbury from the south.

GLASTONBURY – CHEPSTOW (55 miles)

Glastonbury is where the Central Route coincides with the West Route and it provides Western walkers with a second introduction to King Arthur. While Tintagel is associated with the birth of the legendary hero, the Isle of Avalon (Glastonbury) is where King Arthur was supposedly buried. The Tor, topped by St Michael's Chapel, and the Abbey, which Joseph of Arimathea is supposed to have visited after the Crucifixion, are fascinating places; but the main street can be choked by traffic, and become a little over-run with a combination of camera-clicking tourists and New Agers.

To reach the Mendip Hills (often referred to as simply 'Mendip' by local people) leave Glastonbury by a quiet lane across the open fields to Godney. At Lower Godney the Sheppey Inn offers accommodation, shuv halfpenny and a skittle alley. From here you can either head straight for the hills via Henton or Wookey, or else pay a visit to Wells. The latter is recommended: shops, banks, beds, and a fabulous cathedral. The Bishop's Palace is worth an inspection, and Vicars' Close is claimed to be the oldest complete street in Europe, with houses dating from 1348; but it is the Cathedral Church of St Andrew which steals the show. The dramatic West Front, twice as wide as it is high, carries 293 pieces of medieval sculpture, and has undergone years of painstaking restoration work.

Between Wells and Cheddar follow the West Mendip Way, a 30-mile route from Wells to Weston-super-Mare devised by the Rotary clubs of Weston-super-Mare to commemorate the Queen's Silver Jubilee. The route is useful not least because it is an attractive path, but also because it is mostly waymarked. Head for Under Wood Quarry, then up and over a wooded hill to Wookey Hole, where the popular show caves are to be found. Continue along the road a short distance, turning off on to a footpath marked 'Priddy', and enter the quiet and unspoilt Ebbor Gorge. This national nature reserve is an example of a typical Mendip valley, carved out of the carboniferous limestone over the centuries by a river. The undisturbed, leafy glades contain many badger setts; and excavation has identified the remains of bears, wolves and lemmings. Your route is up a steep, stepped path to the right of the actual gorge. At the top, although the route continues on to Priddy, a short path to the left will bring you out on to open grass above the cliffs – a wonderful viewing station, and a fine place for a spot of lunch. However, if you crave a hot meal then press on to the New Inn at Priddy (2 miles), the highest village on the Mendips. Nearby are Swildon's Hole and Eastwater Cavern, popular with cavers. This windswept plateau once housed a Roman leadworks, and much later hosted an annual fair during the days of the Black Death, when local residents climbed the Mendips to escape the plague.

The hills rise to over 300m, and the open fields and wooded valleys offer good walking – and for our friends below good caving. As a result, B&Bs and campsites are fairly well represented; for instance, there is a site (with shop) at Mendip Heights, half a mile north-west of Priddy.

The West Mendip Way now takes you back down the scarp slope to Draycott, and from there to Cheddar (this area is renowned for its strawberries, by the way). At Cheddar there is a youth hostel, shops and cafés, and probably a lot of people looking for cheese or caves or both. Or they may be queuing for the working rural theme village. It is unlikely that you will, so instead leave the hubbub by taking the path up and along the attractive green top of Cheddar Gorge by Pavey's Lookout Tower. This was built ninety years ago by Ronald Pavey, who was convinced that he could fly, and miraculously survived several practice flights from the cliffs above the gorge. As you stroll along the top there are places where you can glimpse the scenes below – over 120m down! Cross the road and enter Black Rock nature reserve, one of a group of four managed by the Somerset Trust for Nature Conservation. Here the West Mendip Way continues straight on through the larches and pines of Long Wood.

Leave the Way by turning north via Tyning's Farm to Black Down (there are many tracks to choose from). Once at Beacon Batch there are wide views over Blagdon Lake and Chew Valley Lake. The latter is not only popular with trout fishermen, but also with wintering wildfowl. Avon Wildlife Trust manage a reserve here, and from late February up to 4,000 ducks of twelve different species may be seen at one time, including internationally important numbers of shoveler and gadwall. The village of Blagdon has a post office and a few shops, and B&B at the Seymour Arms. The outskirts of Bristol are only about six or seven miles away, and to reach them it is really a question of picking any one of a dozen small lanes from the OS map. However, a more attractive route, if slightly longer, is to walk along the top of the Mendips to Dolebury Warren, a huge lump of a hill that is crowned by an ancient fort and a sea of wild flowers, and which commands spectacular views across Avon. Skip over the A38 near Churchill, and continue along Lyncombe Hill to Sandford, where the Cheddar Valley Railway Walk takes you across the Levels to Yatton. Minor roads over Kenn Moor lead to the exotic woods of Clevedon Court (part semi-natural, part Victorian landscaped), and from Clevedon there is a 4-mile footpath along the coast to Portishead. The M5 bridge over the River Avon has a safe foot/cycle path.

Bristol is a particularly attractive city: setting, history, facilities – there is much to recommend it. Both the youth hostel and tourist information centre are to be found close to the city centre by the renovated docks, and close to Bristol Cathedral, the Maritime Heritage Centre, and SS *Great Britain* (the first propeller-driven ocean-going iron ship in history, designed by Brunel and now fully restored). Even better, you can follow the Avon Walkway from the city centre along the banks of the river to Pill, by the M5 bridge at Avonmouth.

Cross this in safety, if not solitude, and take the main road left, through a huge industrial sprawl, towards the River Severn. If you have not entered Bristol city centre this massive complex will come as something of a shock after so many miles of rural peace. But it is short-lived; in one stretch the authorities have developed a walkway back from the road with new saplings and hedges, and a footpath can cut out another section of the road. However, beware of the thundering HGVs.

At Severn Beach, a quiet and lost settlement that died once the Severn ferry was decommissioned, you will be uncomfortably aware of the Second Severn Crossing. The plan is for this new bridge to open in 1997, taking much of the pressure off the existing Severn Bridge. Unfortunately, the short-term effects are noise and disruption, so that what should be a fairly quiet few miles along the shore may be disturbed (although this is still the course of Avon

County Council's projected Severn Way Path). Make up for it with a healthy feast at either the Boar's Head in the village of Aust, or at the M4 service station nearby – whatever your stomach or budget dictates.

Directly ahead are the gigantic 120m towers of the Severn Bridge, presenting an airy and – if the fog has crept in – an eerie mile's reverberating walk over the huge spans to Chepstow. As with the East Route crossing of the River Humber over the awe-inspiring Humber Bridge, it is a satisfyingly definite way to finish one stage and enter the next, and in this instance leave one country and enter another. You should feel pleased at the achievement, but the adventure is only just beginning. Welcome to Wales!

10

KINGLY FOOTSTEPS

Chepstow – Chirk

CHEPSTOW – KNIGHTON (79 miles)

Chepstow makes an obvious overnight stop. It is only a few minutes' walk once you step off the Severn Bridge, has the full range of amenities, and allows you to catch your breath before striding out into a new country and a refreshingly different landscape. Ahead is the Offa's Dyke Path, a varied and stimulating 176-mile swathe of glorious Welsh countryside (although the End to End West Route leaves the Dyke at Chirk, after 132 miles).

Although the official route begins at Sedbury Cliffs, on the Severn, it is probably easier to begin by the River Wye road bridge in Chepstow, where the Norman castle looks on imposingly and is well worth visiting if you have a few minutes to spare. The first section of the trail to Monmouth is along the handsome Wye valley, winding and deep-cut, and coated in attractive mixed woodland. After so many days of the open pastoral scenery of Somerset and Avon this switch to steep, rich forest is striking. The Offa's Dyke Path largely keeps to the high rim of the valley, whereas the parallel Wye Valley Walk follows the lower ground and river bank. Either route can be taken, depending on whether your penchant is for trees or water – or whether your legs need a rest. My suggestion is to combine the two routes: the Offa's Dyke to Tintern, then a riverbank section, and so on. But take your pick. The paths are generally in good repair and the waymarks regular.

From Chepstow the Offa's Dyke Path climbs via paths and pavements to the top of limestone cliffs, from where there are dramatic views of the lower reaches of the meandering, chocolate brown river (this is caused by a vigorous two-way tidal flow); then you plunge into the trees and for 2 miles follow the actual Offa's Dyke earthwork. Although it is not quite as dramatic as first hoped, particularly since the trees and undergrowth are so thick, the course of the ditch is reasonably clear – which is more than can be said for what we know of its history. It is believed to have been built by King Offa some time around the late eighth century as a frontier between Mercia and the Welsh kingdoms, but it is not entirely clear whether it was a boundary marker or a defensive work. There is also speculation as to whether some of the man-made ditches were in existence before King Offa's time. Today, the continuous earthworks can be traced for about 81 miles in total.

Between Plumweir Cliff and the Devil's Pulpit the trees thin out, and from this lofty position there are breathtaking views of the valley below, and in particular of Tintern Abbey. The Offa's Dyke Path clings to the hilltop, but it is worth descending one mile down a waymarked path to visit the Abbey. Founded by Cistercian monks from France in 1131, Tintern Abbey remained a centre for monastic prayer until Henry VIII's Dissolution in 1536. The vast shell that remains is rather haunting, but you will need the informative guidebook to help bring the place back to life. (It is also a sure bet that you will not be the only visitor.)

From Tintern, where a welcome pot of tea may be found, follow the Wye Valley Walk upstream to Bigsweir Bridge. This meadow and riverbank walking is straightforward and relaxing, and gives a different perspective of the valley. Then rejoin the more elevated Offa's Dyke for glorious beech and bluebell woods near the village of St Briavels, which was once the capital of the Royal Forest of Dean. Nowadays the youth hostel occupies what was formerly the gatehouse of St Briavels Castle, from where the constable administered the Forest. It is a most imposing building, and in 1993 the present wardens celebrated its remarkable 700th anniversary with medieval banquets, encouraging visitors to dress in period costume! In the semi-natural broadleaved woodland nearby, coppice management is gradually being revived, providing a habitat for natural woodland creatures such as the dormouse, which have suffered over the last few decades through mass conifer planting, and insensitive woodland management.

From the small settlement at Redbrook you can either follow the

Wye Valley Walk along the river bank (quite pleasant, until you meet the sewage works), or else take the Offa's Dyke Path up Duffields Lane to Kymin Hill. From this well-known viewpoint, perched above Monmouth, and with an odd-looking building that was originally built for dinner parties, there are extensive views towards the Brecon Beacons and the miles of path ahead.

Monmouth offers shops and accommodation, including a campsite and youth hostel. The town is associated with Charles Rolls (of Rolls-Royce fame), Lord Nelson and Henry V – an interesting combination. With its famous public schools and unique thirteenth-century gatehouse over the river, Monmouth is the largest place that you will meet for some time, so it is worth stocking up. It is also decision time. From Monmouth there are two possible routes to Hay-on-Wye. Either continue with the Offa's Dyke Path (which I will describe), or loop northwards along the Wye Valley Walk.

The Monmouth–Hay section of the Wye Valley Walk is 59 miles long, and mostly in England. It follows the river north-east via Symonds Yat to Ross-on-Wye, then on to Hereford before swinging west to rejoin the Offa's Dyke Path. (It actually continues into the heart of the Cambrian Mountains to Rhayader.) And there is also the 'Offa's Dyke Three Castles Alternative', which makes a detour to visit the local Norman remains of Pembridge, Skenfrith, Grosmount and Longtown.

To reach Pandy, at the foot of the Black Mountains, the national trail route wanders over the low, rolling countryside of Gwent. King's Wood and Dingle Wood provide peaceful woodland walking, and on a sunny morning in May I walked here in the company of singing blackcaps and coal tits. However, this section of the walk has one particular drawback: stiles. There are 710 on the entire route, and my landlord in Pandy reckoned that 72 of them block the way between Monmouth and his house, a fine test of equilibrium for the top-heavy backpacker. A pub and a ruined castle provide the highlights in this section: the Hostry (CAMRA's Gwent Pub of the Year 1992) at Llantilo Crossenny, and White Castle, 2 miles further on, so named because its outer walls were originally painted white. This Norman fortification also has a well-preserved and filled moat, and there is endless pleasure to be had watching disobedient youngsters slide helplessly down the steep grassy bank towards an early muddy bath.

There is little else at Pandy besides the A465, a few B&Bs, a hotel, and the walker-friendly Lancaster Arms, where the lamb and apricot 'Lancaster Pie' is recommended, as is the Cardiff-brewed Brains beer. However, there is even less in the way of amenities between here and Hay-on-Wye (18 miles). Indeed, many stretches of the Path traverse remote and sparsely populated areas, and so if you require fixed accommodation it is worth booking ahead.

From Pandy the path ascends the flanks of Hatterrall Hill and on to the Black Mountains, in effect the eastern edge of the Brecon Beacons National Park. Unless it is raining and the cloud is down it should be an uncomplicated and exhilarating march for the fit End to End walker. However, the Black Mountains offer the wildest section of walking that you will probably have experienced since Land's End, and they *are* the wettest place in the Welsh Borders, so be prepared, for it is entirely exposed once you leave the valley. The toughest bits are at the beginning, where the stiff climb through the pasture can be painful after a large cooked breakfast; and towards the northern end of the ridge, where the broad track is becoming broader as successive walkers try and dodge the patches of bog and mire (like some of the Pennine Way it can be atrocious after very bad weather). Apart from this, the track is direct and unmistakable, and the views from the elevated ridge are spectacular: west to the nearby Brecon Beacons, north to the hills of Shropshire, and east to the Golden Valley, Hereford and the distant Malvern Hills. The Black Mountains are actually made of a hard sandstone known as brownstone, but the peat is most definitely black.

The second-hand bookshop capital, Hay-on-Wye, is a natural place to stop for the night. If you arrive late and seek a B&B address, the tourist information centre has an ingenious computer screen fixed inside their main window that can be operated 24 hours a day by touching squares on the outside of the window. Earlier in the day however you will have to push through a load of people who have no interest in the addresses of local paragliding centres or hairdressers but simply want to press little bits of the window and make electronic pictures.

Rejoining the Wye once more, follow the west bank through some thick woods and then fields (one is a campsite), and where you cross the busy A438 there are terrific views back down the river towards Hay Bluff and the Black Mountains. A mile or so away is Clyro, home of the Reverend Francis Kilvert, mid-Victorian diarist and keen observer of rural life. For the next few miles you will be walking the same deserted lanes and fields that the curate took to visit the tiny communities and sheltered villages that he preached to daily. It has rather predictably become known as Kilvert country. The Royal Oak at Gladestry offers food and beds, and there is also a tiny post office store. But the real gem of this section is Hergest Ridge, rising above the village. It is a narrow, grassy ridge that stretches a modest three miles to Kington, and yet it is quite wild on top and there are superb views north to the shy hills of Radnorshire. If you missed out Hatterrall Hill and the Black Mountains, enjoy the safer and more junior (but no less enjoyable) Hergest Ridge.

The national trail acorn posts are out in force on Hergest Ridge; you really shouldn't get lost. Eventually they lead you down to a long surfaced lane that runs into the small town of Kington, where the basics of life are to be found (banks, a SPAR supermarket, fish and chip shop, etc). The local tourist blurb tries to cater for all comers: 'From sheep to shirts, maps to material, you can buy it all in Kington.'

The next quiet but scenic stretch to Knighton comprises further gentle hills and farmland. It also requires you to cross the highest golf course in England and Wales (on Bradnor Hill, above Kington). Make sure that you scrutinise the tees and fairways, and what their occupants are preparing to do, before you step out. A whizzing golf ball is a dangerous object.

Just before Dolley Green there is a treacherously muddy approach to the footbridge across the River Lugg. But overall the going is firm and fairly straightforward, and the efficient waymarking allows you to relax and appreciate the views of Radnor Forest and rural Powys. It is also pleasing to note the reappearance of the Dyke, which can be walked either on or alongside, although this can sometimes be complicated by the close attentions of the local livestock, which not unnaturally find the trees and bushes along the earthwork an ideal place either to take sixty winks or use as a toilet.

This section ends as it began with a golf course, and includes a very steep and potentially slippery descent among trees to enter Knighton, roughly half way along the Offa's Dyke, and in many ways the spiritual centre of this majestic path.

KNIGHTON – CHIRK (52 miles)

Knighton is the home of the Offa's Dyke Centre, next door to the youth hostel, and is where Lord Hunt officially opened the Path in

1971. Indeed, Knighton's Welsh name – Tref y Clawdd – means town on the dyke, and the Centre is a fascinating well of information on all aspects of the Dyke, including the historical angle, its development and maintenance as a long-distance footpath, and the communities it traverses. There is a campsite just along the river, or else plenty of accommodation in the town itself, where Ginger's Café and the George and Dragon provide good value-for-money fare.

However tough you think your legs are, the next section across the Clun hills can be a real effort. Apart from the village of Newcastle, there is nothing on the path in the way of facilities until near Montgomery, and in between there are 15 miles of strenuous and often rough up-and-down hillwalking. From Knighton the steep climb up Panpunton Hill and Cwm-sanaham Hill will no doubt leave you puffing, but the views are panoramic, and soon you are rewarded with one of the finest surviving sections of continuous Dyke. It rolls up and over the open hillside, scenically flanked by a few stands of pine, and provides a clear and enticing way forward. However, there is one section in particular where erosion has taken place and it has been fenced off (walkers are asked to follow a track beside it). The culprits appear to be not so much walkers as rabbits, undermining the grassy banks, and the long-term effects of overgrazing by sheep. But the approach to Edenhope Hill is typical of this section of the route. First there is a long, slippery and taxing descent among conifers to Churchtown (it has a church, but no town); then to clamber back out of the tiny valley requires an instant and near-vertical struggle up the rough grassy hillside.

On the slopes of a large grassy hill known as Hergan, a few miles from Clun there is a new waymark, a buzzard in flight, which denotes the circular Shropshire Way.

The Shropshire Way runs for a total distance of 140 miles, and if you feel like varying your route, or if you want to see some of Shropshire, then here is a perfect opportunity to leave Offa's Dyke for another waymarked trail, and rejoin the West Route further north near Whitchurch. From its meeting with the Dyke, the Shropshire Way wanders over quiet and rolling countryside via Bishop's Castle and the Stiperstones to Shrewsbury, then north over Grinshill to Wem, where there is a 12-mile extension to Grindley Brook, near Whitchurch, where the End to End West Route has just completed the Maelor Way and is about to embark on the Sandstone Trail. Overall, the Clun–Grindley Brook Shropshire Way alternative is just under 50 miles. If you want to savour Shropshire's green hills this is the route to take, but King Offa still has plenty of attractions ahead.

From the crest of the hill above Cwm there are glorious views over the lush, flat Vale of Montgomery ahead. Pause and enjoy it – your legs certainly will. And for the next few miles the walking reverts to a less demanding sequence of woodland and field-hopping, following the level and direct course of the Dyke. Just off the path is Montgomery, a small but extremely attractive town with some well-preserved Elizabethan and Georgian buildings, plus a ruined castle on the hill above and several cheery pubs at ground level.

After a couple of flat miles of fields and a few hundred yards of road, head up a shaded, high-hedged lane and on to the wooded and sometimes muddy flanks of the Long Mountain. Leave the unspectacular Offa's Pool behind and plod up the side of a long grassy field to the dense crown of trees on Beacon Ring. There are wide views over Welshpool and the Severn valley from this ancient and well-sited hillfort, although it is now juxtaposed with obtrusive modern TV masts.

After a steep, grassy descent, which I found to my cost can be extremely slippery in wet weather, head for the busy road junction in the valley below, which entails going past the new and rather improbably named Offa's Dyke Business Park. If you want to reach Welshpool, a mile further on, use the towpath of the Montgomery Canal, which avoids the hideously busy A-road. This section of what was previously known as the Shropshire Union Canal has been recently restored, and at Welshpool Wharf there is a museum and visitor centre. Here, too, the Offa's Dyke Path also links up with the Glyndwr's Way, a circular route that you will already have crossed at Knighton. However, if you simply seek lunchtime refreshment then the Green Dragon at Buttington is just the ticket.

From Buttington the Path shadows the course of the canal and then the River Severn, and not surprisingly it is mostly flat and undemanding. Across the river the Breidden Hills rise strikingly, and unless you are feeling particularly energetic I would imagine that you may be thankful for these easy but nonetheless scenic miles. At Four Crosses join the canal once more and follow the towpath into Llanymynech, where shops and accommodation may be found.

The remaining few miles to Chirk begin with a stiff pull on to Llanymynech Hill, making sure that you do not stray into the disused quarry. On the far side of the hill is a golf course, and as with those that have gone before be alert to the hazards. The Path loses its hard-won height and drops down to a messy stretch through the former mining area around Nantmawr. However, just beyond is one of the best viewpoints on Offa's Dyke, the 285m Moelydd Hill. Even the Long Mynd can be seen on a clear day.

There are some facilities at Trefonen, but for a greater range I suggest you make the short detour to Oswestry, less than three miles' walk away. Oswestry, or Croesoswallt, was reputedly where 'Oswald's Tree' was planted to commemorate the place where St Oswald, King of Northumbria, was killed by the pagan chief Penda. This busy market town is actually in Shropshire, but you will hear both Welsh and English intermingling on every street corner.

North of Trefonen climb through Candy Wood. The line of the Dyke is once more obvious ahead, although there are sections around Baker's Hill where lack of any public right of way means that you can only look and not explore. After using some tarmac and farm tracks, round Selattyn Hill and – presuming you are not walking all the way to Prestatyn – enter the last few miles of the Offa's Dyke Path. As you drop down to the Ceiriog valley (purpose-built steps have made this descent easier) there are fine views of medieval Chirk Castle ahead.

The Offa's Dyke Path then skirts Chirk Castle before swinging west to Llangollen, after which it crosses the Clwydian Range to arrive at the Irish Sea, another 45 miles away. Some may feel that such a splendid trail deserves to be walked in its entirety. If this is your opinion then from Prestatyn return east on the Cestrian Link Walk and rejoin the End to End West Route at Beeston, or continue all the way to Edale if you want to switch routes. Otherwise, your happy association with Offa and the Welsh Borders is at an end, for now it is time to strike out for Cheshire and North-West England. The 54 miles of quiet and unspoilt countryside ahead (Clwyd, Shropshire, and then the sandstone ridges of southern Cheshire) incorporate two relatively unknown long-distance paths, and it is this fact – especially after two long and fairly well-used national trails within a month – that is recommendation enough.

11

NORTH-WEST PASSAGE

Chirk – Arnside

CHIRK – FRODSHAM (54 miles)
From Chirk there are in fact two routes that can be followed to near Whitchurch. The Maelor Way, the preferred route, is 24 miles long and waymarked, and offers a pleasant variety of walking. *The alternative is to follow the towpath of the Llangollen Canal via Ellesmere. This is slightly longer, and it may be advisable occasionally to divert for local footpaths in order to diversify what could be an all-day towpath tramp. Ellesmere is worth pausing over, since it is at the heart of Shropshire's 'meres'. These small lakes were formed by glacial action, and today are fed not by rivers and streams but by drainage from the surrounding soils. The canal touches both Blake Mere and Cole Mere, and there is always an abundance of wildlife on and in the pools. At Cole Mere it is best to take the path into the woods of the country park in order to avoid a section of overgrown and eroded bank, or alternatively follow the obvious path around to the open, grassy southern shore where yachts are moored.*

The Maelor Way follows a more northerly course to Grindley Brook, near Whitchurch. The route was devised many years ago by the late Jack Baker, founder of the Mid-Cheshire Footpath Society, but only opened officially in 1991. It is well-maintained, and Gordon Emery's guidebook provides a comprehensive and entertaining companion. The Way begins at Bronygarth, just south of Chirk Castle. Wave King Offa goodbye, and unless you want to visit the castle (there is a permissive summer path from Castle Mill) follow paths close to the River Ceiriog until Chirk Bank. Nearby is the dramatic Telford-designed Chirk Aqueduct, 30 metres above the valley; and the railway viaduct, just above, is no less impressive. A short detour north along the canal to view the spectacle is recommended, although the scale of the constructions can be better appreciated from the A5 below. Otherwise follow the Llangollen Canal south to Gledrid Bridge, then green tracks to Glymorlas.

The course continues north-eastwards across farmland and quiet country lanes to Overton, keeping just south of the River Dee. The yew trees in Overton churchyard are particularly impressive, as is the handsome White Horse (food and accommodation). There are more paths across fields and scattered woodland to reach Penley, a modern-looking village but with a thatched schoolbuilding and a picturesque pub (the Dymock Arms) dated *c.* 1550; then via a long curving lane to Hanmer. This is dominated by the Hanmer estate, the family having been resident since the time of Henry III. The Hanmer Arms, which dubs itself the 'village hotel', serves food and afternoon teas.

From the village proceed to Lyn Bedydd which, like the tree-lined Hanmer Mere, is another of the area's distinctive 'meres'. After Bronington the route switches north to Whitewell and Higher Wych. Grindley Brook is less than 2 miles away, and the Maelor Way emerges on to the B5395 only a few hundred yards from the Horse and Jockey public house. This is within sight of the Llangollen Canal, where the Sandstone Trail begins (and where canal-walkers from Chirk will enter). Whitchurch is only a couple of miles away, where there is a good range of shops and other facilities. Whitchurch regards itself as the centre of the Cheshire cheese industry, and local farmhouse produce can be sampled each Friday, market day. The Black Bear is a useful place to rest weary legs, being at the top of the main street next to the Church of St Alkmund. The church probably had Saxon foundations, but was rebuilt in the late eleventh century in 'white' stone, which gave the town its name.

Grindley Brook is also where the South Cheshire Way begins. This 31-mile waymarked trail runs diagonally across the county to link with the beginning of the Mow Cop Trail at Mow Cop Castle.

Here is a splendid opportunity, if you desire, to switch from the West Route to the Central, since from Mow Cop it is barely ten miles to Rushton, where the Central End to End Route emerges after strolling up the Staffordshire Way, and where it then embarks on the Gritstone Trail and heads for the Pennines.

The South Cheshire Way traverses low-level farmland and canals, but the Sandstone Trail takes a far more varied and higher course above the Cheshire Plains, and more than one End to End walker has praised the Trail's bouncy wooded heights, as well as its satisfyingly direct course northwards. There is everything to be gained with keeping the west coast in view.

However, for the first three miles the Sandstone Trail follows the towpath of the Llangollen Canal once more, then at Willeymore Lock it cuts across fields via Chad's Chapel, and so the Triassic Sandstone begins to rise. Formed 300 million years ago, this Central Cheshire ridge carries the Trail for 30 miles through the county, and from numerous points allows superb views of North Wales and the Mersey. There are also a number of ancient fortifications along the Way, including the dim outline of Maiden Castle, an Iron Age hillfort, near Larkton and Bickerton Hills.

The Sandstone Trail is waymarked by yellow circles bearing a black bootprint and the letter 'S', as well as occasional finger posts. Follow these to Raw Head, at 227m the highest point on the Trail (great views over the Dee plain), and where the steep woodland slopes flank dramatic red sandstone outcrops. The rocks bear signs of both wind erosion and past quarrying, and the large cave known as the Queen's Parlour probably resulted from the excavation of sand used to scour cottage floors.

Descend the sandy slopes of Bulkeley Hill. At Higher Buwardsley the Pheasant offers excellent food and expensive accommodation, and has its own herd of Highland cattle, oddly enough. On the other side of the lane is the Cheshire Candle Workshops, a popular tourist destination.

At the northern end of the Peckforton Hills, where pine and larch give way to attractive oaks, pheasants are likely to be strutting loudly and absurdly about; and conditions can get muddy in bad weather. Here there is a tale of two castles. Peckforton Castle, Norman in style but built only in the 1840s, was where *Robin Hood, Prince of Thieves* was filmed. It is privately owned, but open during the summer. However, the real gem is Beeston Castle, which stands on a spectacular rocky crag opposite Peckforton. The romantic remains are not enhanced by an ugly modern concrete bridge, nor by the briskly efficient English Heritage ladies who insist on telling you where exactly to walk, but nevertheless Ranulf, Earl of Chester, picked a truly stunning site for its construction in 1337. On a clear day it is possible to see the Clwydian Range (west), Liverpool Cathedral (north), Jodrell Bank telescope (east), and the Wrekin (south).

At one of the two car parks by the entrance there is a useful refreshments kiosk, and a Sandstone Trail noticeboard. You will see quite a few of these display boards along the way. Each shows the local section of the route marked on a large-scale map, which can be quite useful for lazy map-readers.

Should you consider switching from the West to the Central End to End Route before the Mersey and have not taken the South Cheshire Way, then here at Beeston Castle consider the aforementioned Cestrian Link Walk. The idea of walking two of the best routes in Wales and England in full is attractive, but in practice Prestatyn is rather off-course as far as overall direction is concerned, and to reach Edale from the Irish Sea requires 112 miles of walking. If you want to connect the two heavyweights then it may be wiser to join the Cestrian Link Walk at Beeston. From here it heads due east to Bunbury and Calveley, then uses the Shropshire Union Canal towpath for a while, until field paths and lanes lead to Warmingham, north of Crewe. The route utilises a number of quiet country lanes, then after Marton the land rises and beyond Gawsworth joins the Gritstone Trail, and the End to End Central Route for a short distance. If you want to extend the Central Route to Edale, the Cestrian Link skirts Wildboarclough and Errwood Reservoir, before crossing the plateau of Combs Moss and approaching Edale from Peak Forest and Castleton.

Keeping west of Tiverton, cross the combination of railway (Chester–Crewe), river (Gowy), and canal (Shropshire Union). The Shady Oak is a popular haunt, judging by the number of boats moored by the public bar, and its good beer and imaginative menu also makes it popular with walkers. Then over pastureland to the west of Taporley (accommodation), and the ground rises once more to Primrose Hill above Kelshall. Most of the houses and horrible modern bungalows are avoided, as the path winds its way over the hilltop and through small thickets, crossing the main Chester road at Gresty's Waste. Now there is a stretch of extremely pleasant woodland walking. Delamere Forest may only be modest in size, but there are enough open patches of bracken and deciduous woodland not to induce conifer claustrophobia. Although other forest trails are waymarked, Sandstone Trail signs are evident, but I still managed to

A stimulating start to the walk: the South-West Coast Path at Chapel Porth (*above*) and the wide sweep of Woolacombe Sands (*below*).

The Somerset Levels offer gentle, peaceful walking. King's Sedgemoor Drain at Greylake (*above*), leading to the splendid architecture of Vicars' Close, Wells (*below*).

The up after the down: the Offa's Dyke Path between Knighton and Montgomery may leave you breathless.

Beeston Castle (*above*), amid the tree-covered ridges of Cheshire; and (*below*) the view towards the Mersey estuary from the end of the Sandstone Trail above Frodsham.

It's over the top for the walker, as the Trent and Mersey Canal towpath (*above*) ends abruptly at Preston Brook Tunnel near Dutton. In southern Cumbria (*below*) the Furness Way weaves its undisturbed course through Lowick Bridge.

The mountains of the Lake District can attract snow well into the year: the Langdale Pikes (*above*), and the summit of High Pike, south of Caldbeck (*below*), both on the Cumbria Way.

The Southern Upland Way traverses the rounded Lowther Hills near Moffat (*above*); but beyond Glasgow the West Highland Way enters real mountain scenery (*below*), Buachaille Etive Mor, Glencoe.

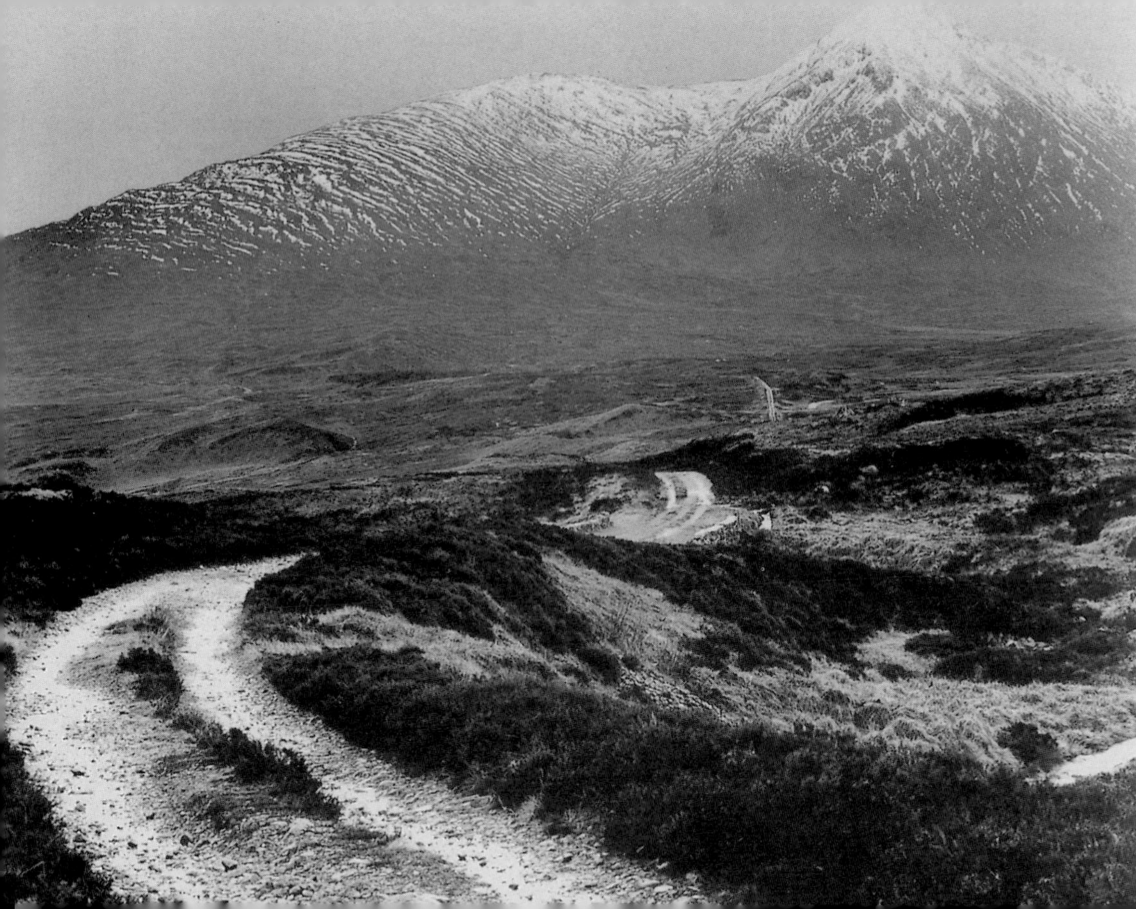

And the path leads ever on . . . the West Highland Way follows the old military road across Rannoch Moor towards Glencoe.

get lost. The route is north along tracks to the public conveniences at Barnesbridge Gates, then over the road and via paths taking a broad westwards curve towards Manley.

From Simmond's Hill the huge craggy lump of Helsby Hill is evident further west, but the Trail has Frodsham in its sights, so skirt the thickly wooded hillfort above Woodhouses. The occasional views from the sandstone outcrops get better all the time. Follow a clear track around the tree-clad hillside to Dunsdale Hollow, where there is an unmissable signpost indicating Beacon Hill (up Jacob's Ladder to the right) and Frodsham (straight on). The official route is to Beacon Hill, but this is a poor finish since the path sweeps recklessly across two large fairways of a golf course and ends at a car park with no view, café or pub in sight. I recommend that you continue along the Frodsham path from Dunsdale Hollow, and unless you want to descend hurriedly into the town follow the steep cliff sides through woods north. It is not very far, but paths shoot off in many directions, and you must maintain your height and emerge from the canopy at the war memorial on a wildflower meadow overlooking Frodsham. Despite the presence of the Mersey View Country Club behind, this is a wonderful viewing platform. Below lies the Mersey estuary, with Liverpool in the distance. Although the industrial complexes at Ellesmere Port and Widnes are all too evident, what is also apparent is the wide green coastal plain and miles of undeveloped farmland. Munch your sandwiches and watch the planes taking off from Liverpool airport (7½ miles away). Another section of the End to End route has been successfully completed.

FRODSHAM – PRESTON (62 miles)

Frodsham is where the long-distance footpaths end, at least for the moment. It is a small town with shops and pubs, but few places to stay. Leave by the pavement of the A56 in the direction of Runcorn, turning right at Frodsham Water Sports Shop by the bridge, where there is a clear public footpath sign (do not cross the river yet). Now proceed up the southern bank of the River Weaver. It is likely that one or more of the shop's customers will be out in loud boats making splashes and whooping noises. However, peace and quiet soon return, and even the distant growl of the M56 is soon replaced by the quacking of waterfowl and the twittering of finches.

The bankside path is rather overgrown in places, but nevertheless it is perfectly walkable, and after some shady woodland follow yellow arrows that direct you through Pickerings Lock Caravan Site to where a well-used bridleway to Dutton begins. As you walk through the meadows by the river towards Dutton Railway Viaduct, among a few docile Fresians lazily chewing the cud, you may wonder where all the smoke and industry of Runcorn and Widnes that was evident from the hill above Frodsham has gone.

The River Weaver is the only large river to rise and flow its full course within Cheshire, and the original object in canalising it was to accommodate the salt trade around Winsford and Northwich. Today the Weaver Navigation hosts pleasure cruisers and narrow boats. At the parallel locks at Dutton switch bank, and once over the white wooden footbridge by the sluice a short bridleway links with the Trent and Mersey Canal, barely half a mile away. Here turn left, towards the hamlet of Dutton, and passing the massed ranks of Cheshire anglers follow the grassy towpath alongside fields and into woodland. Before long, Preston Brook Tunnel approaches. The British Waterways notice states the hours that northbound boats are permitted to enter. No such restrictions on the walker! Take a glimpse inside the tunnel – the light from the other end is just visible – and leave the canal temporarily for the lane above.

Unfortunately, this inviting lane leads only to the A533, and there follows a short diversion of a couple of miles until the canal is rejoined near Preston Marina. At the Talbot Arms, opposite the lane's entrance, you can either turn left and scurry down the main road. There is a pavement, but there is also a fibreglass works and a large Guinness brewery. At the roundabout at the very end turn right, and the canal is almost in sight once more. A far better option, if slightly longer, is to turn right at the Talbot Arms, and after a hundred yards take the left fork at a three-way junction. The relatively quiet road you have now joined cuts across fields a safe distance from the industrial works, and there are interesting views over Runcorn and the Mersey estuary. At Preston on the Hill turn left down the lane marked 'Chester', which emerges opposite Claymore Navigation (boat hire) by the canal bridge. Take the left-hand bank underneath the motorway bridge, and via the mouth of Preston Marina. As the canal curves gently eastwards, the cooling towers of Fiddlers Ferry power station, over the Mersey near Widnes, lurch into view. But this is only a glimpse of industrial Merseyside; the End to End route shows you the scene, then whisks you away through the fields once more.

At Preston Marina join the Bridgewater Canal, generally agreed to be the country's oldest, and certainly the first to be built in England as a commercial waterway. Its pleasant, open towpath, popular with local ramblers, now heads east through Moore and Higher Walton, and skirts the southern edge of Warrington. Walton Hall Gardens and the nearby Church of St John the Evangelist (sitting alone with a neat graveyard in the middle of a field) are well worth a short detour to visit. Around Hillcliffe and Stockton Heath the surroundings are certainly residential, but all the while this unassuming, watery corridor manages to avoid the grime and bustle. There are constant reminders of the canal's past activity, as well. From London Bridge, in Stockton Heath, two packet boats specially built for the Duke of Bridgewater in 1774 made regular trips to Manchester. Here you will also find Thorn Marine, which among other things operates a friendly little shop stocked with everything that a mariner – or walker – might need.

Continue along the towpath to Grappenhall, an attractive village with cobbled streets and stocks. The Ram's Head and Parr Arms offer refreshments, and on the tower of the sixteenth-century church is the figure of a grinning cat, appropriately for Cheshire. Then Warrington is left behind, although it is hard to ignore the mighty M6 as it thunders overhead and on to Thelwall Viaduct over the Manchester Ship Canal. Almost immediately afterwards you reach Lymm, where there is a beautiful row of cottages beside a round pool and weir. Lymm Dam, in woodland to the south, provides a relaxing evening's stroll.

After these eastbound canal miles the course now reverts to a more satisfactory, northerly direction, and there are a few roads and some field miles before reaching the Leeds and Liverpool Canal near Wigan. For those who dislike towpath-walking the Cheshire–Lancashire section may not be among your favourite on the Walk, but unless you want to make a lengthy diversion east it must be said that these historic watery arteries offer probably the quickest, and usually quietest, ways of negotiating the urbanised North-West. Many are still navigable, and some quite popular. There are often pubs and small stores at the major locks or junctions, and all the time lessons in industrial archaeology and the early transport revolution go hand in hand with those in natural history, especially birdlife. Also, some canals have been incorporated into new country parks and outdoor leisure areas, and it is one of these, Pennington Flash, that you are aiming for now.

To cross the Manchester Ship Canal requires a pavement mile to Warburton, then over a high and rather spectacular girder bridge. There is a princely toll of 10 pence for car drivers, but walkers are graciously allowed a free passage. On the other side it is worth fleeing the A57 as soon as possible. A five-minute walk will take you to the Rixton Claypits, where Nature has been left to take over some abandoned clay excavations; and it has succeeded to such an extent that part of the area is now an SSSI.

To avoid the pull towards Warrington take the quiet and more scenic route to Glazebrook, then a few yards up the B5212 turn off right at New Farm, and for 2½ miles follow a delightful path along the east bank of Glaze Brook. There is a bridge over the M6, otherwise all the traffic stays a suitable distance the other side of the Brook. Worsley and Salford are far enough away across fields to the east not to worry about; instead, the signposted (if occasionally overgrown) footpath directs you past the handsome Woolden Hall to Moss House Farm, and then before the railway turn left down a cobbled lane and rejoin the road at Glazebury.

Another option is to take a short footpath across open fields from Rixton to near Hollingreave Farm. From here you can follow the farm track north-west, over the railway, to Hoyles Moss Farm and then on to Culcheth. This allows for a detour to visit Risley Moss, one of the last unexcavated peat mosses in the North-West.

Unless you pause at the George and Dragon at Glazebury, which has an all-day menu and public vaults, do not turn left but right on to the main road, and proceed under the railway for a hundred yards. Leave by Hurst Lane and follow this past the cricket club towards Hurst Hall. Despite the 'Private Road' and 'Trespassers will be blah blah' signs, this is a public right of way, a fact confirmed by public footpath signposts at the end of the lane. Take the track to the right, which crosses fields and the county boundary. The A580 dual carriageway has a gap in the central reservation – but take extreme care when crossing this road. Then shrink into the high grass and shrubland west of Land Side, and along footpaths to the eastern end of Pennington Flash Country Park. (The newly built A580 link road may not be featured on some maps and can disorientate; it is safely negotiated at the traffic lights.)

Pennington Flash is a surprisingly large lake that was originally formed by mining subsidence. It now hosts yachts and ducks in equal numbers, and there are even birdwatchers' hides north of the visitor centre. The 1,100 acre park also has a municipal golf course, and your way is around the edge of this to join with the Leeds and Liverpool Canal on the park's northern rim. Ahead, beyond Leigh and Westhoughton, is the unmistakable lump of Rivington Moor, with the distinctive collection of masts and transmitters perched on Winter Hill.

It is about six miles to Wigan, and the firm and sandy towpath will allow a good head of steam. This is perhaps fortunate, since these are not among the most attractive miles you will walk. The Plank Lane Lift Bridge is an interesting feature, even though it is situated on Slag Lane. There are some largely innocuous and grassed-over remains of old spoil heaps, and a number of lakes and pools that, like the Flash, owe their origin to mining (but now host ducks and geese). Yet it is not so much an ugly, despoiled place, rather a strange wasteland where Nature is slowly creeping back.

At the canal junction at Chapel Lane lock a signpost reads: Blackburn 21, Leeds 92 (east); Burscough 11, Liverpool 35 (west). Here the End to End West Route turns left, westwards, and after visiting Wigan Pier it follows the Douglas Valley Way by canal and river to reach Longton, near Preston.

However, there is an alternative route over the higher and wilder ground to the east; through Wigan to Haigh Hall Country Park and Rivington Reservoir. Either follow the canal, or waymarks for the Douglas Valley Way (eastwards, towards the Pennines). At Rivington, on the reservoir's eastern shore, clear paths and quiet minor roads lead north along the slopes of Rivington and Anglezarke Moors (there are wide views across the Lancashire coastal plain from the top, even to Anglesey and the Clwydian Range on a clear day). After White Coppice there are about another 9 miles of lanes and local footpaths, until you enter the Lower Ribble Valley, and the outskirts of Preston.

If you stick to the spirit of the West Route, which means resistance to all forays eastwards, then turn left at Chapel Lane and pass the moored canal boats sitting snugly before Trencherfield Mill. This is part of the Wigan Pier development. There isn't of course a pier, instead a large and newly renovated canalside and mill heritage site, which includes the world's largest working mill engine (in steam hourly) and the unimaginatively named 'The Way

We Were' exhibition. Or you can simply pop in the Orwell for a drink.

There is no need to enter the centre of Wigan, since the Douglas Valley Way takes you out west along the canal. The arrow for Appley Bridge confirms the route. The towpath is clear and firm, but not until Crooke do the trees begin to encroach and urbanisation is fully left behind. The Gathurst (M6) Bridge remains audible for some time, but peace gradually returns, and the canal and River Douglas go hand in hand until Parbold. The Way now leaves the canal and mostly follows the embankment of the Douglas Navigation northwards. However, there is nothing stopping you from continuing along the Leeds and Liverpool Canal until Burscough Bridge, then swinging north to Rufford. Industrial Lancashire seems far away; all is now quiet and agricultural. From Burscough the path is grassy rather than sandy, but still firm and not overgrown. After Rufford, however, it is a different matter. Both the canal and Navigation channel route can be covered with high, coarse vegetation. Be prepared to make use of a mile or so of tarmac if conditions are too bad. At Bank Hall use the pavement of the A59 until Carr House, where you can return to the embankment and walk above the marshes towards the mouth of the River Douglas.

At the Dolphin, a public house isolated in the middle of flat, empty pasture, the Douglas Valley Way ends and the Ribble Way begins. There is a small waymark indicating this fact, depicting a letter 'R' above wavy blue lines. The route continues across fields to the embankment above the River Ribble. These embankments are testimony to the considerable land reclamation that has occurred, although they were originally constructed in an effort to keep the Ribble channel free for ships. The flatness and emptiness of the landscape is quite startling; and there is the odd sight of white sails gliding through the pasture and salt marsh, as yachts make their way up from the Irish Sea. Soon the buildings begin to draw closer, a power station looms, and you are at Preston docks.

PRESTON – ARNSIDE (55 miles)

Lancashire's modern county town offers the chance to replenish stocks, perhaps visit the launderette, or even admire what I have been told is Europe's largest bus station. But your thoughts will not be with buses. By now you should be feeling fit and in the groove. Behind you the South-West, Wales, the industrial North-West;

ahead lies the coast and hills of Lancashire and Cumbria, and then the challenge of Scotland.

If you are feeling ambitious, or if the Pennines seem simply irresistible, there is now the option of veering north-east along the Ribble Way, which from Preston follows the course of the river upstream through varied and ever more rugged scenery, via Ribchester, Gisburn and Settle. The overall distance from Preston to the Ribble's source on Gayle Moor is about 62 miles. From here, a few miles to the north of Pen-y-Ghent, in the Yorkshire Dales National Park, it is only half a mile to the Pennine Way. The temptation is then to join the End to End Central Route across the High Pennines all the way to Scotland. However, a more appealing option, perhaps for the connoisseur long-distance walker, would be to pick up the Dales Way (it is coincidental with the Ribble Way on Gayle Moor) and return to the West Coast along this glorious 81-mile route via Dentdale and the Howgill Fells to Windermere, in the Lake District.

Another attractive option, if the thought of a further towpath is dismaying, is to cross the M6 and head for the Forest of Bowland. Possibly make for Beacon Fell Country Park, an isolated hill comprising 185 acres of rough moorland and woods, and then take the path from Bleasdale Tower over to Langden Brook; or around the south side of Wolf Fell to Dunsop Bridge. The low but quite rugged heather-clad tops and hidden valleys provide good walking, especially since they are usually devoid of the rambling hordes descending on the Dales and Lakeland Fells. However, public access has always been a problem here, especially on the fells north of the Trough of Bowland. Despite this, there is a direct moorland track (the old Hornby Road) from Slaidburn over Croasdale Fell to Crosgill, with great views of Pen-y-Ghent and the Yorkshire peaks. Then drop down to Caton and rejoin the West Route on the banks of the River Lune near Halton.

Back at Preston, the Lancaster Canal, the main West Route until Lancaster, originally started behind Corporation Street, but now you must venture a little way down the Fylde Road before coming across the canal basin. Ahead is just over thirty miles of easy and relaxing walking, and as at Wigan it is only a matter of minutes before the houses begin to thin out. The Lancaster Canal is another that has seen welcome renovation in the last couple of decades. It was constructed in the 1790s to transport limestone from south Westmorland and north Lancashire to be burnt into the arable land in the south, and at one stage extended as far north as Kendal.

Once under the M55, the canal swings round northwards to Bilsborrow. If you fancy a change of scene then take the lane through Catforth and Woodsfold to St Michael's on Wyre, an attractive village with some fine stone buildings and a church recorded in the Domesday Book. Footpaths to Nateby, on the edge of Rawcliffe Moss, allow you to rejoin the canal near Garstang, a pleasant and unassuming market town that makes a useful overnight stop. There is even the Lancaster Canal Museum for the suitably interested.

The towpath is generally well-kept and easy to follow, but is sometimes muddy in bad weather. However, this is by and large manageable mud. Think yourself lucky that you are not wading through the oozy quagmire on Bleaklow or Black Hill, early on the Pennine Way. This relatively short section of canal-walking (under two days) may not be as dramatic as the Pennines, but your legs will thank you for the respite and you can relax as far as routefinding is concerned. Besides, the End to End Walk is about enjoying the rich variety of Britain's scenery. It is not only about the sea cliffs, moors and mountains, but about discovering the hidden countryside: old railway tracks, drove roads, forgotten lanes, and canals. Along the length of this largely unknown canal you will meet a few fishermen, perhaps a farmer now and then, and maybe just the occasional walker. And, of course, a boat or two. But there will not be a procession of orange cagoules ahead. You are not in the midst of a national park nor on a national trail. This is a bit of real, ordinary rural England, and it is all the more charming for that.

However, it will have become clear, since Preston, that you are not the only north-bound traveller about. As the northern Lancashire coastal plain narrows, the roads (A6 and M6), the railway (West Coast main line) and the canal occasionally squeeze into sight of each other. It makes for an interesting visual history lesson of the transport revolution in all its stages. Where the canal and A6 rub noses, there is often a conveniently placed pub. The Plough in Galgate is open all day and serves a good pint of Boddingtons. Before long, however, bungalows can be glimpsed among the trees, and the occasional jogger will stumble past, signifying that Lancaster is at hand. The canal runs through the top of the town, but it is worth venturing into this historical centre to visit the Priory Church and castle, the massive fifteenth-century gatehouse of which is a stupendous sight. Looking north there are new and exciting views over the Lune valley and estuary, the expanse of Morecambe Bay, and on a clear day to the distant Coniston range of mountains. Lancaster also offers a wide range of shops, restaurants and accommodation.

An alternative way of reaching Lancaster is to leave the main canal before Galgate for the arm to Glasson Dock. At this tiny, picturesque port join the newly-formed Lancashire Coastal Way north via Conder Green. This trail will eventually stretch for 137 miles around the coast, and for this short burst to Lancaster it takes the form of the Lune Estuary Path (a dismantled railway), arriving in the town via the handsome St George's Quay.

Which direction now? Certainly the Lune valley looks inviting. The river meanders its way across the wide, lush meadows to Kirkby Lonsdale and Sedbergh. There is a riverside walk to the former, and then quiet lanes to the latter. From Sedbergh, take the Dales Way along Dentdale to the Pennine Way – an option for those uninterested in the Lake District. But one of the highlights of the West Route is the Cumbrian section. How could you get this far and then shun the Lakes?

Returning to the original route, there are two ways to reach Carnforth from Lancaster. The first is to continue along the canal, which crosses the river valley by the Lune Aqueduct, a superb construction rising nearly 20m above the Lune. After this, the elevated banks give wide views over Morecambe Bay, and since the coast is so close the whole perspective changes.

If you have had enough of canal-walking then choose the second route. Initially, at least, it is up the Lune Way cycle path (the former Lancaster–Wennington railway line), which sticks to the river's eastern bank and passes under the M6. At the village of Halton cross the narrow road bridge above a dramatic wooded ravine known as the Crook of Lune. For the next 2 miles it is necessary to follow quiet minor roads to Nether Kellet, then over the rumbling M6 and into Carnforth.

Carnforth is the home of Steamtown, a small but noisy working train museum. You will either call in and end up staying several hours inspecting the busy engine shed, riding one of the locos in steam, or choosing which 'engine driver' cap to purchase; or else you will hurry past, shaking your head sadly. Either way, a succession of attractive lanes lead around the edge of Morecambe Bay to Silverdale. At the RSPB's Leighton Moss reserve there is a chance to sit and observe dunlin, snipe, bitterns and, if you are very lucky, otters. The reserve is an extension of the mudflats and marshes that sweep for miles around the north-west edge of Morecambe Bay. In the excitement of mistaking a crow for a marsh harrier, you may also miss the fact that just beyond Silverdale the intrepid long-distance pedestrian enters Cumbria. Lancashire is a large county, and it may have felt like it, but now the Cumbrian fells are reaching out, and after that the Scottish border!

Before plunging ahead, however, take stock of the countryside about. The Silverdale-Arnside area, a small, wooded coast of low limestone hills and bays, is an unspoilt gem of the North-West. Most holidaymakers seem oblivious to its existence, as they sit steaming in queues for the Lake District on the nearby motorway. All the more reason for you to linger. Arnside Park is dotted with winding footpaths, and Arnside Knott, although only around 140m high, provides a glorious panorama of southern Cumbria. The small resort of Arnside has one of the world's shortest promenades, an even shorter pier (rebuilt in stone, after the original was washed away in the storms of 1982/83) and offers plenty of accommodation, including a youth hostel. It is an ideal place to dally on a warm, sunny evening, and contemplate the 650 miles of walking now behind you . . . and the amount still ahead.

12

ENGLAND'S FINEST MOUNTAINS

Arnside – Carlisle

ARNSIDE – CONISTON (51 miles)

The next stage of the Walk may come as something of a surprise, since the approach to the Lakes is both scenic and very peaceful. Skirting the Kent estuary, the route winds its way through ancient woodland and unspoilt villages, past stately homes and the odd castle. All the while it creeps nearer to the mountains, and yet the low relief offers mostly undemanding walking. What is particularly striking is the relative quietness and emptiness of southern Cumbria. Aside from Barrow, Ulverston and Grange-over-Sands, there are few settlements of any size, and the Cartmel Peninsula in particular appears to escape the hordes that seem so determined to stay within three square miles of Windermere and Grasmere. Also, the route adopts long-distance paths once more: the Furness Way, from Arnside as far as Coniston, and then the Cumbria Way to Carlisle. These are not bustling national trails, but local, thoughtful routes. Yet they are certainly long-distance (75 and 70 miles respectively) and there is much to see. The walking is varied, some along quiet lanes, but it is seldom difficult (although there is plenty of scope to bag a few mountains later on). Those without a tent should not find accommodation too hard to come by, although central Lakeland may need booking in advance if it is peak holiday time.

From Arnside, the Kent viaduct stretches across the estuary in a tempting fashion. Unfortunately this is strictly a railway bridge; your route does not cross the river until Levens Hall, 6 miles to the north. Of course there is nothing stopping you catching one of the local trains from Arnside to Grange-over-Sands, the next station over the bridge. There will have to be a little route adjustment, but it is only a mile or so from Grange to Cartmel, where the route can be picked up once more. But how much of a purist are you? By what means did you cross the River Camel at Padstow, for example, all those miles ago on the north Cornish coast? Naturally there are strict rules prohibiting mechanical transport for those End to Enders challenging the clock. But ultimately the record-breakers are not too dissimilar to those walkers intent on the more leisurely approach, since all have embarked on a very personal journey, and in the end you must be truthful to yourself. Some walkers shun the use of *any* roads or tarmac between Cornwall and Caithness. On the other hand, many long-distance walkers are quite happy to use a local bus or train to visit a place or person along the way – say, on an appointed 'day off' – so long as they return and resume walking at the exact spot they left off previously. The question is, in X number of years' time, as you once more recount the tale of your marvellous walk from one end of the land to the other, will you deliberately leave out the bit about the train across the Kent estuary?

So, feeling decidely self-righteous, leave Arnside by foot and give the bridge barely a glance. Besides, you will now be too busy route finding. The Furness Way is indicated only by standard public footpath or bridleway signposts – where it is at all. Follow the road up through the village and then via footpaths across wide fields towards Dallam Tower, a curious old mansion that began life as a pele tower. Skirting Milnthorpe, the route then follows the direction of the A6 for a while, but fortunately misses most of the traffic by detouring through Heversham. Before plunging into Levens Park above the winding River Kent, take a look at Levens Hall, a well-preserved stately home set in glorious grounds. From the Park, the troublesome A6 is crossed for the last time, as you head up through narrow lanes to Sizergh Castle (photograph time again) and then via footpaths to the attractive village of Brigsteer. Enter the Lake District National Park; and perhaps a minor celebration would not be out of place.

After a succession of quiet country lanes the route reaches Crosthwaite (pub and post office; some accommodation) then swings abruptly south, via Whitbarrow Scar and Witherslack to Lindale, about 9 miles away. It may seem odd that you are now heading south, but it is only a minor detour to take in the delights of Cartmel, 3 miles on from Lindale. First ascend Hampsfield Fell, a splendid little hill with a curious viewing station known as The Hospice, built by a local pastor last century. For shops and B&Bs, Grange-over-Sands is only a mile away, but most walkers will take the cross-field path direct to Cartmel, where the ancient Priory Church, founded in 1188, is worth a visit. Cartmel is a village of unique character and charm; it does not seem to have been ruffled by the gaudier side of twentieth-century life, and must be one of the few villages to have its own racecourse – which the route now crosses to Park Wood.

Pick up a quiet lane all the way to Howbarrow Farm, then heading north once more, follow the broad ridge of Ellerside from Howbarrow to Bigland Tarn. There are great views west across the Leven estuary, but this will be the last time you will smell the sea for many miles. After the tarn, follow a path through Bigland Woods and then veer west along the banks of the Leven to Roudsea Woods. The paths here offer good, firm walking; but this is also a nature reserve, so a silent passage might win you a sight of some deer or a woodpecker.

There are now four villages in the next four miles: Greenodd, Penny Bridge, Spark Bridge and Lowick Bridge. They are all on or close to main roads, but you will be able to avoid the traffic by using a path along the banks of the River Crake, once busy with bobbin mills for the Lancashire cotton industry, or by taking alternate minor roads.

The feel of Lakeland will be stronger than ever, and Coniston Water is only a mile away, but if you stick with the Furness Way the approach demands a little huffing and puffing over Bethecar Moor, at the heart of the Furness Fells. It may be time to get the trusty compass out. If the paths seem indistinct, take a bearing for Top o'Selside, almost due north from Low Bethecar Farm. It is certainly worth the effort. The 335m summit of Top o'Selside may be modest, but it offers great views over the Coniston Fells, and it is the first close-up view of the high mountains.

There are only six miles to the village of Coniston, but this will begin to escalate alarmingly if you get lost in Grizedale Forest. Try not to. There is a clear track from Low Parkamoor, north of Top o'Selside, that enters the thick conifer plantation. Stick with it, consult your OS map, take a left turn, and try to emerge from the sea of green on the bridleway above Brantwood, John Ruskin's house, which overlooks Coniston Water. John Ruskin, Victorian art critic and social reformer, was a dynamic but rather odd fellow. He was divorced by his wife after six years, who complained that he was incapable of normal sex and had never consummated the marriage. Then he became totally besotted with a nine-year-old girl. He ended up virtually insane, and died at Brantwood in 1871. The house has a fine collection of Ruskin's drawings and paintings, and enjoys a tremendous view over Coniston.

Coniston marks the end of the Furness Way as far as the End to End walker is concerned. It actually extends for another 25 miles to Ravenglass, on the quiet shores of the Irish Sea, but now you must pick up the Cumbria Way for a scenic journey through the heart of the Lake District. However, the slate buildings of Coniston offer a useful resting point. There are the usual shops, two youth hostels, the Ruskin Museum; and you can even take a cruise around the lake on the Victorian steam yacht *Gondola*. But if you don't feel that restful, you can always scale the Old Man of Coniston for a little exercise.

CONISTON – CARLISLE (60 miles)

In devising the End to End West Route I had a few concrete ideas in mind. It had to include some of the Cornwall and Devon coast; it must try and reflect the grandeur of Wales – a sizeable chunk of the Offa's Dyke, at least; the rather neglected north Lancashire coastal lowlands should be represented; and, of course, there is the Lake District. Seasoned walkers will need no guide to central Cumbria. For the End to End walker, the Cumbria Way is basically a suggestion. The variations on a south–north route are too numerous to mention, and with such a proliferation of campsites and youth hostels, plus all the amenities available for outdoor types in places such as Coniston and Keswick, this can easily become a stage for you to fashion according to your own fancy. But in staying faithful to the Cumbria Way, the West Route enjoys a variety of scenery from tarns and woodland to open fellside, and yet remains attractive and accessible to the backpacking long-distance walker. And an added advantage is that the Cumbria Way is shown on the Ordnance Survey's excellent Outdoor Leisure maps of the Lake District.

From Coniston village, head north through the scattered woodland about Yewdale Beck to Tarn Hows, about 2 miles away. Tarn

Hows is a curious place. It continues to grace countless place mats and postcards, and it does have a certain prettiness. But it is neither breathtaking nor inspirational (like the view south from the top of Great Gable, or being out on a rowboat on Ullswater and watching a storm rush in). Tarn Hows is a place to visit once. And as soon as you have, continue north along clear footpaths, cross the busy Coniston–Ambleside road, and then turn left down a track for High Peak Farm, then right to Skelwith Bridge. There are B&Bs, a campsite at Little Loughrigg, and a youth hostel nearby.

It is unlikely that you will be alone as you stride up Great Langdale towards the Pikes, but it is footpaths all the way, and the presence of such mighty mountains so close at hand will lift any walker's heart (provided the weather allows you to see them). It has been several hundred miles since you have been among such sturdy hills.

From the Old Dungeon Ghyll Hotel, a well-trodden track leads purposefully up Mickleden, until the Cumbria Way chooses the right fork and zig-zags up on to Stake Pass. The track is steep in places, but you will want to pause to look behind, for the Langdale valley is every geography teacher's dream, a classic U-shaped glacial valley, replete with hanging valleys, truncated spurs, moraines, etc. Now is a great opportunity to use the height gained to nip up Crinkle Crags or Bowfell, perhaps even the Langdale Pikes themselves. If the weather is favourable and you feel strong, why not consider a short detour to ascend Scafell Pike, the highest piece of land in England? In a few weeks' time you might even have the opportunity of crowning this achievement with the ultimate: Ben Nevis. Land's End to John o'Groats, plus the highest mountains in England and Scotland (and with the latter, of course, the highest in the UK). Now there's a thought.

On Stake Pass proceed north, across some marshy ground, and then straight over and down by Stake Beck. This is a significant watershed for the south-north traveller in Lakeland. Until now, all the streams and rivers have flowed south into Morecambe Bay, but now they all drain north and west into the Solway Firth. This can also be a tricky area in mist or rain, where map and compass should be employed, but in clear weather there should be no problems.

From one outstanding valley to another. While Langdale is stern and spectacular, Borrowdale opens up as a verdant garden of meadows and mixed woodland, but still ringed with high, imposing fells. From the King to the Queen. After descending by Stake Beck into Langstrath, keep to the left-hand bank of Stonethwaite Beck for Longthwaite Youth Hostel, campsites and Seatoller; or the opposite bank for the pub and post office at Rosthwaite.

Upon leaving Rosthwaite, take the fenced footpath down to the river, crossing it by the stepping stones if you feel daring, or by New Bridge, a few yards further downstream, if you want to play it safe. The Cumbria Way follows the river north for a short while, then heads up into trees and around the flanks of Castle Crag. If your impulse is to stay by the banks of the amiable River Derwent then do not resist it. You may have the odd scramble as the valley narrows and the banks steepen, but pause among the silver birch and you may be rewarded by the sight of a dipper bobbing on a rock amid the rushing water. I have even seen deer along this stretch.

A choice of footpaths will either take you above the hamlet of Grange and bring you out on the lane a little further on, or else into the middle of the clustered buildings, conveniently close to the tearooms. Barely half a mile down the minor road turn off at Ellers Beck, and follow the open path down to Derwentwater. Although a more direct path now heads through the woods inland, the scenic, winding path around the bays and promontories of the lake's western shore is a delight that should not be missed.

After two or three miles' wandering the path emerges at the foot of Cat Bells, and there take the footpath signposted 'Portinscale' through gentle mixed woodland. The lane past the hotel to the right leads to a suspension bridge and a footpath across the floodplain into Keswick.

Keswick is generally a busy place, and at times it is a very busy place. But, as the northern centre of the Lake District, it has all the amenities that the self-reliant long-distance walker eventually needs. Additional choices here include restaurants, a pencil factory, a police station, an information centre, a tiny cinema, and a nearby stone circle. There are apparently more B&Bs in Keswick than in any other town of its size anywhere in the country. But there is also a large youth hostel and a good lakeside campsite; and try the Dog and Gun for an evening's refreshment.

Well-stocked once more, heave the pack on, locate Station Road, and stay on it across the River Greta for half a mile until a rough track leads off right by Briar Rigg. Once over the footbridge across the A591, follow the bridleway around the flanks of Latrigg, then contour Lonscale Fell and climb steeply up Glenderaterra

Beck. The track then makes for the lonely Skiddaw House Youth Hostel.

From here to Caldbeck, very roughly 10 miles by foot, the route diverges. The western alternative avoids the high ground (useful if the weather has closed in) and offers the chance to visit Bassenthwaite village for food, drink or possibly accommodation. Follow the clear track north-west from Skiddaw House, down by Dash Beck to the minor road. The village is to the left, otherwise proceed along what is usually a fairly quiet road for just over 2 miles to Longlands, where a green track leads on to Branthwaite and eventually via Nether Row to Caldbeck.

The other route ascends High Pike which, at 658m, is actually the highest point on the Cumbria Way. The fells around here are bare and unpopulated, which generally makes for invigorating walking. From Skiddaw House, follow the bridleway above the babbling River Caldew for 3½ miles, until a track leads off the now metalled road to the left, up to Wolfram mine. Head up the hillside to the hut on the skyline, then north along the path to the flat summit of High Pike. This is the northern edge of Lakeland, and there are extensive views across the Cumbrian Plain to Carlisle and the hills of south-west Scotland. The border is almost in sight! However, there are a few more miles to be trod yet, so descend the northern slopes of High Pike to Nether Row and Caldbeck.

The remainder of the route to Carlisle is along the gentle banks of the Caldew, a maturing river that eventually joins the River Eden at Carlisle. The walking is generally easy, although it can be extremely muddy in bad weather, when the banks can become hazardous. Minor detours may be necessary to avoid patches of erosion, and at one place there are signposts around a section of the path that has been washed away in a landslip. Beyond Caldbeck Churchyard cross the bridge over Parkend Beck and turn right into woodland, then follow the Beck, which joins the Caldew, until Sebergham, where it is necessary to cross and join the other bank until Bellbridge. A mile or so on, Rose Castle stands in neat grounds, the residence of Bishops of Carlisle since the thirteenth century. The road through Hawksdale Hall then brings you to modern civilisation at Bridge End and Buckabank. From here, either follow the eastern bank of the river into Carlisle, or if it looks too waterlogged and eroded, journey through Dalston and follow the railway track via Cummersdale into the town centre.

At last! Only a few miles from Scotland, and the sense of achievement will be profound. Forget the rigours ahead for the moment; reflect on so much already achieved, and allow yourself a moment of self-congratulation. Your body is now fine-tuned, an efficient walking machine. It has managed to get you from one end of England to almost the other, and it is now ready for the final challenge ahead.

13

THE BARE HILLS

Carlisle – Strathblane

CARLISLE – WANLOCKHEAD (76 miles)

The first couple of hours' walking from Carlisle to the Scottish border across the Esk and Eden floodplain are flat and rather featureless, and some may find it uninspiring. As before, don't worry too much – it will give you the chance to make quick miles and, with the Scottish hills looming, the scenery will soon improve dramatically. The main thing here is to avoid walking on or near the desperately busy A74; and the A7 for that matter. Since there are few satisfactory public footpaths in the area the best option is to follow the network of quiet minor roads east of the A7, linking hamlets such as Scaleby, Kirklinton, Easton and Scuggate, and crossing the border east of Rowanburn. From Claygate there are intermittent tracks, including the bed of an old railway, up the Esk valley; or if you feel more energetic follow Tarras Water upstream and ascend Whita Hill where, from the massive monument to the poet and co-founder of the Scottish National Party, Hugh MacDiarmid (Langholm's famous son), there are great views over the town and the narrow, wooded Esk valley.

Langholm, which introduces itself as the 'muckle toon', enjoys an attractive situation at the confluence of three rivers, yet the dark stone buildings can be rather severe. Although there are shops, accommodation is limited, so booking ahead may be advisable. Stay with the Esk for the next 6 miles or so (there are more tracks and lanes along its eastern bank). By the side of the road at Bentpath is a memorial to Thomas Telford, born near here in 1751 and apprenticed to a stonemason in Langholm.

However, it is now time to head west and out of the Esk valley, keeping south of Castle O'er Forest to Boreland and, although there is a path of sorts through trees above Bentpath, it is best to leave the road a little before the hamlet, close to a narrow stone bridge near Hopsrig. The unsurfaced track that you should follow has a rough wooden sign declaring 'Boykenhopehead 3 miles'. Go past fields of black, woolly-haired Galloway cattle and countless sheep, and at Calkin ignore the newer, higher track around the hillside (not marked on the OS Landranger). Continue along the track underneath Ward Hill, altogether a gentle and peaceful place, and finally emerge on to a lane near Whitecastles. Take the minor road via Corrie Common to Boreland, where there is one B&B and not much else. This is an unspoilt and out-of-the-way place, where farming and timber are more important than tourism. There are a few tracks, and scope for some cross-country navigation, but by and large it is quicker and easier to stick to minor roads. Most are fairly wide, and all agreeably quiet. A good example is the lane from just outside Boreland to Moffat, through hamlets such as Gillespie, Wamphraygate and Woodfoot. It runs for almost 12 miles, is open and scenic (with pleasant views over Annandale), and although there are no services along the way it is a very direct and purposeful route. This, I suggest, should be your means of reaching Moffat.

Moffat's early importance was partly due to the development of its spa waters, and also to the woollen industry. The Moffat Ram, a giant statue in the centre of the main street is testimony to this, as is the existence of woollen shops and a mill that pulls in the tourists (they are also sucked in by the famous Moffat toffee). Accommodation and hot meals are also plentiful. From Moffat, Annandale stretches green and invitingly north towards the steep-sloped natural depression of the Devil's Beef Tub, but unfortunately there are few tracks of any length that provide a smooth way forwards. Of course there is plenty of scope for making your own way across the hills to Talla Reservoir, and to the impressive summits of Broad Law and Cramalt Craig above Meggat Reservoir, but bear in mind that all the time you will be swinging away from the west coast and closer to the Central Route.

The best way to proceed to the West Highland Way is to walk a short (but nevertheless tough) section of its less-popular sister route

– the Southern Upland Way. All three End to End routes borrow sections of this twisting 212-mile trail, and despite its overall coast to coast direction it provides a useful step north-west towards Glasgow. The Southern Upland Way often traverses wild and remote land, and this 20-mile chunk is no exception. Although it is excellently waymarked, there are just a handful of buildings between Beattock and Wanlockhead, certainly no shops or cafés, and, with miles of dense forest and some high and open hills ahead, it is as well to be adequately prepared and informed about weather conditions.

Leave Moffat for Beattock, on the A74, preferably via the quiet lanes that the SUW takes past Barnhill House. The A74 at this point is not strictly a motorway, but it may as well be (its roar is audible for miles around). Do not attempt to cross its surface; rather, go underneath it on a path where it spans Evan Water. At Beattock House Hotel there is a licensed campsite, and opposite its entrance follow the lane over the London–Glasgow mainline railway and up Beattock Hill. There are more impressive views over Annandale, but your way is now north, into the Forestry Commission's dark rows of conifers. The SUW signs are clear (a white thistle inside a hexagon), and for the most part the surface is firm, but the corridors among the evergreens inevitably deny decent views, and it is not until the top of Beld Knowe and Hods Hill that the perspective widens. Now there are new views north and west, over the bare Lowther Hills, and more immediately to Daer Reservoir. Approach this down open, bumpy hillside. The path is not always distinct, but the unbroken fence will offer reassurance in poor visibility. Daer Reservoir is a large and rather gloomy tub of grey drinking water. Visitors are not welcome, so the Way is forced to squelch around some woodland and past a short terrace of drab houses that belong to reservoir workers.

After a short burst of tarmac between more trees, the Way clambers out on to rough pasture and heads along a well-defined track to the Sanquhar–Elvanfoot road. From here the radar station on the top of Lowther Hill should become more apparent. If it does not then you are either looking in the wrong direction or else the clouds are down. If the latter is the case, then consider carefully the relative merits of navigating by compass over steep and exposed hillsides, or following the course of the road to Elvanfoot, then minor roads to Crawford and Abington.

On reaching the fairly quiet A702 turn up past Over Fingland

and follow clear signs across the hillside. Apart from chickens and a couple of excitable dogs at the farm, only sheep, larks and mewing buzzards are likely to accompany you. These hills are not well-populated, and since the SUW is among the least-walked of Britain's long-distance paths it is quite likely that you will have the countryside to yourself. Relax and enjoy it, since Glasgow is only a few days away!

By the time you have struggled over Laght Hill and are plodding up Comb Head to Cold Moss, relaxation may be replaced by perspiration. These steep, grassy slopes bring back memories of the middle section of Offa's Dyke, so make sure you have frequent stops to 'admire the view' (this means 'get your breath back' in walkers' parlance). At the top of Lowther Hill, which at 710m is the high-point of the entire Southern Upland Way, skirt the Civil Aviation Authority's massive white golf balls (radar station) and admire the panorama. On a clear day many of southern Scotland's hills are revealed, including Cairn Table and Tinto Hill, plus the distant Grampians.

Follow the access road down from the summit for a short way, then along a rough track and into the hotch-potch of buildings that makes up Wanlockhead, the highest inhabitated village in Scotland. Remoteness and isolation, rather than height, are perhaps the first impressions. There is a youth hostel, a B&B, and the dilapidated Walk-Inn Mountain Lodge, on the site of the former railway station, which may or may not reopen for business. Otherwise amenities are rather scarce, and it is the Museum of Lead Mining that gives a clue as to why there is anything here in the first place. Gold was one of the first discoveries in this area (as early as the Middle Ages), and in 1992 the World Gold Panning Championships were held here! But lead ended up as the principal deposit worked, and the whole village bears this out – the youth hostel was once the mine surgeon's house, and the mine forge is now the visitor centre. At nearby Leadhills is the Allan Ramsay Library, founded by miners in 1741, and the oldest subscription library in Britain. Wanlockhead-Leadhills is a fascinating place to end your brief encounter with the Southern Upland Way, and to look ahead to the crossing of the Clyde valley and the larger hills beyond.

WANLOCKHEAD – STRATHBLANE (61.5 miles)

At this juncture give some thought to Glasgow and how to get through or around it. The route that I propose makes use of the city's country parks and former railway lines, and skirts Glasgow's eastern edge via Coatbridge to join the West Highland Way near Strathblane (about 5 miles after its start at Milngavie). Much of this route has been described in an excellent guidebook by Erl Wilkie, called *Glasgow's Pathways*. I recommend it should you also wish to consider a route around the west of the city, possibly crossing the Clyde via the foot tunnel. As for the main West Route, it approaches Glasgow via Douglas and Strathaven, and from Chatelherault Country Park crosses the River Clyde to Strathclyde Country Park. However, it is hoped that an even better route will soon be possible from New Lanark, using the Clyde Walkway. But bear in mind that like the environs of any large city there must inevitably be a certain amount of urban walking – remember Bristol, Wigan, Preston and Carlisle. Buildings, cars and people will have to be tolerated for a while – so grit your teeth and look forward to the delights of what lies beyond.

The immediate destination is Duneaton Water, south of Mountherrick Hill, which can be reached by tracks from either Wanlockhead or Leadhills. One particular path follows the length of Snar Water. Here, a mile south-west of Crawfordjohn, begins a pleasant, airy lane signposted 'Douglas 6¾ miles', which wanders over low hills then drops down through a gradually flatter landscape of open pasture and young conifer plantations. Douglas was the home of one of the most famous Scottish families. Sir James the 'Black Douglas' created the family's power base in the fourteenth century, and was a close ally of Robert the Bruce, fighting at Bannockburn. Many tales surround Douglas Castle, some of which are described in Sir Walter Scott's novel *Castle Dangerous*. Unfortunately the building was demolished in 1938 due to subsidence, and all that remains is a ruined tower. However, the Douglas and Angus Estates have signposted rights of way through the parkland by Douglas Water, allowing the castle remains to be visited, and this offers walkers a perfect opportunity to continue downriver via tracks and lanes to where Douglas Water meets the River Clyde. Near here, in the Scottish Wildlife Trust's reserve, the Falls of Clyde thunder through a wooded gorge, and kingfishers and willow tits can be seen. In this unspoilt haven south of New Lanark the Clyde Walkway begins its journey to Glasgow. At present, the 37-mile-long Walkway is complete only in parts, but the plan is to form a continuous trail from New Lanark, and when this is finally achieved it will make a superb path that is an obvious route for the West Route End to Ender to adopt.

Unless you are already drawn by the Clyde, for the moment I suggest that you leave Douglas in a north-west direction and use tracks and local lanes to reach Strathaven; or if you want to take a more direct course head for Glassford and omit Strathaven. The landscape becomes slowly softer but, unless you stray into Coalburn or Lesmahagow, conditions remain rural and pleasant. Strathaven is a small market town whose history extends back to the early Middle Ages, when it was granted a special Charter and became a Free Burgh of Barony. There are plenty of cafés and shops, plus a tourist information centre. From Strathaven take the lane through Glassford to the River Avon at Millheugh, west of Larkhall, from where there is a footpath (a right of way) to Chatelherault Country Park. As with the Clyde Walkway, the Clyde and Avon Valleys Project is also developing the Avon Walkway, which follows the river's deep, wooded course for over two miles through the attractive grounds of Chatelherault. The parkland of the eighteenth-century house includes a total of 10 miles of footpaths, with regular waymarks and 'storyboards', and abounds with all manner of wildlife; and from the high grassy ridge by the visitor centre there are wide views over the Clyde valley and central Glasgow, and towards the Campsie Fells.

Leave Chatelherault on the Avon Walkway across the Old Avon Bridge, and passing underneath the M74 join the pavement of the A723 road bridge over the Clyde. Then immediately cross the road and enter Strathclyde Country Park. Opened in 1978, the Park's 1,650 acres host all manner of outdoor activities, especially water sports on the huge surface of Strathclyde Loch, which was the venue of the canoeing and rowing events in the 1986 Commonwealth Games. But it also contains nature reserves that incorporate mature woodland and carefully preserved marsh and wetland. Of more practical interest for the long-distance walker, perhaps, is an official campsite (with showers and a small shop), which is situated at the north-western end of the tree-lined loch.

The centre of Glasgow is little more than seven miles away, but unless you want to make for the inner city head for Drumpellier Country Park, north of Coatbridge, and then swiftly via Moodiesburn to Kirkintilloch and Milton of Campsie. Here the Campsie Fells rise up, and the welcome feeling of unspoilt countryside and open hillcountry returns. The West Highland Way is then only a few miles away. This passage around Glasgow's eastern edge is not particularly long, and there are a surprising amount of quiet minor roads and paths, but of course you will have to negotiate built-up centres such as Coatbridge, sites of former industry, and cross several main roads. If doubts arise over routefinding either consult Wilkie's guide or a map, or ask locally.

On the north-eastern side of Strathclyde Loch, by the remains of a Roman fort and bathhouse, take the access road out of the park, under the A721, and join a path by South Calder Water. Leave the Water before it curves around to the south and work your way through Mossend, following the A775 towards Holytown for a short distance, then left along either a path or small lane to the A8. Cross with great care, and once over North Calder Water join the Monkland Canal near Calderbank for two miles to Coatbridge. There are short cycle routes and walkways through the town, many of which are along disused railway lines that served the town's former heavy industry. This district of Monklands used to be known as the 'Workshop of the World', but nearly all the industry has disappeared, and it is left to Summerlee Heritage Trust on the site of the former ironworks to display the area's industrial heritage, including the first preserved electric tramway in Scotland.

Aim for Drumpellier Country Park, west of Blair Road on the edge of the town. Once a private estate, this small oasis of wildlife comprises two lochs, one an SSSI, plus a tropical butterfly house and visitor centre. To reach Moodiesburn take first a road then a path by the railway from Gartgill, around old industrial works, and cross under the M73 north of Marnock. Again, disused railway lines prove useful, and you should follow the former Monklands–Kirkintilloch line for a number of pleasant miles. The Kilsyth Hills and Campsie Fells have been drawing ever nearer, and after arriving at Milton of Campsie via a track from Kirkintilloch, the last of the built-up Lowlands are almost behind you. Now it is a question of continuing along this excellent thoroughfare – the old Gartness–Kirkintilloch Railway – westwards to Strathblane, via Lennoxtown. As befits an old railway, the route is firm, flat and direct, and the walking is most enjoyable. Across the A891 the Clachan of Campsie conservation area has a small arts and crafts community, and from here the more ambitious may like to ascend the Campsie Fells for spectacular views over the city, or simply to forge a route northwards to Fintry and beyond. South of the old railway track is Lennox Castle, now a hospital, and Lennox Forest, which offers enjoyable woodland walking and affords fine views over Glasgow – now behind you.

14

HIGHLAND GRANDEUR

Strathblane – Inverness

STRATHBLANE – FORT WILLIAM (91 miles)
The full length of Scotland's best-known long-distance footpath is only 95 miles, but between Glasgow and Fort William the West Highland Way takes in a wealth of fine scenery, and includes the highest piece of land in Great Britain. Although the trail is generally low-level and avoids the actual mountain tops, there is every opportunity to bag a few Munros along the way. Experienced walkers enjoying reasonable weather may like to adapt their route to include the likes of Ben Lomond and Ben Vorlich, Stob Ghabhar and Clach Leathad, Carn More Dearg and Ben Nevis.

A vocal lobby among Scottish hillwalkers and outdoor types still maintain that long-distance trails are alien to their nation, and that the 'wilderness' element should be carefully preserved. But this does not disguise the fact that since the West Highland Way opened in 1980 – Scotland's first official long-distance path, in fact – it has proved immensely popular (far more so than the Southern Upland Way, which you came into contact with a few days ago). And while many of the boots and packs lying in the corner of Crianlarich Youth Hostel or the bunkhouse of the Kingshouse Hotel will belong to sundry climbers and other backpackers, there will inevitably be plenty of company along the Way. But this must be put into perspective: by now you are a seasoned veteran of the long-distance path, and – presuming that you want to share your great adventure with others – it is *your* tales to which people will be listening around the stove or in the bar. Whilst others around you are contemplating the last 50 or 25 miles, you are still contemplating around 300. And of course that is with around 700 miles already under your belt. You may feel justly proud, but the end is not quite in sight yet, and there are some rather large hills ahead.

The WHW officially starts at Milngavie (pronounced 'mull-guy'), now a quiet northern suburb of Glasgow but in the depressed 1930s it was the conduit of escape for many hundreds of city dwellers keen to discover the countryside for the first time. The first few miles of the Way are through Mugdock Country Park, then it is more a question of the WHW joining *your* path, for at the foot of Dumgoyach, an ancient basalt plug that rises out of the ground, the Way follows the course of the former Blane Valley Railway, an extension of the line that you have been following since near Moodiesburn. The direction is obvious, and routefinding is made even easier with a fair sprinkling of official waymarks – a thistle within a hexagon (the same as that for the Southern Upland Way).

At Drymen there is plenty of accommodation and shops, and since they will be thin on the ground for the next few days it is as well to stock up now. At this point the West Highland Way really begins in earnest, and the first proper ascent is ahead. Conic Hill may only be 358m, but from its aptly named summit a wonderful panorama reveals itself: the dim tops of Glasgow southwards, to the distant mountains of Arran in the west. Below lie the deep blue waters of Loch Lomond, with which you will keep company for the next 13 miles. The Loch contains no less than 38 named islands, and its 27.45 square miles also boasts the most species of fish than any other loch, including the unusual powan, a type of freshwater herring; and there also used to be a naturist colony on Inch Murrin, known to the locals as the Danglers.

The long journey by Loch Lomond's eastern shore can be rather dull amid the blanket conifer plantations, but there are some pleasant views across the Loch and a certain amount of scrambling and scrabbling along the wooded shoreline is necessary. A Forestry Commission campsite at Cashel, or Rowardennan Youth Hostel two miles further on, make obvious halts. Apart from a couple of hotels, there is little else in the way of accommoda-tion, bar camping, on Loch Lomond's eastern shore, although ferries do link up with Inveruglas and Tarbet across the water. Above you is the massive shoulder of Ben Lomond, the most southerly Munro, and the main path to its summit begins at Rowardennan.

The last few miles of lochside from Inversnaid are arduous. There is little in the way of path; rather, a jumble of boulders and tree roots, where Rob Roy is supposed to have had a hideout. It can be particularly hazardous in wet weather when the rocks become slippery and especially dangerous for those carrying large packs, so treat this section with caution. Once refreshed at the Inverarnan Hotel, an old drovers' inn, follow the Way along the occasionally boggy but thankfully flat floor of Glen Falloch, past scattered remnants of the ancient Caledonian pine forest and the noisy Falls of Falloch, to Crianlarich. Here there are a few shops, a couple of bars, and a handily placed youth hostel with an invaluable drying room, though my sodden boots never fully recovered from their Glen Falloch experience.

Now the big hills are all about. If you are feeling adventurous or energetic you might like to leave your pack at the youth hostel and scale Ben More. But don't underestimate these forays. If all you can see is a blanket of low cloud then it is probably best to continue north along the tracks and forestry roads of Strath Fillan to Tyndrum. Here the route veers right, together with the A82 and the railway. Tyndrum owes its existence to local lead-mining, first developed in the 1740s, and also to cattle droving. Strath Fillan was one of several routes used by drovers to bring their herds south from the West Coast and Islands. But now, in the height of the summer at least, the formidable army of drivers are in charge of caravans and coaches, and it can be quite daunting. If you do not need the general stores or hotel, when the crowd pulls in, it is time to pull out.

The next 7 miles to Bridge of Orchy are direct and satisfying. The firm track underfoot is an old military road, constructed around 1750, under the direction of Major Caulfeild. It allows for the working-up of a good head of steam as Rannoch Moor approaches. The same can be said for the trains that rumble up the strath, and with whose route the Way jockeys for position. The line contours around Auch Gleann and continues along the base of the hills, where walkers and passengers alike can enjoy the superb spectacle of Beinn Dorain rising majestically above.

Bridge of Orchy enjoys an inspirational situation, as befits such a beautiful name, and consists of little more than half a dozen buildings, which include a hotel and bunkhouse. Non-campers should beware, and book ahead as far as possible, certainly in the popular holiday period. Consult the annual West Highland Way accommodation list published by Scottish Natural Heritage.

From the Inveroran Hotel at the western end of Loch Tulla, 2 miles by path from Bridge of Orchy, the bleak inhospitable morass of Rannoch Moor stretches east for many miles. The WHW skirts its western edge, choosing a combination of a firm and unmistakable old drovers' track and an old military road 9½ miles to Kingshouse, at the foot of the Pass of Glencoe. It is invigorating walking, and the views are tremendous, but it is also bare and exposed. There is virtually no shelter for over 6 miles, and the average annual rainfall in this area is around 120 inches. Regrettably, this Bridge of Orchy–Fort William section is also used for annual motorbike trials in the first week of May. However, a good-weather alternative for the experienced hillwalker is the superb high-level ridge walk over Stob Ghabhar and Clach Leathad to Kingshouse, although – like other hilltop excursions along the way – you should first check locally if the deer stalking season is in progress.

Civilisation, of sorts, returns with the sight of the A82 ahead, and to your left the lift of the White Corries ski centre takes people 650m up the flanks of Meall a'Bhuiridh. Indeed, as you proceed along the flattish track to Kingshouse and the eastern approach to Glencoe, more and more peaks line up ahead. Of them all, Buachaille Etive Mor ('the Great Shepherd of Etive') stands the proudest, being possibly the most handsome mountain you will see on the whole of the Walk. If the weather allows, an evening wander in this spectacular setting is highly recommended. The famous hotel (which now has a bunkhouse) has been visited by a wide range of outdoor enthusiasts over the last 200 years, from Dorothy Wordsworth to Sean Connery. So add yourself to the worthy list.

Leave the car-bound tourists intent on Glencoe and follow the old military road up the hillside in a series of steep zigzags known as the Devil's Staircase. Taken at a measured pace it should present no problems, despite all the dire warnings that you have heard. As you approach the 550m col, the views back to the Three Sisters of Glencoe repay all the huffing and puffing; and northwards the Mamores and Ben Nevis massif take shape for the first time. The track stretches out clearly ahead, to the east of the Blackwater Reservoir, where Robert Louis Stevenson set some of his novel

Kidnapped. But, as on the Rannoch Moor section, have both map and compass ready if the clouds descend.

Kinlochleven comes as something of a surprise. No tourist shops here; rather, a large aluminium plant and rows of drab houses. The B&B I stayed in was cheap and accommodating, the people friendly, but this industrial microcosm in the mountains still jolts after so many miles of unspoilt natural beauty.

However, the West Highland Way is almost at its end, with only 14 miles left to Fort William. They begin with a stiff climb out of the houses, rewarded by magnificent views down Loch Leven to Sgorr na Ciche (the Pap of Glencoe). After several miles of valley walking along a steady track, still the old military road, Ben Nevis heaves into view. If the weather is foul you can join a quiet metalled road at Blar a'Chaorainn, which runs all the way into Fort William. Otherwise there are some messy Forestry Commission paths that have to be negotiated before you descend to Glen Nevis, and to the foot of the Ben. Fort William is a mile down the road, Ben Nevis 1,343 metres above. Which way for you?

FORT WILLIAM – INVERNESS (68 miles)

Fort William has the air of a frontier town, but at the same time seems rather anonymous. It has been remarked that everyone seems to be getting ready to go somewhere else. If the youth hostel in Glen Nevis is overflowing with loud, pimply youths (often the case) then try the Backpackers Guest House on Alma Road, which has the advantage of being three minutes and not three miles from the town centre. For books, maps, outdoor equipment, plus a café and bar, visit the Nevisport shop at the end of the main street.

This is an important moment in your Walk, for a whole number of reasons. First, the West Route abandons its western options and uses the Great Glen to switch to the east coast, where it joins the End to End Central Route. Second, as the situation stands at the moment, the conclusion of the West Highland Way at Fort William signifies the last official or unofficial long-distance footpath used on the overall route. Although there is a waymarked route from the Fort to Inverness, the Great Glen Cycle Route is not primarily for walkers (although, as you will find, it is an ideal pedestrian thoroughfare, especially as the proposed Great Glen Way still hovers on the drawing board). Third, it may occur to some walkers to consider the overall direction now, with a view to possibly striking off on their own. For those adventurous and experienced walkers who are used to mountainous terrain and are competent in every aspect of outdoor life, there are countless routes that can be plotted through the North-West Highlands to John o'Groats. Published End to Enders have taken a variety of courses, with mixed results. Chris Townsend enjoyed clear skies and sunshine in the mountains around Torridon, but John Hillaby came unstuck in the mists on Ben More Assynt. Meanwhile the redoubtable Hamish Brown took a tortuous but highly enjoyable wriggling route over the tops that enabled him to complete his sixth round of Munros. The options really are endless. At the same time, and by its very nature, the wilderness of the North-West Highlands is best left like that: unspoilt, remote, spectacular. There is a strong case for arguing that the region should not be a place for waymarked trails, although there are plenty of good guidebooks on high-level routes that can be consulted, and if you are well-equipped and have studied the relevant maps, a route over and through the North-West Highlands should be an exhilarating experience. However, if you are crossing in late summer, bear in mind the twin problems that can afflict any walker in the Scottish Highlands at this time of year: midges and the stalking season. The dreaded midge can make life hellish, despite the array of ointments and sprays; and stag hunts can put large tracts of hillside out of bounds and add many miles to a route.

It should be stated that the West Route does not switch east just because it is daunted by mountains! Since you are aiming for the far north-east corner of the land it is obvious that sooner or later you will have to swing eastwards, and the Great Glen offers the perfect opportunity to move swiftly and scenically across country. The means to do this is presently provided by the Great Glen Cycle Route, managed by the Forestry Commission with cooperation from British Waterways, and intended to help both cyclists and walkers avoid the hazardous Fort William–Inverness road as much as possible. Most of the route is along existing forest tracks, with some brand new sections created, plus a few miles of the Caledonian Canal towpath. However, there is another, parallel route still at the planning stage which may ultimately offer walkers an even better passage. The Great Glen Way is being prepared by Scottish Natural Heritage, and it is hoped that eventually it will become a waymarked route along the lines of the West Highland

Way and the Southern Upland Way. Since the Great Glen Way is to be specifically a walkers' route, this may eventually turn out to be the better option for crossing the Great Glen. Ask at Fort William Tourist Information Centre for more details.

The Great Glen Cycle Route is excellently waymarked by brown signs on roads, and green on the forest sections, both of which give destination and mileage. Short sections of the route are still under development, and at the time of writing a little roadwalking is necessary until new tracks are opened and access arrangements finalised.

From Fort William take the A82 Inverness road east, then turn left for Mallaig (pavement all the way), leaving the highway at the Caledonian Canal swing bridge. Walk up and past a flight of eight locks known as Neptune's Staircase, from where there are impressive views across to Ben Nevis and Aonach Mor. The canal was engineered by Thomas Telford between 1803 and 1822 with the object of providing a safe east–west coast short-cut. It links the three inland lochs of the Glen (Lochy, Oich and Ness), and although sea-going fishing boats still make the journey you will see mostly yachts and pleasure cruisers.

Take the right-hand towpath (south bank) and head for Gairlochy. The flat, easy walking makes a welcome change from the ups and downs of the previous days, but the mountainous spectacle remains. After Gairlochy there is a short stretch of B-road until Clunes, then single-track road and forest highway along the northern shore of Loch Lochy until Laggan. Now a section of purpose-built cyclepath takes you away from the main road and provides a well drained gravel-based passage for cyclists and walkers, although when I followed the route (on a September weekday) walkers outnumbered those on two wheels.

There are more forest roads up and down the hillside between Laggan and a pot of tea at the Invergarry Hotel, and afterwards hairpin tracks lead steeply up the hillside above Loch Oich. Where the trees have been cleared the path almost seems to float on the high slopes, and there are brilliant views up and down the Glen. Among the trees wood ants build themselves huge nests and, if you are quiet enough, you may also spot some deer; but you will have to use much more stealth even to catch a glimpse of the elusive pine marten.

It is also possible to walk along the southern shore of Loch

Oich, following the route of the former Fort William–Fort Augustus railway, a scenic but short-lived line, and some of General Wade's Military Road. Since the Great Glen Cycle Route rarely visits any of the shores of the lochs that it passes this may be an agreeable alternative.

At Oich Bridge join the towpath of the canal once more (left/north bank) all the way to Fort Augustus, where there are B&Bs and a large campsite, plus a café by the bridge for cheap scoffs. This is the mid point of the Great Glen, and now you must follow the A82 by Loch Ness for a little while. The loch is your companion for possibly the next 24 miles, depending on which route you take. It is Britain's largest body of fresh water (three times the volume of Loch Lomond, even though the latter has a greater surface area), and the freshwater system around Loch Ness is massive, drawing water from almost 700 square miles (nearly 1,775 sq km).

Enjoy the changing views of the Loch as the cycleway follows rising forest tracks once more, and then down into Invermoriston.

Inverness is still nearly 40 miles away, but for those that are reluctant to follow the Great Glen all the way to the Moray Firth there are two alternative routes that will effectively cut off Inverness and allow you to take a scenic short-cut, and join the End to End Central Route at Strathpeffer for its solitary march to the finish. The first alternative breaks off here at Invermoriston, and is a rough and more remote route that heads for the open hills. The second leaves Loch Ness further on, past Drumnadrochit, and is a gentler affair involving lanes. The main route keeps with the Great Glen all the way to Inverness, where it joins with the Central Route and heads north.

The first alternative, from Invermoriston to Strathpeffer across the hills via Glen Urquhart and Strathglass, is approximately 40 miles in length. Follow the A887 up Glen Moriston for 3 miles. It was in this area that Bonnie Prince Charlie was sheltered as he fled after bloody defeat at Culloden in 1746. Turn off by the road bridge at Bhlaraidh for a steep and winding track up the forested hillside to Bhlaraidh Reservoir, and a little further on to Loch Liath. The track finally ends at Loch ma Stac, where you should make your way around its shores and pick up another track that descends by the River Enrick to Corrimony in Glen Urquhart. The chambered burial cairn near the settlement is worth a visit, enclosed within a ring of eleven standing stones. Cannich, an hour's walk away, has shops and a youth hostel. A single-track lane takes you down the narrow bottom of Strathglass towards Erchless Castle. Near Struy, by Maud Bridge, is the Chisholm Stone, which marks the spot where William Chisholm took leave of his wife for Culloden, where he was a standard bearer. He never returned. The Clan Chisholm Burial Ground is nearby. Follow the track via Erchless Forest Cottage up to Loch Balloch then over Allt Goibhre at Tighachrochadair.

Like the area around Loch ma Stac earlier, this is rough and exposed land, so pay attention to your map-reading and compass technique. The track emerges on to a tarmac lane by Aultgowrie Bridge, where there is a choice of a simple tarmac walk to Marybank, then across the River Conon at Moy Bridge and over hillside to Strathpeffer. Or a more interesting alternative is to follow the River Orrin upstream past the Falls of Orrin (ask permission to enter the Fairburn Estate at the lodge first). The dam by the power station at Loch Achonachie can also be reached by a public road from Marybank; then there is a popular track around the foot of Torr Achilty to Contin. Further up the Conon are the Rogie Falls, and a fish-ladder for salmon, but your route is over wooded hillside north-east of the village. Follow the waymarked forest trail via View Rock fire lookout, from where there are panoramic views of Ben Wyvis, Strathconon and the mountains of Mid Ross. Leave the trail for a track to Loch Kinellan and Strathpeffer – where you join the End to End Central Route.

The main West Route continues beyond Invermoriston (the old Invermoriston Inn was where Dr Johnson and Boswell stayed before they set off on their Hebridean journey) and along the Great Glen above Loch Ness. The steep but surfaced lane behind the newer hotel leads back into the conifers, then out on to cleared land high above the loch. There are numerous vantage points, and even an isolated wooden picnic table. Should it start to rain you can take shelter in a tiny stone cave set in the hillside by Estate workers last century. The track then descends to the shore road, emerging opposite Loch Ness Youth Hostel at Alltsigh, from where you can indulge in an evening of Nessie-watching from the lounge window. The next 5 miles begin with a seemingly endless uphill track that weaves its way across open land to a height of 300m. The views over Loch Ness are terrific, but all too soon you lose height and return to the road. The remaining miles to Drumnadrochit are at present along the A82, past the ruins of Urquhart Castle, a walk which can be decidedly uncomfortable when a coach or a caravan lurches past. However, there is a handy lane from near Bunloit to Drumnadrochit, although this can be difficult to locate through the trees; otherwise a lochside passage may be feasible until such times as the authorities have developed a better route.

There are cafés and B&Bs around the triangular green at Drumnadrochit, plus the Loch Ness Monster Exhibition Centre, with audio-visual tours all day long, ending in a sumptuous gift shop which sells Nessie tea towels, key rings, mugs, shirts. Everything, in fact, except signed photos. Just beyond the Centre turn left up a steep lane signposted 'Drumbuie', and after the tarmac finishes there is a track (a right of way) to Loch Glanaidh. Conditions may be rather damp underfoot, but soon you reach a firm forest road that bounces down through a corridor among the conifers to a minor road near Loch Laide. It is here that you must choose whether or not to visit Inverness. If you would rather skip the busy town (there are shops, banks and launderettes at Beauly, Dingwall and other places ahead), then take the second of the two short cuts to Strathpeffer.

The corner-cutting exercise begins with a pleasant lane north to Kiltarlity, a descent which affords expansive views of Erchless Forest. Follow the 'Beauly' sign to Kilmorack, then either through the centre of Beauly or via lanes above the town. The former is useful if you are in search of B&Bs, but the latter is a quieter thoroughfare, even if the minor roads twist and turn a bit. There are a few more shops at Muir of Ord, which you should leave on the lane that passes the Glen Ord distillery (free tours, free dram!) and continue to Aultgowrie Bridge. As described earlier, either follow this quiet lane among the trees to Marybank and Strathpeffer, or make for Loch Achonachie and then tracks to Contin, and via the waymarked trails of Torr Achilty Forest to Strathpeffer.

For those intent on Inverness turn right on to the minor road and continue past Loch Laide. Take the left fork at Abriachan, through another large Forestry Commission plantation, and out across the open hilltop. The unfenced lane is quiet and direct, and drops steeply to the A82 at the bottom of the Glen. Although Inverness is only a couple of miles away, I suggest minimising the use of the main road by joining the Caledonian Canal towpath behind Dunain Park Hotel, which leads into the town centre. The Great Glen Cycle Route is presently incomplete from Drumnadrochit to

Inverness, although part of it utilises the minor road via Abriachan as I have done. Since further route developments may occur, watch out for signs, and ask for details in local tourist information centres.

THE EAST ROUTE

15 SUNNY SOUTH COAST
Land's End – Plymouth
by the South-West Coast Path
158 miles

16 THE ENGLISH RIVIERA
Plymouth – Lyme Regis
by the South-West Coast Path and the East Devon Way
132 miles

17 WALKING THROUGH HISTORY
Lyme Regis – Ivinghoe
by the Wessex Ridgeway, Imber Range Perimeter Path and the Ridgeway
216 miles

18 THE FLAT EAST
Ivinghoe – Oakham
by the Icknield Way and the Hereward Way
207 miles

19 THE GENTLE HILLS
Oakham – Filey
by the Viking Way and the Wolds Way
209 miles

20 ALONG THE TRACKS
Filey – Heddon
by the Cleveland Way, Esk Valley Walk and railway paths
153 miles

21 A COAST TO YOURSELF
Heddon – Edinburgh
by local paths
143 miles

15

SUNNY SOUTH COAST

Land's End – Plymouth

LAND'S END – FALMOUTH (84 miles)

It may seem a little unusual to begin a mammoth journey to the north of Scotland by heading south, and then east, but the East Route does not hold with convention. If minimising time or distance is paramount, then look at the Central or West routes. The East provides a wandering, sometimes quirky but always fascinating journey across southern England and up the east coast. In End to End total it is several hundred miles longer than the other two, but its richness and variety should appeal to the more unhurried and discerning walker who favours the gentle Wolds to King Offa's blustery hills; or the springy chalk downlands of Wessex to the slimy peat bogs of the southern Pennines.

The East Route, above all else, should be a relaxed route. Think in terms of days and not miles. There are several opportunities to switch to the Central Route, if the fancy takes you, plus the lure of other short- and long-distance paths that either cross or branch off from your course. But by sticking with the East Route you will walk the downs and the moors, along the cliffs of the Atlantic and the scarp of the wolds. There is the prospect of a thrilling walk ahead.

And so to Land's End. Don't let your nervy elation at the prospect of finally beginning the Walk be tempered by the gaudy theme park or gawping tourists. Wave them all goodbye (or good riddance) and stride out purposefully along the cliff path. After all the planning and preparations it is finally time to begin.

The first six miles to Porthcurno are thankfully straightforward, along easy-to-follow clifftop tracks. Basically, keep the sea on your right and watch your footing. This is the South-West Coast Path which, maybe with a few diversions inland, you will be following as far as Lyme Regis in Dorset. In many respects the route has evolved quite naturally, with the linking-together of paths trod by local coastguards since the eighteenth century. The coastguard patrols were introduced after new excise duties on imported goods led to widespread smuggling. Later the lookout was kept in the interest of bona fide shipping, as the toll of wrecks grew and grew. The idea for a long-distance path was first voiced in the 1940s, and took a great advance with the National Trust's Enterprise Neptune two decades later, when sizeable chunks of the coast were purchased for the nation, and public access guaranteed. The South-West Coast Path was officially opened, as a whole, in 1978, but in fact it consists of four separate paths: Somerset and North Devon, North Cornwall, South Cornwall, and South Devon and Dorset. The Cornwall Coast Path was opened as long ago as 1973, and is an exhilarating and often strenuous walk, full of interest and variety. But, especially at this very early stage, do not overreach yourself. The constant ascent and descent involved in climbing up to the clifftop then descending to the bays and coves can be very tiring. So take it easy to begin with – there are many miles ahead!

Along this early stretch the high granite cliffs have broken into pillars, arches and steps, over which the powerful Atlantic surf crashes. There are a number of lovely, unspoilt coves and bays, such as Nanjizal, Porth Chapel and Porth Curno. At the last, below the Minack open-air theatre, a large sand bar developed to the east of the bay in 1992, and was a popular destination for the curious and carefree at low tide. However, not all the bays are easily accessible, and if you clamber down to investigate it can often be a steep and awkward climb back up on to the path. Some facilities are available in Treen, Penberth and Lamorna, but Mousehole offers the whole range.

The southern coastline enjoys plenty of fixed accommodation, more so than most of the north Cornwall shore (West Route). Of course in peak season the holiday crowds exert considerable pressure, but if you take good care to precede the summer rush, most of the B&Bs and youth hostels will have beds to spare. See the South-West Way Association's annual guide for a comprehensive and up-to-date accommodation list. Campsites are not quite so plentiful; and some backpackers may be put off by the larger, louder campsites that also welcome caravans. Away from the towns it is usually the case that polite enquiries will yield some sort of pitch, but in only a few places is there scope for wild camping. Nevertheless, many walkers find the rigours of cliff-walking particularly exaggerated if the weight of a tent, sleeping bag, etc, is added to the load, so give careful consideration to your as yet unhardened limbs. Some End to Enders prefer to walk the South-West Coast Path using B&B and youth hostel accommodation, then collect camping gear once the cliffs are finished with and the switch to the gentler plains and hills inland takes place.

The path can be tricky around St Loy's Cove, where rocks and boulders make the going rough, but a return to the clifftop is swift. Beyond Lamorna Cove is Carn-du, a rocky headland giving spectacular views across Mount's Bay to the Lizard. Newlyn and Penzance (the two virtually run into each other) are reached after a walk along the coast road from the colour-washed cottages of Mousehole (pronounced 'Mowzel'). Penzance is now a busy commercial and tourist centre, but in 1595 uninvited Spanish visitors virtually destroyed it. The town offers the chance to purchase all those little things that you forgot to pack before leaving. The maritime influence is everywhere: the Trinity House National Lighthouse Centre boasts the world's largest and finest collection of lighthouse equipment; and on Chapel Street the Museum of Nautical Art and Man O'War even has a display of sunken treasure (opposite, the Admiral Benbow public house appears to have even more). For those not stopping, the best way through is along the promenade, around the harbour, and out by the heliport, where there are regular flights to the Isles of Scilly. A level path runs by the side of the railway, parallel to the beach, emerging at Marazion where the much-photographed St Michael's Mount can be reached by causeway at low tide or else by boat. The fourteenth-century castle and church was originally given to monks by Edward the Confessor, but is now in the hands of the National Trust, and is undeniably attractive.

The 10 miles of clifftop and fieldside walking from Marazion to Porthleven are not complicated, but care must be taken, as along the rest of the path, where landslips and erosion have made the going unstable (minor re-routing may be taking place). From Marazion to Perranuthnoe there is an alternative route inland should a high spring tide and heavy seas make the shore path dangerous. Then after several miles of straightforward cliffwalking descend to the smooth Praa Sands (cafés and camping). Porthleven is a small but useful centre, and it is a place where you will have to make your first routefinding decision. Ahead, the official coast path continues its southwards curve around to the Lizard peninsula. Some End to End walkers have found, especially so early in the Walk, that this deviation away from the 'crow's flight' north-eastwards is exasperating; there is a sense of walking extra, unnecessary miles for no overall gain. If you feel this, then I suggest you head inland from Porthleven, around RAF Culdrose, and using minor roads head for Gweek (about 7 miles away). This route will also eliminate the problem of negotiating the Helford River estuary.

However, there is much to recommend sticking with the coast path, and continuing past the Loe (Cornwall's largest lake) via Loe Bar, an endless shingle bank on which sea holly and the rare horned poppy can be found, and around the Lizard. This is a delightful place, mostly quiet and unspoilt, its sandy heathland attracting many rare flowers and insects, and its unique rock structure famous for serpentine, a distinctive greenish rock, with red and black veins, which is easily shaped and takes a high polish – but this can make the Lizard's stone stiles slippery in wet weather! After rounding the southernmost tip of Great Britain, follow the clifftop to Cadgwith and Coverack (youth hostel). There are now several miles where quarries have despoiled the scenery, and a new route has had to be sought. Follow the official signposts.

The creek at Gillan may be waded one hour either side of low tide ('the wading window'); otherwise there is a 2-mile walk upstream via Carne and Manaccan, where the New Inn, a beautiful thatched cottage, is well worth a lunchtime visit. But the estuary at Helford is another matter. A seasonal ferry, which must be summoned by operating a sign, runs to the wooded shore opposite, although if you are walking before April or after October you face a long detour inland to Gweek. The South-West Way Association estimate the inland alternative to be 8.5 miles long. Then again, you may not *want* to use ferries. Many who look on walking from one end of the country to another as (quite rightly) a deeply personal experience/challenge eschew all notions of mechanical assistance. If you use a ferry to cross a river, why not take a bus to cut out an urban section or a dull bit of countryside? Basically, it's up to the individual whether he or she has a 'foot power only' policy. Nevertheless this south Cornwall/Devon coastline is riddled with probing estuaries, and many diversions, often entailing lanes and roads, will be necessary if ferries are out of bounds.

If you have ended up in Gweek, where there is a pub, a SPAR supermarket, and the Cornish Seal Sanctuary and Marine Animal Rescue Centre, follow minor roads via Constantine back to the sea at Helford Passage, or else make your way direct to Maenporth or Falmouth, a bit further along the coast. Otherwise the coastal path via Rosemullion Head is very straightforward, the only problem coming from a little cliff-edge erosion. Pendennis Point offers great views over Falmouth Bay and Carrick Roads, and is the site of a sixteenth-century castle, used in the Civil War as a Royalist stronghold, but now home to more peaceful youth hostelling types. Falmouth itself is a hive of boating activity. The deep, natural harbour – in size second only to that of Sydney, Australia, it is claimed – provides shelter for craft of every size and shape. And there is plenty in the way of accommodation and refreshments.

FALMOUTH – PLYMOUTH (74 miles)

For the End to End walker there are further dilemmas on reaching Falmouth. The official coast route takes the ferry from Falmouth (Albert Quay) to St Mawes, then a seasonal ferry across the Percuil River to Place. In its absence some walkers have apparently obtained lifts from other, local boats, but difficulties persist in finding a combination of ferries for this crossing, so be warned. If you are not in the business of employing ferries, then there is a long detour of around 8 miles upstream – the South-West Way Association's Guide has a detailed route description. But you could use this excursion inland to visit Truro (and possibly join the Central Route); there are plenty of quiet lanes via Tregony to Portholland, or even to Mevagissey or Dodman Point. Consult the Ordnance Survey map!

If you have successfully reached Place, then you have the prospect of 20 miles or so of relatively unspoilt coastal scenery, beginning with St Anthony Head, complete with lighthouse and naval battery. There are great views back across to Falmouth, and to the flotilla of vessels bobbing in and out of Carrick Roads. Continue to Portscatho via undulating but not difficult cliffs, then around Gerrans Bay to

Nare Head. It is generally quiet and pleasant, but the gradients slowly stiffen towards Portloe and Portholland, and there are some steep scrambles. Boswinger (youth hostel and campsite) is half a mile off the path. Make your way out to the fine headland of Dodman Point, with its stark granite cross. This was constructed in 1896 by the local rector, but it failed to prevent the unhappy toll of wrecks and drownings. Dodman literally means 'dead man'. The lane from Hemmick Beach via Penare neatly cuts the headland off if time or foul weather presses. There are refreshments and some accommodation at Gorran Haven, but there is more at Mevagissey another 3 miles further on. This is a likeable fishing and tourist centre, but it can get a bit hectic at the height of summer. Once upon a time, however, it was not trippers but pilchards that made life hectic. Shoals approached the coast in late summer, spotted by clifftop lookouts. The whole community sprang into action, and after the fish were netted, unloaded and cured, most were barrelled for export to continental Latin countries for eating over Lent. The industry stopped about a century ago when the shoals disappeared.

After the gruesome caravans at Pentewan, there is some exhilarating but tiring up-and-down walking via Black Head before you arrive at Charlestown, which leads into St Austell. The old harbour at Charlestown was built originally to handle local ore and china clay, and was fashioned out of solid rock. Unless the dock gate is open, cross at the harbour mouth.

Unfortunately the St Austell–Par stretch of coastline is pretty grim, mainly due to the china-clay workings, but not helped by the Cornish Leisure World development at Carlyon Bay (which, at first sight, could be taken for an extension of the mining complex). Around this area decomposed granite has produced kaolin, a fine white clay used in many modern products and only found in the UK in Devon and Cornwall. The resulting mining and processing works have on the one hand spawned an important local industry and large employer, especially welcome with the demise of traditional tin and copper mining, and on the other have despoiled the countryside and coast.

There is some roadwalking necessary through Par, but after Polmear the mess is left behind and there is a pleasant and very relaxing cliff-edge walk to Gribbin Head. At Polkerris, a former pilchard-fishing village, stop for a pot of tea and admire the old harbour. Then, after 4 miles of fairly steep cliffs, pass St Catherine's Castle, another defence built by Henry VIII, and enter Fowey (pronounced 'Foy'), erstwhile haunt of pirates and smugglers. In 1346, Fowey furnished forty-seven ships and 770 men for the siege of Calais. There is a regular ferry service across the harbour to Polruan, otherwise be prepared for another long trek inland. But this is not as bad as it sounds: you can join the course of the Saints' Way upstream until Milltown, passing Golant Youth Hostel at Penquite House. The route is waymarked by orange arrows with the distinctive Cornish cross, and continues for roughly 30 miles to the north Cornwall coast at Padstow. It traces the route of Celtic saints from Ireland and Wales who favoured an overland journey through Cornwall rather than a hazardous sailing around Land's End. From Lostwithiel take quiet lanes back to the coast via Lerryn and Penpoll.

There are some stiff but scenic miles after Polruan on the east bank of Fowey Harbour, along a generally wild and unpopulated cliffline to Polperro. It can be arduous in adverse weather conditions. To some, Polperro is the perfect Cornish village, with narrow streets and attractive clustered buildings. But on a sunny Saturday in July it becomes a victim of its own popularity. Polperro is not alone in suffering a summer invasion, and herein lies a problem. If the End to End walker sets off too early in the year, the crowds may be absent but the ferries may not be running and the B&Bs shut. Yet bear in mind that even if the ice cream and sandals brigade frustrate you, there is plenty of unspoilt coastline ahead – and plenty more miles ahead altogether.

At Looe, a further 5 clifftop miles later, there is ample accommodation, and East and West are easily joined by bridge or ferry. From Hannafore you can see St George's or Looe Island, which has had a curious history. Joseph of Arimathea allegedly stayed there; two monks certainly did in the twelfth century; a whale grounded itself there in the 1930s, and had to be blown up with explosives; then in the Second World War the Germans bombed the deserted island, mistaking it for a warship. Today it is inhabited by two sisters.

The cliffs after Looe become higher, and near Downderry they reach 150m (the highest on the South Cornwall coast). But the route from Downderry to Rame Head is rather messy and in places unclear: it is 'undefined' in one stretch and there is roadwalking involved. Then the walker has to cut inland to avoid Tregantle Fort, an odd-looking firing range ('do not enter when red flags and lamps are showing' is the MOD's helpful advice). The South-West Way Association say that at low tide it is possible to walk along the beach below the fort, but only when the range is not in use. Watch out for waymarks and possible re-routing. Rame Head can be eliminated by an inland diversion via a path to Treninnow Farm and then Rame Lane. Otherwise the path to Plymouth ends near Mount Edgcumbe Country Park at Cremyll, where there is a ferry (all year-round) across to Stonehouse and Plymouth city centre. If you have a few minutes to wait, relax at the Edgcumbe Arms (B&B), where sailors and navigators such as Sir Francis Chichester and Sir Alec Rose have been entertained over the years.

For those avoiding ferries, leave the coast path after Downderry and take roads via Polbathic and Tideford to reach Saltash and then Plymouth. However, this involves some uncomfortable walking along the A38. You may consider using the network of country lanes to the north of this highway and crossing the Tamar upstream at Gunnislake, so avoiding Plymouth altogether. From Gunnislake I suggest you work your way east on to Dartmoor and towards Princeton, then join up with the Plymouth–Exeter inland alternative route (see next section).

16

THE ENGLISH RIVIERA

Plymouth – Lyme Regis

PLYMOUTH – EXMOUTH (98 miles)
Plymouth is the largest place that you have encountered or are likely to encounter for some considerable time. A naval port since the Middle Ages, it is of course famous for Francis Drake and the Armada, and the sailing of the *Mayflower* in 1620. There is a youth hostel in Stoke, near the dockyards at Devonport; and by crossing the River Tamar you enter the second county on your walk: Devon.

However, the size and position of Plymouth (the Rivers Plym, Tavy, Tamar and Lynher all eat into the land) makes navigation tricky. If you do not take the ferry from Cremyll a long and circuitous walk is necessary, and even if you do there are several miles of tarmac before resumption of the coastal path at Turnchapel, on the River Plym (the South-West Way Association's Guide suggests a route). Mind you, if mechanical transport is out then much of the next 90 coastal miles to the River Exe will be extremely awkward, since river mouths and estuaries will demand innumerable detours, often involving roads, and even some of the smallest, fordable points can be impassable in bad weather. As an alternative, I have suggested an inland route from Plymouth to Exmouth via Dartmoor and Exeter. This is preferable in many ways: it takes a more direct route and cuts off the whole Salcombe/Start Point peninsula; the tourist mecca of Torbay can be totally avoided; and it offers a rest from the relentless switchback and salt spray of cliffwalking, giving you a chance to get your breath back and enjoy quite different moorland scenery. However, this route necessitates some roadwalking, although the quiet country lanes are on the whole very pleasant and, depending on how far you penetrate, the empty moors require careful navigation.

But for those content with ferries, and keen on sampling some more superb South-West coastline, I have described the shore route as well. This is *your* adventure, and *your* feet will be walking it, so choose the route with which you feel happiest.

Plymouth – Exmouth, via the coastal path

If you choose to stick to the coast the first problem you will face is exactly where to leave the city of Plymouth. Likely it will be a question of how fast can I leave? The official route resumes at Turnchapel, and to get there you must walk the busy A379, then head through a dreary urban patch (the guides say 'catch a bus' – what an unthinkable idea!). You may end up simply scuttling down the main road until you can bear no more, or else carve a route through the houses and head for the water.

There are good views over The Sound from Staddon Heights, and walking conditions are generally easy, although diversions are sometimes necessary when the naval firing range at HMS Cambridge is operational. At the mouth of the River Yealm there is an extremely limited-service ferry; otherwise a long and frustrating detour via Newton Ferrers to Noss Mayo is demanded. You may want to cut out this section from Plymouth altogether, for sake of time and convenience, and simply take lanes direct from the city's edge to Newton Ferrers. Next is a lovely stretch of quiet and unspoilt cliff around Stoke Point, although a little strenuous in places. The River Erme at Mothercombe can be waded an hour either side of low tide. The alternative is a 7 mile journey to Sequer's Bridge along sometimes steep minor roads. To avoid this lengthy detour consult tide tables in advance, and try and time your arrival accordingly.

Now the cliff path becomes more rugged, with some stiff pulls. At Bigbury-on-Sea, popular with holidaymakers, there is accommodation and refreshments. At low tide it is possible to walk over the sands to Burgh Island, and to the Pilchard Inn, a wooden fourteenth-century smugglers' tavern, or continue by the shore to the mouth of the River Avon. Here is another river served by a very occasional ferry. The alternative is a walk along riverside paths and the odd lane to Aveton Gifford, then back downstream to Bantham, a total distance of 9 miles. Informed commentators advise against wading the Avon. It is not a good idea to find yourself floundering in a rising tide wearing boots and a heavy pack, and even when the water is low there are hidden channels and patches of soft sand.

Resume the coastal path near Bantham, rounding Thurlestone Golf Course and Warren Point. Between Bolt Tail and Salcombe some of the most stunning cliff scenery on the South Devon coast is revealed, with one fine view after another. Beyond Bolt Head the path makes its way up Salcombe estuary into the town. This busy yachting centre has a youth hostel and other amenities. Kingsbridge Estuary runs for nearly 5 miles inland, providing safe moorings for hundreds of craft.

After a ferry across the harbour there are two fabulous headlands: Prawle Point, Devon's most southerly tip, is reached after some rough walking among the heather and thrift (or sea pink), then around the unspoilt Lannacombe Bay to Start Point, a place to have the cobwebs blown out! This whole section is refreshingly wild, with no tourist villages to negotiate, so stock up well before leaving Salcombe.

Both direction and scenery now alters abruptly. Start Bay stretches out gently and peacefully ahead. The path clings to the straight and low shoreline, past the deserted village of Hallsands, and to Torcross, where there is accommodation and refreshments. The Start Bay Inn's fish and chips are renowned. Then walk alongside the A379 for the duration of Slapton Sands. You may not like being close to traffic, but your legs will welcome the level ground. Slapton village was evacuated in 1943 in order to allow American soldiers to train for D-Day.

To reach Dartmouth you have to negotiate a short inland section from Strete to just after Stoke Fleming, approaching Dartmouth via the castle at the mouth of the estuary. Dartmouth was an important medieval maritime centre, and today still houses the Royal Naval College. It is a busy but likeable place, and there is a short ferry-ride to Kingswear (where the Torbay and Dartmouth Steam Railway terminates). Head back to the coast through woodland. There is a memorial to Lieutenant Colonel H. Jones, who was killed in battle in the Falklands, and this stretch of coastal path was opened in his memory. The 11 miles to Brixham are once more scenic but strenuous, with virtually no amenities. If the weather is clear you may be treated to a view across to Lyme Bay, where the End to

End East Route begins its inland journey. Nearer at hand the urban sprawl of Torbay is evident.

Once round Sharkham Point you are virtually in Brixham. This is where William of Orange landed in 1688 and began the Glorious Revolution. He might have second thoughts if he landed here today, since Brixham soon leads into Paignton, then into Torquay. (In an administrative sense, the three combined in 1968 to become Torbay.) This short stretch of coastline is referred to by tourist officials and travel agents as the English Riviera. It is inevitably urban and desperately commercial, but the palm trees and seafood kiosks on the promenade do have a peculiar charm. There is a ferry across the bay, but really the best option is to walk briskly through it.

Beyond Hope's Nose, continue along the coast past Babbacombe, underneath the cliff railway at Oddicombe, and follow endlessly rolling cliffs to Shaldon. From here there is a regular ferry to Teignmouth, or else cross the bridge in sight upstream. At Teignmouth and then at Dawlish bear in mind that high tides can make the walk along the sea wall impassable, so follow the inland alternative if that is the case. For long periods you accompany the Brunel-designed mainline railway as it hugs the shore and tunnels through the vivid New Red Sandstone. At Starcross there is a ferry to Exmouth, or else follow the road and then the Exeter Canal towpath to Topsham (another ferry) and into Exeter.

Plymouth – Exmouth, via Dartmoor

The alternative route from Plymouth to Exmouth is across the south-east of Dartmoor and involves no ferries or mechanical short cuts. Head for the River Plym at Longbridge, on the eastern edge of the city, and from here follow the Plym Valley Cycle Way (the disused Great Western Railway) through the woods of Bickleigh Vale to the delightfully named Hoo Meavy, a distance of about 6 miles. You are now in Dartmoor National Park. A minor road will take you to Meavy, and here the Royal Oak serves excellent home-made food. It is worth relaxing on the green at the front of this sixteenth-century pub for a leisurely and well-earned break. The pub takes its name from a nearby oak tree, which is roughly 500 years old. Much refreshed, follow roads and tracks around Burrator Reservoir until you come out on to access land and the open moors. The woodland around the reservoir is owned and managed by South-West Water, who are in the process of planting oak, wild cherry, beech and ash to break up the conifer blanket.

It needs to be emphasised to those unfamiliar with the largest open space in South-West England that Dartmoor can be deceptive, for many people have lost their way on the bare and sometimes featureless moors, and in bad weather care must be exercised. Make sure map and compass are to hand. If the mist is down an alternative route would be to follow the road from Yelverton to Princetown and then Dartmeet. If you are camping, remember that this is essentially private and not public land. The Dartmoor National Park Authority's guidelines are: don't pitch on moorland enclosed by walls; on the roadside or within 100 metres of the road; anywhere within sight of houses or roads; in reservoir catchment areas; or on heavily used 'recreational' commonland.

Follow the bridleway east from Burrator Reservoir to the remains of Whiteworks Tin Mine, then on to Hexworthy and Dartmeet. Unfenced roads lead over the moors to the attractive village of Ponsworthy where the post office stores sells hot pasties, although if the weather is clear it makes far greater sense to plot your own course over the access land. At Ponsworthy join the Two Moors Way as it heads north up West Weburn River. This is a 102-mile route from Ivybridge, on the southern edge of Dartmoor, to Lynmouth, on the north Devon coast in Exmoor National Park. Here the Way crosses Hamel Down, and is worth following until Grimspound, a well-preserved Bronze Age enclosure. However, in bad weather the maze of small tracks may be confusing, and so a good alternative is to follow lanes to Widecombe in the Moor. Here there is some accommodation and tea rooms, plus the impressive St Pancras Church, dubbed the Cathedral of the Moor and a fine example of the Perpendicular period. Bear in mind that this picturesque village gets congested with the cream tea mob when the sun comes out. Afterwards, skirt Easdon Tor and make for Moretonhampstead, where there are more facilities.

To reach Exeter, about 11 miles away, either take short footpaths and woodland tracks (although they are not particularly prevalent) or stick to minor roads as they wind their way through Dartmoor's eastern flanks. Bear in mind that the Moretonhampstead–Exeter road can get uncomfortably busy, and there are few verges or pavements. The youth hostel at Steps Bridge, near Dunsford, provides a handy overnight halt, although there are many B&Bs dotted about the area.

The city of Exeter can be avoided, although you will have to scrutinise the map carefully, as it not unnaturally acts as a focus for most local roads, including the M5. However, the return to the coast requires some roadwalking through Topsham to Exmouth, where walkers who crossed by the Starcross ferry will be met. A quieter, surfaced route from Exeter would be to take lanes via Woodbury Common to the coast near Otterton.

EXMOUTH – LYME REGIS (34 miles)

If you want an altogether more varied inland route to Lyme Regis, or if you simply have had enough of coastal walking, consider taking the East Devon Way, which at 38.5 miles is only about four miles longer than the coastal route. This new, scenic trail begins at Exmouth, popularly regarded as the flattest town in Devon, but it can be picked up just south of Lympstone by those walking down the Exe estuary from Exeter. It soon enters the East Devon Area of Outstanding Natural Beauty, swinging north across open heather slopes to Woodbury Castle, an Iron Age hillfort, and the RSPB's Aylesbeare Nature Reserve. The heath and broken woodland supports birds such as nightjar and stonechat. Follow the East Devon Way's foxglove logo past Newton Poppleford to Harpford, after which there is a puffingly steep climb up to the 220m Fire Beacon Hill (Harpford Common). The Saxon village of Sidbury offers shops, pubs and beds, plus an imposing hillfort and a Saxon church. Then take a northwards loop through low and often wooded hills, via the small settlements of Farway and Northleigh to Colyton, besides the willows of the gentle River Coly. Cross Seaton's electric tramway and the meandering Axe and make for Musbury; then over soft rolling hills to Uplyme, a mile from the coastal path at Lyme Regis.

If you decide to stay by the sea, and the wooded combes and spectacular landslips of the south Devon coastline are certainly worth seeing, then from Exmouth continue along cliffs via Budleigh Salterton, where the River Otter is best crossed by the nearby bridge, and not waded. Altogether it is about 11 miles of generally peaceful and attractive walking, with the well-defined path sticking close to the sea all the way. Across the Otter, Sidmouth is home to the famous Donkey Sanctuary which, since its inception in 1969, has cared for over 4,000 animals.

After Sidmouth the cliffs steepen, with a number of deep-cut valleys to negotiate; and the steep ups and downs should not be underestimated. The thatched cottages and Saxon church of Branscombe are worth a diversion, and once over Beer Head, the westernmost chalk outcrop in Britain, relax in the sheltered fishing village of Beer, which has a youth hostel. The path drops down to Seaton Bay; where there is plenty of accommodation. Once over Axmouth Bridge climb back on to the cliffs and enter a stretch of dense woodland that extends for about 5 miles. This is Axmouth–Lyme Regis Undercliffs National Nature Reserve, a fascinating jungle of trees (ash, sycamore, hazel, beech) and undergrowth, which sprawls over a series of sizeable landslips. The most dramatic slip occurred on Christmas night in 1839 when a colossal 8 million tons of land subsided, forming 'Goat Island' and 'the Chasm'. Bear in mind that there is no permitted access inland or to the sea in this stretch, and the path, although well-waymarked, can be arduous and muddy in wet weather. Nevertheless the peaceful shade, with ferns and bluebells all about, provides a welcome change from the miles of open clifftop, even if the views seaward are often limited.

When you finally emerge from the foliage admire the views ahead to the Golden Cap, the highest spot on the entire south coast, and descend through fields to Lyme Regis. It is worth pausing and reflecting on a few facts: the next few steps will take you from Devon into Dorset, your third county since leaving Land's End, although by now it will probably feel like you've clocked up half the length of the country. This is also the last time that you will see the south coast, intermittently your companion for the last few weeks. From Lyme Regis the direction is north-eastwards, and so inland. The next time you will see the sea is at Filey, on the coast of the North Sea, after another 630 miles. So take a good look now.

[illegible]

[illegible]

[illegible]

17

WALKING THROUGH HISTORY

Lyme Regis – Ivinghoe

LYME REGIS – SHROTON (59 miles)

It is worth pausing at Lyme Regis, not least because there is abundant accommodation in and around the handsome little town. The ancient quay, known as the Cobb, has seen ships set sail to fight the Spanish Armada, and to explore and trade with the New World. Sir George Summers, Mayor and MP for Lyme as well as occasional buccaneer (supposedly the inspiration for Shakespeare's *The Tempest*), headed off at the close of the sixteenth century and discovered Bermuda. He died there in 1610, but so attached was he to his native town that his body was pickled and sent back for burial. Latterly the Cobb has witnessed actress Meryl Streep staring moodily into the rain in the film *The French Lieutenant's Woman*, a book written by Lyme resident John Fowles.

The means of crossing southern England to reach the east coast is provided by a route often referred to as the Great Ridgeway. It follows ridges of chalk downland that stretch across from the present Devon/Dorset border on the English Channel to the Wash, and includes the Wessex Downs and Chilterns. The route has been in existence for thousands of years, as generations of hunters and traders found the high downs much easier for movement than the wooded or swampy valleys. Indeed, the Great Ridgeway appears to have evolved as simply a series of paths and trackways that have enjoyed a pattern of continual use; and even today there is no single, continuous path that runs the whole distance, rather a number of connecting walking routes.

The first 130 miles, to Avebury in Wiltshire, are along the Wessex Ridgeway (not to be confused with the Ridgeway National Trail, which follows immediately afterwards). There are a number of points to bear in mind about the Wessex Ridgeway. First, the original guidebook is written for those walking in the opposite direction, which makes it downright difficult to work out some of the route directions. Second, this is not a national trail and county council waymarking is still in progress, so don't expect a signpost at every turn. Yet you may feel that it is refreshing or challenging *not* to be kid-gloved with signs and arrows every step of the way. (The Dorset section is currently being waymarked with the Wessex Wyvern symbol – a green dragon.) Third, if you feel that something is missing then it may well turn out to be the sea. The crashing surf is now behind; ahead lie the green hills and open plains of Dorset and Wiltshire.

Should this thought appal you, or if you simply want to walk more of the South-West Coast Path, then continue along the shore as far as Swanage, and from here follow the 103-mile Wessex Way via Corfe, Salisbury and Stonehenge to Avebury.

Leave Lyme Regis by the River Lim and take footpaths and a lane inland for Penn. Here, cross the busy A35 and follow paths across rolling fields to Wootton Fitzpaine, a village that is as lovely as it sounds, but offers no facilities for walkers. The narrow Dorset lanes are by and large pleasant to walk along (barring the occasional vehicle). This is just as well since not all the footpaths are either clear or obvious to find. There may be times when walking 2 miles of lanes seems more sensible than floundering in a muddy field or overgrown copse, and I would heartily concur with a modification of the official route in such circumstances. But often the Wessex Ridgeway makes use of short stretches of minor road, and one such is the approach to Coney's Castle from Wootton Fitzpaine. A short way along the ridge is Lambert's Castle, and from the modest elevation of 256m there are terrific views, particularly east over Marshwood Vale. These two hillforts, built some time around 500 BC, are now just grassy mounds topped with hawthorn and bluebells and relatively unvisited, but in many ways this actually enhances their appeal.

The route makes a short detour north to avoid using the fast, rather winding and pavementless B3165 to Coles Cross, north of Birdsmoorgate. The goal is Pilsdon Pen, the highest hill in Dorset, and like so many around bears the traces of an Iron Age hillfort.

There is a bridleway to Lewesdon Hill, south of Broadwindsor (where there are shops and a post office, and where the White Lion provides food and B&B), then after the open slopes and pleasing viewpoints of Gerrards Hill descend to Beaminster, former centre of the Dorset Blue Vinney Cheese producing district. Around the attractive square there are shops and cafés.

A track leads to Langdon Farm, then lanes via Toller Whelme, Hooke and Lower Kingcombe to Maiden Newton. The last has a few facilities but is rather dull, so you may want to press on to Sydling St Nicholas where there is a pub and a couple of B&Bs.

The route now climbs up on the hilltop once more, and heads north along an unswerving lane towards Gore Hill, before turning east for Up Cerne. However, you may consider staying on the road from Sydling St Nicholas to Cerne Abbas in order to inspect the village and its famous giant. The medieval houses are undeniably attractive, and each flower border meticulously tended. You may have to book ahead for accommodation at weekends. Meanwhile the Giant stands erect with his club and unsheathed member on the hillside above. The public are not allowed to walk over this 55-metre-long chalk fertility symbol for fear of erosion, although I suspect that only one piece of his anatomy would attract most visitors' attention. The National Trust's information board is most tactful: '. . . the semi-naturalistic style in which he is portrayed suggests a Romano-British origin.' The 2,000-year-old Giant has recently had his nose (six feet long) remodelled, using sterile chalk. Sheep keep the surrounding grass short, but their droppings need to be regularly swept up to stop soil forming.

Clear tracks lead over the open hillside to just north of Alton Pancras, then continue over Church Hill and along hedged (and sometimes muddy) bridleways to the Dorsetshire Gap. The Gap is partly man-made and partly the result of erosion, and despite references to its magical and spiritual aura it is really just a small and rather unspectacular-looking junction of five ancient tracks in the chalk escarpment. There are a couple of sunken lanes, with grassy banks on which the weary traveller can rest, plus an intriguing fixed green box that houses notebooks for visitors to the Gap to sign. Those passing through have included local ramblers, long-distance walkers, and the paw-mark of 'Tessa the Dog'.

A diversion to the Fox Inn at Ansty (marked Lower Ansty on some maps) is recommended, since the food is excellent and they permit camping in the adjoining field. The village also has one of the country's tallest maypoles, and you may even be unlucky enough to experience Morris dancers at work.

The steady pull up Bulbarrow Hill might leave you a little breathless, but the vista from Woolland and Ibberton Hills repays the effort. Apart from an undistinguished-looking pub, there is little else to make the steep descent to the village of Ibberton worthwhile. Far better to stay on the road at the escarpment top as long as possible, drinking in the views across Blackmoor Vale. You will also pass the improbably-situated Baker's Folly restaurant, which now serves afternoon teas and snacks.

Branch off right and battle through the wind as it howls over Bell Hill. The descent to the Stour valley through Blandford Forest is especially beautiful, after which Shillingstone makes a sensible place to stop. The Willows is a particularly handy B&B/tearoom, since the Wessex Ridgeway continues down Holloway Lane, 50 metres away. The footbridge across the River Stour is ugly but functional, and now swing north by the river and make for the imposing bulk of Hambledon Hill, with its massive Iron Age fort. The two grassy ramparts around the crest of the hill enclose nearly twenty-five acres, with views across the Stour to the Mendips in the west. There is even evidence of a Neolithic long barrow on the top which predates the actual fort. Members of the Durotriges tribe inhabited the camp at some stage, and with evidence of over 200 platform huts it is thought that as many as 1,000 people may have lived here at one time.

The tracks are clear and easy to follow. Descend to Shroton, also known as Iwerne Courtney, a sprawling village with a pub (the Cricketers, plus restaurant) and a large green surrounded by inelegant modern brick houses. St Mary's Church was believed to be the last resting place for the body of the Saxon King Edward the Martyr on the way to Shaftesbury Abbey, after he was murdered at Corfe Castle in AD 978.

SHROTON – AVEBURY (72 miles)

From Shroton, either visit the nearby fort on Hod Hill, then cross the A350 and take the pleasantly direct Smuggler's Lane eastwards, or follow the 'official' route across the main road and up into Preston Wood. It then jinks about in a fashion that is likely to confuse, particularly since this area falls in that exasperating zone between three different OS Landranger maps. This is hilly and often thickly wooded countryside – the heart of Cranborne Chase – and your next goal is Ashmore, the highest village in Dorset, how ever you choose to reach it.

Cranborne Chase was originally granted to the Earls of Gloucester by William Rufus, but it later reverted to the Crown. The Chase was a favourite hunting ground of King John, who had a royal hunting lodge at Tollard Royal, which is where the Wessex Ridgeway now heads after crossing into Wiltshire. Tollard Royal is little more than a tiny but pleasant collection of buildings that includes a pub; then continue along Ashcombe Bottom and up on to Win Green before descending to Ludwell. If you are pushed for time, or if it's pelting with rain, you could simply take the road from Ashmore to Ludwell and save a few miles. But the steady climb to the exposed top of Win Green reveals more and more glorious views. Take the straight and uncomplicated flinty lane (signposted 'byway to Win Green') instead of the overgrown valley bottom path, and at the head of the dry chalk valley it curves around the rim allowing views north to Shaftesbury, and to the distant Salisbury Plain, and south to the Dorset coast (Weymouth is 30 miles away).

Leave the kite-fliers and Sunday strollers and follow blue bridleway signs through Elliott's Shed (a small wood) and into Ludwell. There are a couple of rather pricey if attractive pub/hotels, and B&B at the Forester hostelry in Donhead St Andrew, which you reach by lanes over the River Nadder. One of these lanes carries the Wiltshire Cycleway, a council-devised 160-mile route around the county.

Your own route is now north to Hindon, just under ten miles away, but if at all possible it should include a detour across footpaths to Old Wardour Castle, which sits romantically by a lake with a thick wooded backcloth. It was begun in the 1390s by the fifth Lord Lovel, whose experiences in France during the Hundred Years War may account for its hexagon design, unique for an English castle of that period. After some rough treatment during the Civil War, when there were two protracted and violent sieges, the castle was left ruined and unoccupied. But its rather haunting remains are intact enough to allow for a happy scramble, and an educational exploration.

Leave Old Wardour Castle by a public footpath through the grounds of New Wardour Castle, now a school, and use either footpaths or lanes to reach Newtown. Tisbury, a mile east, has a good number of shops and eating places. Then the route takes bridleways via Summerleaze Farm and around the edge of woodland to Hindon; or easier still, take the shaded, up-and-down lane through the woods of Beacon Hill. The Lamb at Hindon and the Grosvenor Arms both offer refreshment.

Take the lane to Chicklade Bottom Farm, turning off just before to skirt Cold Berwick Hill and down a steep grassy field to the busy A303. Cross carefully, and follow the rough farm track via the once handsome Rake Barn into a large area of woodland marked as Great Ridge (the sound of the traffic is present for some time). The guidebook in fact suggests crossing the main road further down at Chicklade, then following a somewhat complicated route through the dense trees and undergrowth. Far better to stick to my suggested route: it is a wide and unmistakable forest track (a right of way) and should offer no routefinding problems. There is a large, young plantation fenced-off on the crown of the hill, but unfortunately the thick covering of maturer trees all around spoil any chance of a view. For this you will have to wait for a few minutes until you leave Rowdean Hill and drop down to the River Wylye.

Ahead, across the narrow valley, are the low but sometimes steep slopes of the south-western edge of Salisbury Plain. The bypassing A36 renders most of the string of little villages along the valley bottom undisturbed. Of these, your path is through Corton, where the newly refurbished Dove Inn sits behind pink-washed thatched walls and is replete with a voluble dovecote. Cross the river and railway to Knook, but keep away from the main road. Proceed for half a mile into Heytesbury, where the waterside Red Lion (residential) is handily placed next to the Greedy Goose delicatessen.

A footpath leaves the houses northwards, dropping to the A36 cutting by a wooden stile and steps. From Heytesbury House it heads up through sloping fields to Cotley Hill, then across to the lumpy heights of Scratchbury Hill and Battlesbury Hill. The last two are examples of late-middle Iron Age hillforts, strategically situated above the valley, but why two such powerful forts should be found so close together has puzzled experts.

From the two hills there are not only views down the valley, but also over the expanse of Salisbury Plain. You are at the western end of the Plain, and for most of the year virtually all of this seemingly unspoilt land is out of bounds. Stark MOD warning signs will already have told you why. In 1943 the land around the village of Imber was designated a military firing and training area, all the residents were evacuated, and public access was permanently denied. Live firing still continues, and tanks and military vehicles are a common sight. However, this has spawned one of the country's more curious long-distance routes, known as the Imber Range Perimeter Path. Its 30 miles encircle the whole military area, and the Wessex Ridgeway joins it from near Heytesbury around the western edge of the Plain to a junction above West Lavington. Walkers should not worry, for this is an official route (there is a leaflet and map available), following clear paths, tracks and lanes, with regular Imber Range Path waymarks. And there are plenty of signs denoting the exact boundary of the range. They include helpful ones such as: 'Warning to public – danger from unexploded shell and mortar bombs. On no account should any object be moved or touched. It may explode.'

If you are seriously worried about walking this section then take a low-level route around the foot of the slopes, through Warminster and Westbury, and rejoin the path at Market Lavington or Urchfont. But there are some fascinating places on the Imber Range Perimeter Path, and always wide and changing views. For all facilities Warminster is virtually at the foot of Battlesbury Hill; then the path climbs to Upton Cow Down, and along a clear track to Beggar's Knoll.

Stay with the track past a huge chalk quarry (it feeds the Blue Circle cement works, sadly unmissable in the valley below) and to the prominent hillfort of Bratton Camp. More famous is the adjacent White Horse. This is the oldest (maybe early 1700s) of six white horses carved into various chalk hillsides throughout Wiltshire. It has become so popular with day visitors that the authorities have had to cement it over to counter worsening erosion. From here you can wander down the steep lane into Bratton, where the Victoria provides both food and beds.

The route now follows the edge of the military range in a clear and obvious fashion, sticking mainly to rough, open lanes which are fairly regularly waymarked with Imber Range Path signs. This boundary route is also popular with mountain bikers and runners, plus the odd sightseer. No doubt you will also be passed by one of the regular police patrols. If firing is taking place there will be red flags raised, or red lamps visible. It goes without saying to stay well clear. At Coulston Hill swing round to Stoke Hill, and then along the former Bath–Salisbury coach road to New Zealand Farm Camp. From close to this inhospitable collection of nissen huts behind barbed wire take the metalled track east to Gore Cross. Away to the south the rough, scrubby heathland contains a few coppices, plus patches of heather and wild grasses. Alas, you can only look, not walk.

Beyond the A360 the lane rises once more. Standing on the high edge of the Plain, the rich farmland of the Vale of Pewsey spreads out at your feet, and in the distance is Devizes and Chippenham, and the southern Cotswolds. Soon you will descend to this flatter land. Unless you want to divert to West Lavington or Market Lavington, continue past a vedette post, which looks more like a public lavatory than a sentry hut, and at Urchfont Hill wander down the track into the village. A path leads from the church across fields to Stert, then on to Etchilhampton Hill, with views over the outer redbrick houses of Devizes. You may have noticed that now and then Wessex Ridgeway waymarks have begun appearing again (a green dragon on a white background).

Leaving the low hillside join a small lane and then the towpath of the Kennet and Avon Canal into the town. Devizes is a pleasant market town with some fine buildings and some fine beer, since Wadworth's Brewery is situated here. Accommodation includes two campsites. If you have a few minutes to spare stay on the towpath, which passes the Kennet and Avon Canal Shop and Exhibition on the Wharf development, and then a little further on is the beginning of Caen Hill Locks, a remarkable series of twenty-nine locks (sixteen in one direct flight) which lift the canal over 600m in just over 2 miles. You will also see signs for the Kennet and Avon Canal Walk.

This towpath walk follows the canal for 78 miles between Reading and Bath, and offers the East Route walker the perfect opportunity to switch to the Central Route at Bath – or even beyond, via the Avon Walkway, to the West Route at Bristol.

Leave Devizes by a lane known as Quaker's Walk, to Roundway, where an obvious track leads straight up the hillside to Roundway Down, near Oliver's Castle. The latter is an ancient hillfort, and the former is the site of a Civil War battle in 1643, after which Cromwell besieged Devizes and destroyed the castle. Take the track over the north of Roundway Down; it emerges as a signposted byway by North Wiltshire Golf Course. The rich, green fairways stand out starkly against the browns and dark yellows of the surrounding fields, which seem to roll endlessly over the bare downland south and east.

Cross the golf course with care, and over Morgan's Hill Nature Reserve. This small site of undisturbed chalkland, which is crossed by the historic Wansdyke, is rich in natural grasses, scrub and woodland. Uncommon plants such as the lesser butterfly orchid and the round-headed rampion may be found here. Then follow the course of an old Roman road over North Down, leaving it after a mile for a path to Cherhill Down. Here is another white horse, although you will have to descend to the A4 to see it properly – which is where a Dr Alsop of Calne (known as the 'Mad Doctor') stood in 1780, giving directions through a megaphone to men on the hillside cutting it. He even had upturned bottles placed in the centre of the 4-feet-wide horse's eye so that it would sparkle in the sunshine, although these have not survived.

Avebury is now in sight as you descend Knoll Down to the A4. Even after visiting so many ancient remains in the last week's walking, Avebury stone circle will leave you in awe. It is the largest stone circle in Europe; indeed, much of the present village is within the double circle of 200 standing stones, which includes a massive bank and ditch. It was constructed in the Late Neolithic period, perhaps around 2000 BC, and may have taken centuries to complete. West Kennet Long Barrow and Silbury Hill are two more fascinating local sites only a few minutes' walk away, and if you have never visited this area you really should allow yourself a few hours to explore.

The Wessex Ridgeway officially runs for another 6½ miles to Marlborough but, unless you specifically want to visit it, it is time to prepare for some invigorating downland miles along the Ridgeway National Trail.

AVEBURY – IVINGHOE BEACON (85 miles)

The Ridgeway National Trail formally begins at the A4 car park by Overton Hill, about a mile and a half from Avebury. But there is really no need to walk along the road to this rather incongruous start, since from Avebury there is a pleasant track, in fact the ancient Herepath, that links with the Ridgeway on Overton Down, a couple of miles north of Overton Hill. The Wiltshire Herepath, as this section is sometimes known, was basically a route used by warring factions in the Dark Ages, although its origins are probably prehistoric. Until the 1700s it was also used as a coach road.

At its conclusion at Ivinghoe Beacon, the Ridgeway runs automatically into the Icknield Way, and together they run north-east for almost 200 miles along the North Wessex Downs and the Chilterns, through the heart of southern England and into East Anglia. The counties simply fly by: Wiltshire, Oxfordshire, Berkshire, Buckinghamshire, Hertfordshire. The chalk downland generally provides good, airy walking, although the elevation never exceeds 280m, and after crossing the Thames at Streatley the route becomes more varied, winding its way through farmland and woods. The sense of history is maintained with the Icknield Way, emerging finally at Knettishall Heath on the Suffolk–Norfolk border.

For the next couple of days you are likely to meet a few horse riders and, if it is a weekend, quite a few mountain bikers. This should not upset you unduly, for as far as Streatley it is a bridleway and they have every right to use the route. Besides, the open rolling track allows ample passing room. However, you will probably need this room in wet conditions, since rain + hooves + tyres = mud. So step out carefully.

The initial 5 miles, to Barbury Castle, are typical of the next two days' walking: quite open and elevated, with panoramic views of southern England. Tumuli and sarsen stones (large sandstone boulders) dot the fields, especially in the vicinity of Fyfield Down National Nature Reserve, and ahead are a succession of dramatic prehistoric hillforts perched on top of grassy summits. The first is at Barbury, where the warden of the country park sells home-made cakes from his cottage. Here, in 1985, workmen digging a new ESSO pipeline uncovered a long-deceased body. Tests showed that it dated from around AD 300, and came from a Romano-British farming community. The workmen gave it the nickname Eric ('Early Remains in Chalk'), but when it was discovered that the body was in fact female, Eric became Erica! About 250 years after Erica died, her local tribe were overwhelmed by the Anglo-Saxons in a large battle, and the relative peace that followed led to the formation of the Kingdom of Wessex.

The track from Barbury Castle follows Smeathe's Ridge, narrow and exposed, then loses height to loop around the village of

Ogbourne St George, where there are pubs and some accommodation. After this swing south, the trail returns to the main ridge of the downs, and the line of the original Ridgeway, at Liddington Castle.

Specific route directions are largely superfluous for these first 40 miles. The Ridgeway mostly follows a clear, chalk track which is frequently fenced and often as wide as a road. Many sections are almost dead straight, with the rolling white ribbon visible for miles ahead. Waymarking for this national trail is exemplary, although at times – when there is only one path to take – it is hard to imagine the need for a signpost. OS maps are, as always, useful for identifying features off the path, and since the Ridgeway seldom leaves the unpopulated high ground you may need a map if you descend to the Vale of the White Horse for a meal or a bed.

Liddington Castle is another defensive circle of grass earthworks, and the open, windy hill marks the highest point on the Ridgeway (277m). Below, the M4 is evident, snaking its way past Swindon, and the roar becomes louder as you lose height and cross it near Fox Hill on a road that itself can be quite busy. The Shepherd's Rest at Fox Hill is one of the very few pubs actually on the path – the next is at Streatley 25 miles further on. Since it sports a sign saying 'Walkers welcome' and serves food all day it must be worth a visit.

Although trees and hedgerows restrict views, they do offer protection should the wind pick up, as the next stretch may prove. There is B&B at Ridgeway Farm, otherwise drop down to the likes of Wanborough and Bishopstone for overnight accommodation. A list of B&Bs and campsites, plus other helpful local details, is given in the annual *Ridgeway Information and Accommodation Guide*.

Off the path above Ashbury is a 200-feet long-chambered barrow called Wayland's Smithy; and a little further on is Uffington, a popular venue for those disinclined to stray more than half a mile from their cars. A few come to see the hillfort, but most take a closer look at the white horse. Of all the chalk horses that graze the hillsides of Wiltshire and Berkshire, this is the oldest. It was first referred to over 900 years ago, and it has been suggested that it was cut as a tribute to the Saxon leader Hengist, who had a white horse on his standard.

The track continues its unswerving passage over the downs. Near junctions with lanes and roads there are notices aimed at other users of the Ridgeway, stating a code of conduct to be observed and warning of a road crossing ahead. This is a popular section with mountain bike riders, and while most are polite and respectful it is a good idea to stay alert to the sound of crunching gravel or splashing puddles behind you. If you feel in need of rest or refreshment take the lane down Gramp's Hill to Letcombe Bassett, the 'Cresscombe' of Thomas Hardy's *Jude the Obscure*, where the Yew Tree Inn serves a fine ploughman's lunch.

After Segsbury or Letcombe Castle arrive at a small lane, called Manor Road. The trail turns right into it, then sharply left and back among the fields. However, if you turn left and take the road down the hill towards Wantage (3 miles away) you come to the Ridgeway Centre on Court Hill, where there is a youth hostel, camping facilities and an exhibition centre.

East of Uffington the route becomes even grander, up to 70 feet broad in places, but there are times when you may be glad that it is so wide. This part of the country (you are now in Oxfordshire) is famous for its racehorses, and while there are specific horse gallops near and next to the path, many still use the Ridgeway itself for exercise. Near East and West Ilsley, where pub refreshment may be had, pass safely under the A34 and begin the long approach down to the Thames at Streatley and Goring.

The Goring Gap divides the Wessex Downs from the Chilterns, the wide bridleway from the winding footpaths, the open downs from the woods. It is the halfway point of the Ridgeway in many ways. The Gap is occupied by the Thames, already a confident river, with the two settlements of Streatley and Goring on opposite banks (apparently referred to as 'Discreetly' and 'Boring' by commuters on the Oxford–London line). Goring, in particular, with its trim weirs, is very smart. Both offer shops, pubs and cafés, and there is a recently refurbished youth hostel in Streatley. Once replenished, follow the attractive towpath upstream for a mile, in the company of moorhens and grebes. All tranquil and serene, until a 125 thunders over the Brunel-built Moulsford Railway Bridge and rather disturbs the peace. Along here you will see waymarks for the Swans Way, which is a 65-mile bridleway from

Goring to Salcey Forest, near Milton Keynes; and of course the Thames Path crosses the End to End route at this point as well. Once through the dozing hamlets of South and North Stoke, turn east after Mongewell Park and join Grim's Ditch. (There are full amenities at the handsome town of Wallingford, a further mile upstream.) Follow this mysterious earthwork for a couple of miles, parting company at Nuffield, where the motor car manufacturer and philanthropist William Morris is buried in the churchyard. Then cross a golf course to reach the A423 by the Crown public house. After downland and river bank, now woodland.

The path passes two large houses, Ewelme Park and Swyncombe House. It is a quiet, sedate landscape, and although there are some appreciable ups and downs, the benign Chiltern slopes should not unduly tax your hardened legs! But life in rural Oxfordshire is not always as sedate as it might appear. On a sunny Tuesday in March I was resting in woodland on the edge of Swyncombe Downs, just before the path reaches Dean Wood, munching a sandwich and minding my own business, when cries and yelping became apparent. Then all of a sudden a fox dashed out of the trees a few yards away, disappearing in a red flash into bushes, followed no more than twenty seconds later by frantic, lolling-tongued hounds. Soon after, several horses crashed through the undergrowth, ridden by wild-eyed fellows panting madly. 'The unspeakable in full pursuit of the uneatable.' But within two or three minutes complete peace and quiet had returned; it was like nothing had ever happened.

After Dean Wood turn abruptly north-east along a direct, grassy track lined with hedges. This is in fact the Icknield Way, the ancient roadway that you will be joining in just under 30 miles. As you follow the foot of the scarp north-eastwards there are modest services at Watlington, a mile away, plus a campsite even closer. To your right the sometimes steep, rounded hills of the Chilterns bowl along, punctuated in a severe fashion by the M40 cutting. Take the tunnel underneath the motorway, and continue along a hedged lane that largely obscures Chinnor cement works from view. Finally the route leaves the lane, toys with a couple of small hills, and wanders across to the uninspiring outskirts of Princes Risborough.

A steep ascent of Whiteleaf Hill helps put the thought of urbanisation behind, and once more you can enjoy regarding it from a safe distance. The mysterious Whiteleaf Cross, carved into the slope below your pleasant picnic spot on the hilltop, could have religious or possibly navigational significance. Green woodpeckers, long-tailed tits, and maybe the occasional deer are likely companions through the trees to Lower Casden, and afterwards through the chalk grassland, scrub and patchy woodland that comprise the nature reserve on Pulpit Hill. Near Chequers Knap the North Bucks Way is met, and soon afterwards the path skirts the grounds of the prime minister's country residence, eventually crossing its driveway.

Climb through beech woodland to Coombe Hill, where there are extensive views from the 257m 'summit' of the Chilterns, and where Lord Nugent of Guildford officially opened the Ridgeway National Trail in September 1973. Then make the wooded descent to Wendover, where there are several places to stay, and more to eat, plus plenty of attractive old buildings to admire. Resume by following the signs out of the town towards more low, hilly woodland, along what the map calls Hogtrough Lane. There are now long sections of woodland, and in wet weather the going can become difficult. Despite signs reading 'Ridgeway – path only', I often floundered in disgusting mud that bore innumerable hoofprints.

The break in the hills at Tring is shared by canal, road and railway. The canal is the Grand Union, which it is possible to follow on foot all the way from London to Birmingham.

Of course, you are neither in London nor want to be in Birmingham, but should you want a painless, pedestrian switch from the East to the Central End to End Route, you could conceivably follow the first National Waterway Walk all the way from Tring to Rowington, near Warwick, which the Heart of England Way passes through on its way to Cannock Chase.

Once over the A41, if a cream tea or a pint of Greene King IPA at the Royal Hotel does not appeal, scamper past Tring Railway Station and return to quiet, rolling woodland. There is a newly surfaced section of bridleway, with a gravel and sand base, that leads up to Duchie's Piece, where the Herts and Middlesex Wildlife Trust's nature reserve supports cowslip and lady's bedstraw, and the rare Duke of Burgundy butterfly.

Pitstone Windmill, the oldest dated windmill in England (1627), can be seen in a field south of Ivinghoe. This is a post mill, where the body revolves on a central post in order to face the wind. Ahead, Ivinghoe Beacon's grassy top draws nearer. It is marked by a proliferation of tracks and paths, some scraped out by the feet of model aircraft enthusiasts who flock to the windy hill. It is here, by the airy trig point, that the Ridgeway National Trail comes to an end. Sit in the long grass and gaze out over Leighton Buzzard, Milton Keynes and rural Bedfordshire, and reflect on another long-distance path successfully completed, and the next beckoning at your feet.

18

THE FLAT EAST

Ivinghoe – Oakham

IVINGHOE BEACON – KNETTISHALL HEATH (105 miles)
Retrace your steps down the grassy slopes of the Beacon to the minor road crossing, near where there is a new Icknield Way milestone. Although the Icknield Way officially begins at Ivinghoe Beacon, there is no sudden transformation from one path to the other. And in many ways that is entirely fitting, since the Icknield Way provides a logical and satisfying extension of the ancient route that you have been following since the Dorset coast.

There is also another ridge walk that joins the East Route at this point. The Two Ridges Link (8 miles) connects with the Greensand Ridge Walk at Leighton Buzzard. This route runs for a total of 40 miles to Sandy, along wooded greensand hills and through historic parks such as Woburn.

The next 100 miles or so, to Knettishall Heath in Suffolk, are straightforward: lowland paths, woodland tracks, green lanes, and only a few short pulls up the downland. The main problems are likely to be mud, occasional road crossings and routefinding. The course of the prehistoric Icknield Way is shown on OS maps, albeit intermittently, in gothic lettering to denote a non-Roman antiquity. However, this is not the exact route of the present-day Icknield Way Path, and walkers would be wise to bear this in mind when poring over their maps. Also, there is a new choice of scenic and historic routes near Luton, as well as a Riders' Route under development that is also open to walkers, so that it is sensible to study the latest guide and watch closely for signposts. As is usually the case, it is best to follow the waymarked route if there is any doubt over the correct course, and through the efforts of the Icknield Way Association and the respective local authorities there are plenty of the Neolithic flint axe emblems to be seen along the path.

The village of Ivinghoe, which has a youth hostel, is only a mile or so to the north, but your route curves in a southerly direction towards the huge and eye-catching chalk lion carved in the grass below Whipsnade Zoo. After open fields at the foot of a grass slope enter mixed woodland, where overgrown stinging nettles may make the passage uncomfortable. Once more across open farmland to Dagnall, where the Golden Rule public house serves a delicious 'Piggly Pie', containing spicy sausage, pork, ham and bacon in a cider and apple sauce. Then after a short climb to woodland, cross the first of several golf courses to the perimeter fence of Whipsnade Zoo. Inside you may spot yak and deer, and possibly some of the rare and endangered species that the zoo breeds, such as the Scimitar Horned Oryx and Przewalski's Horse, but ask yourself if you'd recognise them if you saw them.

Emerge from a lane on to Whipsnade village green by the Chequers Inn (hot and cold food), and depart via the unusual Tree Cathedral, an arrangement of trees and bushes deliberately planted and cultivated in the ground-plan design of a cathedral. The waymarking for the Icknield Way is impeccable, and there are also signs bearing the letters 'CR' (circular routes). Return to the open hillside at Dunstable Downs, where there are wide views across Bedfordshire and Northamptonshire. Closer at hand the London Gliding Club fill the air with their silent craft. There is a handy snack bar, and seasonal information centre.

From Dunstable Downs walkers have the choice of the 'historic' or 'scenic' route for the next few miles. The former stays close to the original route, and is the course plotted by the Icknield Way Association. But it also runs straight through the middle of Dunstable and then around the fringe of Luton, which is fine if you want to visit shops or find a bed for the night, but not aesthetically pleasing otherwise. It is well-signposted, even on the urban street corners of Luton. Perhaps the highlight of this section is the Priory Church of St Peter, in Dunstable, where Henry VIII made history by announcing his divorce of Catherine of Aragon – the first divorce in England. However, my choice of route would be the newer 'scenic' one to the north, via the edge of Sewell Manor, the village of Toddington and Sundon Hills Country Park, crossing the busy A6 at Streatley. At Galley Hill the older route is rejoined, and then a pleasant green lane takes you across Telegraph Hill Nature Reserve. Here the poor, thin 'free-draining' soils support a wide variety of wild flowers: horseshoe vetch, cowslip and salad burnet, plus a number of different orchids.

The condition of the path varies considerably. It can be desperately muddy after rain, and although chalk drains relatively quickly, the clay soils are often heavy and sticky. The alternative route around Dunstable and Luton outlined above can be particularly messy, for unlike the original route it passes below the spring line. Of course the mud and mire is aggravated by the passage of horses and bikes, so take care on the bridleway sections. But by and large the tracks are wide enough to allow pedestrians to avoid the real goo, and the green lanes, such as the one over Telegraph Hill, are quite delightful.

You are now in Hertfordshire, and after emerging from a bridleway at the village of Pirton, head east towards more home counties civilisation: Letchworth, Baldock and Royston appear in quick succession, and all offer accommodation and refreshment, plus Hitchin is just off the route. None of them is particularly gripping, but all are sufficiently small to walk through in only a few minutes. The route will be obvious. Letchworth was the first of the Garden Cities (that shows how close London is), but Baldock's history goes back to at least the Romans. From here aim for Clothall Church to the south-east, then via tracks to Wallington, where George Orwell was married and lived for some years (apparently copies of his marriage certificate can be purchased). Field paths and lanes lead to Therfield, and as you approach Royston across the edge of Therfield Heath there is evidence of prehistoric earthworks side by side with the modern golf course.

Royston was founded in the early Middle Ages and is sited on the junction of the original Icknield Way and Roman Ermine Street. County-collectors will rejoice once more as the Cambridgeshire border looms. Follow the drive of Burloes Hall for a short distance; ahead are 2 miles of green lane, after which turn sharply right, and trace the Anglo-Saxon Heydon Ditch south to the village of Heydon.

Now into Essex, briefly, and along easy lanes via Elmdon and

Strethall to Great Chesterford (pub, shop). There is also some accommodation here, or failing that plod 3 miles further on to Linton. From here to the end of the Icknield Way Path the landscape becomes more diverse, with evidence of woodland and heathland. The influence of horse-racing on this area of Suffolk is also fascinating; and towards the end of this section the open sandy fields of Breckland come into view.

However, as Newmarket approaches you may like to pause and consider the route ahead. There are roughly another 30 miles until the end of the Way at Knettishall Heath. Then the East Route, having stayed true to the Icknield Way, has to veer back on itself to join the Hereward Way and head for Ely. If you are in a hurry, because of a tight timetable or a limited budget, or perhaps eager to see high hills or the sea once more, you may wish to cut a corner and save a few days. Or you may simply feel that the East Route is taking too much of a diversion into East Anglia. If this is the case, leave the Icknield Way Path between Stetchworth and Ashley and head for Newmarket, then take footpaths northwards via Chippenham Fen and Fordham Moor to Soham, where the quiet banks of Soham Lode and then the Great Ouse will lead you to Ely, about 6 miles distant. Here you can join the Hereward Way, and with it the East Route once more. Also, since the Hereward Way is only properly waymarked from Ely to Peterborough, and not from Thetford/Knettishall Heath to Ely, this short and convenient diversion may be attractive for those relying on regular waymarks.

But for those enjoying the Icknield Way to its conclusion there is still plenty of interest. Many of the scattered pockets of woodland about the route over the next few miles are remnants of an ancient forest, and you will see them as you pass the villages of Balsham and Stetchworth. At the former is another IWA milestone, and near the latter the Stour Valley Path is joined very briefly. The area's association with racehorse training is also obvious around villages such as Cheveley and Ashley, where there are a number of stud farms. You may even meet some horses being exercised, so naturally be polite and courteous, and you may get a tip direct from the horse's mouth.

Enter Suffolk, the final county of the trail, and after the hamlets of Dalham and Gazeley, pass under the busy A45 and the railway line, and head along a quiet minor road to Herringswell. The church is dedicated to St Ethelbert, King of East Anglia, who had a run-in with King Offa of Mercia in 792 – and came away from the meeting minus his head. After Icklingham the reconstructed Saxon village of West Stow is just off the route, where you can delve about the sunken-floored huts and dark wooden hall – an appropriate moment to reflect that the Icknield Way, like the Ridgeway behind and the Peddars Way a little further on, is steeped in history, and it is instructive to understand that yours are not the first feet treading the route.

The Icknield Way Path originally entered the trees ahead of you at West Stow and skirted the woodland's southern flanks, and if you have an old copy of the IWA's guidebook it still will. But nowadays the route dives into the heart of the King's Forest, which is part of the much larger Thetford Forest, and for a few miles follows the original Icknield Way in the form of a clear and unmistakable track among the trees.

The last few miles, through the estate village of Euston, are along flat and easy tracks. The finish is at Knettishall Heath Country Park, an appropriate end to what has been a generally gentle and scenic wander across southern England. Now, however, a change is at hand. From Knettishall Heath the Peddars Way National Trail heads north to the Norfolk coast along flat and direct Roman paths. But for the End to End walker a more significant change is to occur. After hundreds of miles facing the morning sun, the route now switches westwards and heads for the Fenlands, so beginning a steady course north-west along the Hereward Way via Ely and Peterborough to Oakham, and then northwards along the Viking Way via Lincoln, finally joining up with the Wolds Way at the River Humber. It took many miles to get here, but the East Route has at last begun in earnest.

KNETTISHALL HEATH – OAKHAM (102 miles)

Although the Hereward Way officially begins at Harling Road station, it makes more sense to turn north-west at Knettishall Heath and join the trail at Thetford. Knettishall Heath is an SSSI, a country park that comprises 350 acres of heathland, grassland and mixed woodland, which supports wild plants such as speedwell, agrimony and bird's foot trefoil. A public noticeboard describes short, circular walks around the park, and also indicates the beginning of the Peddars Way '. . . for the more serious walker'. Allow yourself a wry smile. The Peddars Way and Norfolk Coast National Trail is approximately 95 miles long; you have already walked over six times that distance.

Thetford may not look much as you cross the A11 and enter, but it is actually quite an interesting place. There are plenty of shops, a certain amount of accommodation, and a visit to the fascinating Ancient House Museum (which also houses the helpful tourist information centre) is recommended. Here you can learn of the 'Thetford Treasure', a great haul of Roman remains; the Norman-dated Thetford Priory; plus information on Thomas Paine, Thetford's famous son.

Now the Hereward Way follows the Little Ouse River through the heart of Breckland, and through woodland around Santon Downham. At Brandon there is B&B accommodation at the Ram, and another public house called the Flintknapper bears testimony to the area's famous raw material. Many of the local houses and shops are decorated in flint, and indeed it has been used as a building material since Roman times; but Brandon became especially important for the manufacture of gunflints. During the Napoleonic Wars over 200 Brandon craftsmen were employed in the quartering, flaking and knapping of the high quality local floorstone flint, and even today a small trade continues, principally for the flintlock guns used by historical societies in the USA.

After Lakenheath press on along the banks of the Little Ouse, and after some roadwalking via Prickwillow the 'Ship of the Fens' guides you into Ely. Indeed, the flatness of the Fens allows the Octagon of Ely Cathedral, built to replace the Norman tower which collapsed in 1322, to be visible for many miles, and is a useful beacon for anyone who lacks direction. Ely is an attractive and well-stocked town; yet once upon a time it was an island in the marshes, and a base for the Anglo-Saxon Hereward in his fight against the Norman invaders. In 1069 Hereward struck up an alliance with a Danish force, and it was while they were occupying Ely that Hereward rampaged about the countryside and laid waste Peterborough. A year later William the Conqueror bought off the Danes, and most of Hereward's forces surrendered at Ely. Further details from the information centre, which is situated in what I think used to be Oliver Cromwell's living room. Other bits of his house are also open for view.

From Ely to Little Downham you will be following not only the Hereward Way but also the Bishop's Way, a short path that traces the route used by the Bishops of Ely to their Palace in Downham. It is worth looking out for Bishop's Way signposts, for although the Hereward Way is now waymarked until Peterborough, 43 miles on, the trail's logo – a Tiger's Head, which represents the 'Fen Tigers' as the fenmen were known – can be easily missed. Just to really confuse you, the county council use a different waymark (two swords in the shape of an 'H', and what looks like a seagull in flight, which appears quite regularly until Peterborough).

Approaching Welney the flatness, bareness and expansiveness of the Fens become evident. The skies are simply enormous, but keep an eye on the ground as well. Although Dutch engineers drained this marshy land three hundred years ago, there is still much surface water in the form of channels and dykes, and this and the frequent floodwater plays host to an array of birds and wildfowl. You are likely to see swans, shelduck, snipe and redshank, plus many more besides. The Wildfowl Trust have a reserve with an information room and hides at Welney.

The walking is generally easy, although the fieldside paths can be muddy and sometimes overgrown, and some of the straight open roads that are crossed appear to attract fast vehicles. The Lamb and Flag in Welney offers food and accommodation, but there is everything on offer in March, 12 miles further on. From this modest centre, which rather surprisingly once boasted the largest railway marshalling yards in Europe, follow the banks of the River Nene (old course) west via the marina, and out across some huge and incredibly bare fields to Turves, where the Three Horseshoes serves very good food. At Whittlesey there are some amenities, but it is not a good place to look for a welcoming cup of tea at 4 p.m. on a wet Sunday in early spring.

In order to reach Peterborough cross the River Nene (new course) by the Dog in a Doublet public house and sluice. The remaining 6 miles are along the raised embankment of the Nene, which offers direct and uncomplicated grass and gravel walking. Unfortunately it is not particularly scenic. Just when you have decided that the brickyard chimneys are not as bad as the electricity pylons, Peterborough's new sewage works arrests the senses.

Peterborough was officially designated a New Town in 1967, but it has in fact been a site of Christian worship since AD 655. The cathedral is undeniably impressive. Hereward's mob ransacked and destroyed the old cathedral, but of more tangible interest today is the tomb of Catherine of Aragon. B&B accommodation can be found on Lincoln and Burghley streets.

The remainder of the Hereward Way to Oakham, just over 30 miles, offers pleasant if rather unspectacular walking. The flatness of the Fens is replaced by a more green and undulating feel; but you will have to wait another five days until the Wolds of Lincolnshire finally offer some elevation and extended views.

Follow the Nene Way along the banks of the river west from Peterborough for 7 miles (there are City of Peterborough Nene Way markings). The biggest hazard is likely to be mud, or tripping over dozing anglers, and for most of the time you will have the background din of the nearby A1 as accompaniment. There is refreshment at two attractively thatched pubs in Castor, and accommodation in Wansford (the Cross Keys). As you head gradually north-westwards there are pleasant patches of woodland, and it is worth pausing at Burghley House, home of the Cecil family since Elizabethan times, to admire both the impressive house and the deer park designed by Capability Brown.

Bordering Burghley Park is Stamford. There are no less than 500 listed buildings, mostly dating from the late Georgian period onwards, and after you have booked a bed at one of the many B&Bs a wander around the handsome streets is recommended. Leave the town by the River Welland, and once under the A1 make for Easton on the Hill and Ketton; then join the busy A606 for a few yards at Empingham, and all of a sudden Rutland Water appears. This large expanse of East Midlands drinking water was created in the 1970s, and while it may not be particularly beautiful its 2.5 × 4 miles attracts birds and humans in equal numbers. As you wander along the northern shore beware of speeding cyclists and ill-directed frisbees. There are two information centres plus cafés, and at Whitwell the Noel Arms offers accommodation. By turning north at the junction of the A606 near Barnsdale Hall you can switch immediately to the Viking Way and miss out the diversion of 3 miles to Oakham, but if you choose to stroll into the county town of old Rutland, now Leicestershire, for overnight lodgings or provisions there is a paved track away from the road's edge.

19

THE GENTLE HILLS

Oakham – Filey

OAKHAM – LINCOLN (57 miles)

As before, there is no dramatic transition from one trail to the next. You may be stepping out with Anglo-Saxons one moment, then Vikings another, but twentieth-century Leicestershire looks as low and mostly green as the last few miles. Ahead is the Viking Way long-distance footpath, 130 miles long, which takes in one of the finest cities and some of the quietest countryside in eastern England. The walking remains gentle and undemanding, but after Lincoln the Wolds offer some refreshingly elevated and airy miles. The trail was established by Lincolnshire County Council, in close consultation with the Ramblers' Association; and the waymark for the route is a distinctive Viking helmet, sometimes with a round shield.

From Rutland Water head north along quiet lanes to the picturesque village of Exton, where thatched ironstone buildings gather around a wide, tree-lined green. It is well worth pausing over, and the Fox and Hounds, a seventeenth-century coaching inn, is the perfect place to do just that.

There is accommodation a couple of miles on at the Black Horse in Greetham, but it is not a particularly exciting place. Nor is it quiet, for just beyond the path skirts the southern flanks of RAF Cottesmore, and if the jets are feeling frisky it can be absolutely deafening. Hurry on, along a lane that marks the Leics/Lincs boundary to Sewstern, and gradually the scenery ahead becomes more rolling and wooded as you approach Belvoir Castle (pronounced 'Beaver'). The route does not actually go past the castle itself, but there are fine views of its dramatic hilltop position among the trees from the village of Woolsthorpe.

At Brewer's Grave, near Woolsthorpe, the Viking Way meets the Jubilee Way. This was created by Leicestershire County Council to celebrate the Queen's Silver Jubilee, and runs for 15 miles south-west to Melton Mowbray. Brewer's Grave, incidentally, is where an unfortunate brewer ended his days, after drowning in a vat of his own beer.

Accommodation is not plentiful in these parts. There are occasional pubs and the odd farm which offer beds, but if you are in desperate need of a roof over your head then walk into Grantham, just a couple of miles to the east. Otherwise stick to the trusty tent. A few official campsites do exist, but a polite word with the local farmer usually yields a quiet spot in the corner of a field.

The 13-mile stretch north of the A52 crossing to just outside Ancaster is messy, with many twists and turns from field to lane to field again, and if the routefinding becomes tiresome then perhaps stick to the more direct lanes from Marston to Caythorpe or Brant Broughton, and then north towards Lincoln. However, if you persevere to the B6403 you will then be on Ermine Street, the old Roman Road. A mile to the south is Ancaster, which came into existence as a camp for the Roman legions using the busy highway. Today it is a quiet and unremarkable place, but there are a couple of shops and the Ermine Way public house.

The Viking Way now follows Ermine Street northwards for nearly 10 miles, and it is a typically direct and no-nonsense Roman route. For a while you have to share company with the road, but there is a clear and safe path well off the tarmac, then after the A17 junction it is an open unsurfaced track across the fields, and if it is not too muddy you should be able to make quick miles.

On leaving Ermine Street follow paths through a succession of small villages perched on a ridge known as Lincoln Cliff. It is not particularly high, but this is the first sense of genuine elevation for some time, and there are wide views over Newark-on-Trent and Nottinghamshire. Soon the southern edge of Lincoln approaches. This fine cathedral city has plenty of places to stay, including a youth hostel as you enter from the south, and also several fine food outlets. Highly recommended comes Brown's Pie Shop on Steep Hill, followed closely by the Wig and Mitre a few doors down. Both of these establishments are in the old quarter, or

'Uphill', near the castle and cathedral. It may be a stiff climb up the cobbled streets, especially after a long day's walking, but Lincoln Cathedral alone repays the effort. This is one of the finest medieval buildings in Europe, and if you slip quietly in for Evensong you will emerge a different person.

LINCOLN – HUMBER BRIDGE (73 miles)

Keeping strictly to the Viking Way it is about 43 miles from Lincoln to Tealby, near Market Rasen, on the edge of the Wolds. However, the distance is considerably shorter if you omit the large loop that the Way takes to the south east, via Bardney, Woodhall Spa and Horncastle. It is quite realistic to cut out this section by following lanes and footpaths across fields to the north-east of Lincoln, and rejoining the Way around Tealby. However, by doing this you will miss out a significant chunk of the Lincolnshire Wolds, a highly delectable walking area which I would urge you not to skimp on but to enjoy as much as possible.

To reach the hills by the official route follow the south bank of the River Witham east from Lincoln to Bardney. This stretch puts you in mind of Peterborough and the Nene – straight, man-made river banks, with flat surrounds and a cathedral dominating the skyline, except that here you are leaving and not entering the city. There is an alternative route between Lincoln and Bardney, via Barlings Abbey, that has been plotted by the local Ramblers' Association group. Details from the tourist information centre in Castle Square, Lincoln.

Woodhall Spa was once a resort for the wealthy seeking remedies for their ailments. Nowadays there are guest houses where footsore walkers can find relief. Continue via woodland and a canal bank to Horncastle, a small but bustling market town that dates back to Roman times. Beds and shops are in good supply, and from this 'gateway to the Wolds' (as Horncastle is sometimes called) the Way climbs up to the village of Fulletby. There is now a growing sense of space and altitude, although overall height remains quite modest, and gradually the scenery becomes more open and wilder. Paths and tracks lead to Scamblesby, a quiet village with some B&B accommodation; and Woody's Top Youth Hostel is 3 miles to the east.

The 11 miles from Scamblesby to Ludford see a change from the Wold scarp to the valley of the River Bain, through rich and intensive farmland. The route is via Biscathorpe to Ludford, where the White Hart offers accommodation, then once over a small hill, descend to Tealby. The impressive Tennyson d'Eyncourt Memorial Hall is a reminder of this area's association with Alfred Lord Tennyson's family, and there are a number of other handsome buildings in this well laid-out and serene village. For practical purposes, the King's Head and the praiseworthy Tealby tea rooms ('Viking Way walkers welcome') should be located.

The Lincolnshire Wolds remain a quiet and largely undiscovered area. There is nothing like the seasonal tourist assault that villages in the Peak District or on the Cornish coast suffer, so as a result local accommodation is not particularly prolific. Beds can usually be found in the small towns, such as Horncastle or Market Rasen, but there are not that many of them and booking ahead may be advisable at weekends and at other peak times. Outside these centres you will have to plan carefully. But camping is a good option in the Wolds, since there are a number of small, private campsites, with several run by the Camping and Caravanning Club (one such is off the Walesby–Market Rasen road, among the massed ranks of Forestry Commission conifers). There are fewer tea shops, as well, which means that you might have to look to villages and farms off the route, and make sure that the flask is well-filled. If you are sticking faithfully to the Viking Way, then from Tealby you may have to wait 9 miles until Caistor before you can find public refreshment.

The up-and-over path from Tealby to Walesby traverses ploughed fields and woodland. Like much of this high Wolds country, it is intensively agricultural, which means that in bad weather it can be muddy and heavy going. On the way down to Walesby the path skips through the churchyard of the Parish Church of All Saints, or 'The Ramblers' Church'. Since 1932 the Grimsby and District Wayfarers' Association have made annual pilgrimages to this beautifully sited church, and in 1950 the East Window of the Lady Chapel was dedicated in their memory. The stained glass window includes two ramblers walking in the countryside, with below it: 'And it came to pass that He went through the cornfields on the Sabbath Day' (Mark 2:23).

Spiritually refreshed, wander down the lane into the quiet village, and prepare yourself for a steep hike back up grassy banks to Normanby le Wold. Despite its evocative name, only the church and nearby farm buildings have any character. Then to reach Caistor descend by Nettleton Beck along an open, empty grass valley. Halfway down you have to pass through a curious foot tunnel under an embankment among the trees, testimony to the former iron ore mine. There is little left of the mine, and instead walk in peace and quite probably solitude down to the village of Nettleton. Caistor is across the flat fields, and this small settlement of Roman origin retains a pleasant market square that simply begs you to sit on one of the two benches and relax with a tea or ice cream. If you want to stay longer there are a couple of B&Bs, plus a small supermarket and food-serving pubs.

From Caistor, the Way ambles northwards across ploughed fields, along deserted lanes and through scattered woodland and peaceful hamlets nestling under the edge of the escarpment. The occasional pheasant and hare gives way near Clixby to the grunts and squeals from a large pig farm. The succession of villages with the suffix 'by' – Clixby, Grasby, Searby, Bigby – are an indication of their Danish ancestry; all grew up on an important spring line at the foot of the slope.

Barnetby le Wold is a sprawling and unattractive village, after which there is an uneventful 12-mile plod to the Humber Bridge, and the end of the Viking Way. The crossing of the M180 may be the most arresting moment for some time, until the succession of fieldside paths and quiet lanes bring you out by the river at South Ferriby. Make your way down to the riverside, appreciating the views across this wide and commanding river. There is a firm and level track which is also favoured by cyclists along the shore by Barton Clay Pits Country Park, and the route officially finishes just under the bridge on the riverfront. The riverside walking is a pleasant change; and the Humber Bridge – the longest single-span suspension bridge in the world – is a curious phenomenon, particularly when viewed from below. If you do not want to enter the rather sleepy town of Barton-upon-Humber, then join the safe foot/cycle path on the west side of the bridge (from the minor road below).

HUMBER BRIDGE – FILEY (79 miles)

The Wolds Way actually begins opposite the Ferryboat Inn, by Hessle Haven, just downstream of the Humber Bridge. But unless you are something of a national trail purist, or you want to see the bridge from every perspective, take the track along the estuary shore by the railway upstream past the Humber Bridge Country Park to North Ferriby. The muddy Humber is not always one of the most celebrated of our rivers, which is a shame. It once separated two kingdoms, Mercia and Northumbria, and today drains one fifth of England. Technically it isn't a river at all, rather a confluence of the River Trent and the Yorkshire Ouse.

The idea of a long-distance footpath across the Wolds north of the Humber was one that local ramblers promulgated as early as the 1930s, but it took several decades of lobbying and protracted negotiation until the plans of the East Riding area of the Ramblers' Association finally met with official approval. Many new rights of way and access agreements had to be made before the 79-mile trail could be officially opened. However, the hard work has paid off, since the resulting long-distance footpath is an enjoyable introduction for all those to whom the Yorkshire Wolds remain an undiscovered quantity. And they would seem to be numerous. This crescent-shaped range of soft chalk hills are still largely unfrequented, and when others are rushing to the Dales and the Moors, the Wolds walker will likely have sheep, skylarks and shepherd's purse as virtually sole companions.

At North Ferriby the foreshore path is usually flooded by high tides every few weeks, so there is an alternative route inland past the car park. Otherwise, turn your back on the Humber and follow the path through Long Plantation, crossing first the railway and then the main road. The ground rises gently, and once past the edge of a large quarry arrive at the picturesque village of Welton, famous for being the place where the highwayman Dick Turpin was arrested. He was actually apprehended after he had had one too many at the Green Dragon, when he decided to wander outside into the street and take a pot shot at the local poultry. The pub has details recording the event.

Head north up Welton Dale, an attractive and partly wooded valley, then emerge into open fields near Wouldby Dam, and down to Brantingham. There are wide views over Humberside and Yorkshire, for although the Wolds are not desperately high nor craggy, like their Lincolnshire cousins they offer splendid views over the flatter countryside around.

Leave Brantigham Dale amid conifers for a winding track around the hillside between farms. There is food and accommodation at the

Fox and Coney, South Cave; otherwise continue up to Little Wold Plantation, then along to Comber Dale. Here is a short stretch of the former Hull–Barnsley Railway to puff along. Constructed in 1885, the line needed nearly 5,000 people to help dig and tunnel a route through the hills.

The High Hunsley Circuit that you may see identified on Ordnance Survey maps is a 24-mile challenge walk around the southern Wolds, circular from Walkington. However, there is no need to rush the Wolds Way, so make your measured way up East Dale, another thickly wooded dale. Once out, the plantations and thickets are replaced by dry, grassy valleys. This typical chalk landscape allows water to drain easily, and so walkers rarely experience the lasting mud of other long-distance paths, such as the peat bogs of the southern Pennine Way. Indeed, there is only one river, the Gypsey Race, that properly rises in the Wolds (it flows east to Bridlington), and there are so many dry valleys that campers will have to think carefully about the provision of water. Farmers have learnt over the years to tap natural springs and build dew ponds.

Although the Wolds Way shies away from entering civilisation again, Newbald is only a mile distant and is worth visiting, if only to say that you have had a drink at the Gnu Inn. There is a long plod back up the road, and unless you want to continue to Flower Hill, and the Northern Shire Horse Centre, join an unswerving track over the 144m 'summit' to Care Gate. The way ahead is obvious, via Hessleskew to Arras. This area was once settled by the Parisii, a late-Iron Age warrior tribe from northern France, who then gave their name to the capital. A chariot burial and other relics have been found near here.

The Way continues over fields to a road junction by the former Beverley–Market Weighton railway line (now the Hudson Way walking route), then into Goodmanham. This was once an important centre of Woden worship, and the destruction of its Pagan temple in the seventh century signalled the advent of Christianity in the north of England. Things have quietened down a bit now, and if you are looking for more than just pub refreshment then consider bypassing Goodmanham and walk into Market Weighton. All the necessary places that you wish were unnecessary on a long walk, such as banks, a small supermarket, chemists, etc, can be found here. But it is not so big that you can get lost, and it was also the home of one William Bradley, born 1787, who literally rose to local fame as 'the Yorkshire Giant', measuring 2.36 m (7ft 9in) and weighing 172kg (27 stone). The official National Trail Guide gives an alternative route out of Market Weighton to rejoin the original Way near Londesborough.

From Goodmanham follow signposts up the hillside towards a roadside picnic site, usually busy with Bridlington-bound trippers, and into the parkland of Londesborough Hall. The Way follows a footpath past Partridge Hall down into Nunburnholme. Its rector from 1854 to 1893 was Reverend Francis Morris, Victorian conservationist and avid ornithologist. No doubt you will be treading in his soft footsteps as you leave the village under the dense green canopy of Bratt Wood. Out of the cover there are open fields and a couple of farms ahead, then a sharp turn right by Warrendale Plantation, and along the high hilltop above the village of Millington. York Minster is visible from this lofty perch on a clear day, although the enormous power stations arrest the senses rather more. If you fancy dropping down to Millington, the Gate Inn provides a warm welcome. The name refers to the nearby Millington Pastures, and to the number of gates (and therefore land) awarded to each farmer after Enclosure (one gate represented pasture for six sheep). It is also the much more recent site of mass protests by walkers when the intensive ploughing of grazing land threatened traditional rights of way.

Into and out of Nettle Dale; the gradient may be steepish but the soft and rounded hills are not difficult to tackle. Most of the ploughed land of the Wolds is devoted to cereal crops, but bright yellow fields of oilseed rape are also common. Aside from arable farming, sheep-rearing continues as it has done for centuries, when huge sheepwalks dominated the high Wolds. The Way finally emerges along the road from Huggate, where the Wolds Inn provides good food and accommodation. Otherwise cut across the fields and skirt the village for the bridleway into Holm Dale, and to Fridaythorpe.

Fridaythorpe is roughly the halfway point of the Wolds Way, and is the highest village on the Wolds. It was also where the trail was officially opened on 2nd October 1982. The plaque commemorating the event is near the Manor House Inn, in the village, from where the trail heads down the escarpment to Gill's Farm. After crossing a small road enter Thixen Dale, yet another peaceful and enjoyable valley to work your way through. It is also enjoyed by the North Wolds Walk, a 20-mile recreational route through the heart of the hills. Join the metalled lane into Thixendale, a small and isolated community, but with a pub and a conveniently placed youth hostel.

Leave the village by a wide track up the hillside, then after some ups and downs swing abruptly right, towards Wharram Percy. If you do not wish to visit the deserted medieval village then keep to the clear course of the bridleway over and around the hill. However, Wharram Percy is worth the detour. The village was deserted around 1500, and is one of possibly 130 in the region that ceased to exist once the landowner, sometimes local monasteries, switched from arable to sheep farming, a reason to evict all the families. And of course the Black Death also played its grisly part in the preceding century and a half, carrying off as many as one third of the East Riding population.

It is around here that the familiar national trail acorn sign is joined periodically by 'CW' waymarks, denoting the 83-mile Centenary Way from York to Filey. Beyond Wharram le Street the Way continues over open hillside. Duggleby, along the road to the east, has a few amenities, but for the most part this is quiet and lonely countryside, and better walking for all that.

Now the route swings slowly around towards the North Sea, and new views are revealed. Above Settrington Wood, on the rising slopes of Beacon Wold, Malton and the Howardian Hills appear fairly close at hand. After dropping steeply through a plantation there are tremendous views over the Vale of Pickering, and to the soft and inviting skyline of the North York Moors. This is your destination in a few days' time. However, to get to it you must first reach Filey (still 24 miles away), then stride the cliffs and bays to Whitby (a further 30). Of course, there is nothing stopping you forsaking these miles and dashing across to Pickering or Thornton Dale, but the Yorkshire Heritage Coast is reason enough to delay the high moors for a few more days.

From Wintringham climb steeply up the wooded slopes of Deep Dale to a short earthwork on an open hilltop, then veer east above further plantations and stride confidently along the top of the escarpment until the path drops down to Sherburn. It then skirts Ganton, and rises to join a road to RAF Staxton, a radar defence station, but then turns off right over Staxton Wold. Follow field boundaries along the upper slopes of a series of valleys (Lang Dale, Camp Dale and Stocking Dale). These are the final miles of real Wolds before the approach to the sea, the sight of which should now be adding an extra bounce to your step.

Drop down the slope into the houses of Muston, then turn off the road at the signpost before the pub, and after crossing the A165 and a long field enter the back streets of Filey.

20

ALONG THE TRACKS

Filey – Heddon

FILEY – WHITBY (32 miles)

The Wolds Way formally finishes on the cliffs north of the town, by Filey Brigg, but ignore the official route which climbs up a scruffy dirt track behind the lifeboat station. Far better to buy an ice cream and saunter along to the slipway to admire the small 'coble' fishing boats. These craft are unique to the north-east coast, a throwback to the Viking longships. They are flat-bottomed for beach-launching, with high bows and strong clinker planking that is designed to withstand the rough weather of the North Sea. Regain the cliffs by a track past the sailing clubhouse, and almost imperceptibly the Wolds Way gives way to the Cleveland Way. To celebrate both this change in trails, and of course the return to the sea, stop awhile on the grassy clifftop of Filey Brigg, a distinctive finger of dark boulder clay with treacherous gritstone steps below. There are fine views of Filey's unblemished sands, which stretch for miles around the bay towards the chalk cliffs of Flamborough Head.

Notices warning of 'dangerous cliffs' abound. Head for the one (in serious red lettering) indicating Gristhorpe Cliff and follow the obvious path northwards. What a joy to be walking along the coast once more! The North Sea stretches endlessly in a haze of blueness; and the refreshing, salty breeze gives a welcome kick.

After only a few minutes there is a distant glimpse of Scarborough, although it will take a few hours to reach. The path is uncomplicated, sticking within yards of the cliff edge, and apart from being rather overgrown in places you need not worry about routefinding. Linnets and yellowhammers flit among the fields on one side, while herring gulls sit nonchalantly on rocky shelves and fulmars wheel and ride the air currents on the other. In the sea far below, black-flagged buoys mark the position of crab and lobster pots.

It is necessary to skirt a sizeable chunk of caravan park (the rubbish-strewn lawn says it all), then the path curves around to the sands of Cayton Bay. A small cafe serves drinks and snacks by the beach, but Scarborough is only 3 easy miles away. These are through tangly scrub and woodland, where criss-crossing paths may confuse, then around the edge of jumbly landslips until bungalows and redbricks appear. Immediately after South Cliff golf course take the upper path on top of the rough slope. This is because there is a hazard ahead, and the official route has been blocked. The hazard is (was) a hotel, the Holbeck Hall, some of which disappeared over the edge of a cliff one night in Summer 1993. The area was immediately cordoned-off, and at the time of writing the whole section of cliff is undergoing urgent counter-erosion treatment in order to prevent the rest of the street slipping into the sea. Cleveland Way walkers are currently being diverted via back streets around the obstacle, but it is expected that the original course of the Way will be restored at some date in the future. The hotel has since been demolished.

The best route through Scarborough is along the seafront. On a hot July afternoon this is a busy, sometimes rowdy thoroughfare, but it is short-lived and you can kid yourself you are observing living history. For with the discovery of medicinal spa waters in the 1600s, and the coming of the railway a couple of centuries later, Scarborough developed into one of the first proper seaside resorts.

Follow the promenade along North Sands beyond the remains of the Norman castle. A fruit stand bears the legend 'Eat healthy, keep healthy', which seems rather out of place among all the chips and candyfloss. Behind the white-domed Sea Life complex there is a footbridge across a stream, then a flight of sturdy steps up on to the cliff once more. The youth hostel, near Scalby Mills, is a mile inland from here.

If you do not wish to continue with the coast any further, and instead want to see as much as possible of the North York Moors, then take what is called the 'Link through the Tabular Hills'. This newly opened 48-mile route runs from Scarborough along the limestone escarpment of the Tabular Hills, renowned for its wild flowers, through wooded valleys, farmland and conifer plantations to Helmsley. Here you can either plot your own course through the heart of the moors, and there are plenty of splendid tracks and pathways, or join the beginning of the Cleveland Way, past Rievaulx Abbey and over the dramatic Sutton Bank and Hambleton Hills. Rejoin the original End to End East Route at Scugdale, or leave the Cleveland Way at Osmotherley or Ingleby Arncliffe for a route westwards to the Pennines.

From the northern edge of Scarborough, Robin Hood's Bay is about 13½ miles away. Most of this distance is along the cliff edge, and sometimes literally so. The cliffs are steep and fairly high, and it is worth staying alert and watching your footing. On blustery days keep a respectable distance from the edge. At Hayburn Wyke there is a small nature reserve, and several unwaymarked tracks that can lead the unwary through the oak woods inland.

Continue along the double-tiered cliffs, through thickets of blackthorn, to Ravenscar. The place is named, it is said, after a flag bearing a raven's image was hoisted by marauding Danes who landed here in the third century. There is a small amount of accommodation and a tea room, plus a National Trust visitor centre. You may also encounter the odd walker from Osmotherley completing the 40-mile Lyke Wake Walk, which is a challenge walk that is meant to be completed within 24 hours. Now the enticing prospect of Robin Hood's Bay opens up. After a short detour inland the path races back to the cliff edge and passes Boggle Hole, once a corn mill and now an attractive youth hostel tucked away in a wooded ravine.

At low tide the wide reach of Robin Hood's Bay is noticeable for the grooved rock scars that stretch out into the sea. The best view is from the north, above the cluster of red-tiled roofs at the top of a desperately steep lane, which is your route outwards. However, from a position on a bench by the slipway you can watch a steady stream of walkers stride down the main street and straight into the North Sea. They are not mad – well, perhaps that is debatable – rather they have just completed Wainwright's 190-mile Coast to Coast Walk. It is curious to see them limping wearily around the corner, then taking on a look of delight mixed with sheer relief as they spot the slipway and dash forwards for the ceremonial boot-dipping in the sea (the walk begins by dipping your boots in the Irish Sea at St Bees). But how will you answer when, after all their celebrations and self-congratulations have died down, they spot your boots and pack and wander over to casually utter the immortal words: 'So, have you come far too?'

There is a short and attractive stretch of airy cliffwalking north to Whitby. The Coast to Coast Walk shares a mile or so of this route, until leaving the cliffs at Maw Wyke Hole. Before long the haunting skeleton of Whitby Abbey comes into view. The Abbess Hilda founded a religious community here in the seventh century, and also organised the famous Synod of Whitby. Near both the abbey and youth hostel, at the top of 199 winding steps up to St Mary's Church, there is a magnificent view over Whitby harbour. This must be one of the most scenic ports in the country. Shops and houses crowd the steep slopes about the water in a pleasantly unregimented fashion, and from the abbey to the docks to the jewellery shops selling crafted Whitby jet, there is plenty to see. Unshoulder the pack and relax for a few hours.

WHITBY – BISHOP AUCKLAND (89 miles)

The direction of the East Route beyond the North York Moors presents a huge dilemma to the walker used to long, waymarked trails through unspoilt and ever-changing rural landscapes. There are virtually no long-distance footpaths that give a satisfactory south–north progression; and there are several massive centres of industry and people to negotiate. The actual coastline north of Saltburn encompasses the latter, and yet to deviate too far west means treading on the toes of the Central Route as it weaves its way up the Pennines.

The route that I have suggested is just one of many possible variations. I was keen first to include a large slice of the North York Moors, providing a change from the coastline, and a chance to sample a delightful new valley trail that begs to be extended over the wild moorland. This move away from the North Sea allows industrial Teesside and residential Middlesbrough to be kept at a safe distance. The quiet and mostly agricultural Cleveland Plain offers local paths of varying quality, and encounters with some unexpectedly nice villages. At Bishop Auckland there is a choice of routes: the Weardale Way leads either to the city of Durham or the heart of rural Weardale; otherwise a former railway line (now the Brandon–Bishop Auckland Walk and the Lanchester Valley Walk) extends to Consett, where another converted railway provides an excellent conduit to the outskirts of Newcastle.

But you may not want to get anywhere near Newcastle. In fact you may want to approach north-east England entirely differently, for north of Whitby the Cleveland Way extends along the coast for another 20 miles to Saltburn, and includes the highest cliffs on the entire eastern seaboard. Alternatively, you may like to consider following the waymarked, 40-mile Cook Country Walk (named after the famous captain and explorer who came from the area), which takes a dogleg route from Staithes, on the coast near Whitby, through Guisborough to Great Ayton, then up to Marton, near Middlesbrough (Cook's birthplace). An interesting, historical option, and a quick dash through Middlesbrough reveals more coastal walking north of Hartlepool to Seaham and Sunderland. But are you happy wandering through South Shields and Jarrow? If you are, then Whitley Bay and the enticing Northumberland coast are in fact very near; if not, a massive detour around the whole of Tyneside is necessary.

Of course, after savouring the high moors of North Yorkshire you may want to retain the wild, upland spirit and shun thoughts of even approaching the likes of Middlesbrough, Darlington, Newcastle, etc. In that case the obvious direction is west to the Pennines. The Coast to Coast Walk follows a direct course across the northern part of the Vale of York, from Ingleby Cross via Catterick to Richmond, but I suggest that you devise your own route to the Pennine foothills. Unless you want to join the Pennine Way, consider making your way north-west to Barnard Castle, from where there is an excellent route up the Tees valley to Eggleston, then back north-eastwards once more on remote tracks through Hamsterley Forest to Wolsingham and Tow Law, and north to Derwent Reservoir and Hexham – but the options are endless! Spread the Ordnance Survey maps out on the floor and give the matter some serious thought.

Returning to the original East Route, and to Whitby, the next 25 miles follow the quiet River Esk into the heart of the North York Moors. The Esk Valley Walk is a new regional route, and its opening in 1992 was one of many events that were organised to celebrate the fortieth anniversary of the North York Moors National Park. The waymark to look out for is a leaping salmon, although it is unlikely that you will see too many of these since the route rarely follows the actual river bank, preferring instead a mix of fields, woodland and open moor.

The Walk leaves Whitby by the river's northern bank, crosses railway tracks, and before long is clear of the houses and winding through farmland to the village of Ruswarp. Here there are rowing boats by the weir, and a welcome café. After a stretch of road the route enters trees along the drive of Woodlands Nursing Home. Over the bridge is Sleights, which sports a number of B&Bs, plus Radford's the Butchers ('Meat and Mouton, Pies and Puddings . . . Bread and Banter with a Smile').

The bridleway wends its way through patchy woodland and quiet fields up the valley to Grosmont. Although the Walk does not enter the village, a diversion is called for, since here is a chance to see the North Yorkshire Moors Railway puffing enthusiastically backwards and forwards. It runs from Grosmont to Pickering, and when it opened in 1836 as the Whitby and Pickering Railway it was one of the world's first passenger lines. It is now one of the country's most scenic steam railways, and at the carefully preserved station at Grosmont there is a particularly useful platform café.

For the next 6 miles or so the Esk Valley Walk shares the company of the Coast to Coast Walk; and although there are even a few signposts indicating 'C to C, EVW' there are plenty of strategically placed leaping salmon to guide you along the valley. Follow one of these along a farm track west of Grosmont for a mile to Egton Bridge, emerging on the Egton Estate toll road (but nevertheless a right of way). The route now switches banks by means of some large stepping stones. Should these be submerged use the road bridge. A few minutes of road-walking will allow you to admire the gentle, lush valley, which after Glaisdale becomes more open and rugged. To reach this follow a path through Arncliffe Woods, where stone trods help avoid the worst of the mud in wet weather.

Glaisdale, a former ironstone mining village, offers refreshment and accommodation in the form of the Arncliffe Arms and the Anglers Rest. Bear in mind that they are frequented by the Coast to Coast mob, plus other walkers, so demand in high season may be considerable. However, the steepish road into the village may be ignored by through walkers, since the route sticks to the valley bottom as it crosses fields and hops stiles to reach Lealholm. After the Board Inn (B&B), the route ascends by an unmade road across

An attractive alternative to the South-West Coast Path is to cross Dartmoor: enjoy the open moorland south of Princeton (*above*) and scenic villages such as Widecombe in the Moor (*below*).

Those not using ferries face a long detour inland around Salcombe Harbour (*above*). Start Point (*below left*), near Kingsbridge; and the plunging cliffs at Beer (*below right*).

The Wessex Ridgeway passes Old Wardour Castle (*above*), before joining the rolling chalk tracks of the Ridgeway National Trail (*below*).

Ely Cathedral is just visible (*above*) as the Hereward Way heads into the Fens. The East Route then visits both Stamford (*below left*) and the charming village of Exton (*below right*).

The distinctive waymark of the Viking Way (*above*) leads to the Lincolnshire Wolds, where the Ramblers' Church, near Walesby (*below*), commands an imposing position.

Filey (*above*) is where the Cleveland Way takes over from the Wolds Way, and the North Sea shore is finally reached; while at Robin Hood's Bay (*below*) the Cleveland Way and Coast to Coast Walk share company for a while.

The harbour and the abbey on its hill make Whitby a lively and interesting stopover (*above*). Swainby (*below*) nestles at the foot of the North York Moors and heralds a much gentler section of the route.

Dunstanburgh Castle (*above*) is one of several fortifications along the low and windswept Northumberland coast. Across the border into Scotland, however, the cliffs rise once more, as at Coldingham Bay, near Eyemouth (*below*).

Lealholm Moor to Beacon Hill. There are impressive views up and down the Esk, with the remains of Danby Castle evident on the far hillside.

Descend the valley slopes to the National Park Moors Centre, just outside Danby. It has a café, exhibition centre, and everything else you would expect to find at such a place. After Danby, follow a bridleway along bracken-coated valley slopes, then underneath the railway to Castleton, where you should stock up before crossing the moors.

The Esk Valley Walk finishes (or begins, according to the official guidebook) with a loop southwards along Danby Dale and back via Westerdale Moor. The purpose of this twist is to follow the Esk to near its source at the delightfully named Esklets. Either arm can be taken, although the latter will actually take you up to the final gurgles of the river, where the scattered farmsteads and bleak, encroaching hills really convey the wildness of the Moors. At Esklets, on Farndale Moor, join once more with the Coast to Coast Walk along a high and winding former mining railway track to Bloworth Crossing, where another old friend, the Cleveland Way, is met.

An alternative route is to leave Westerdale village by an unfenced road north-west across Westerdale Moor. (Westerdale Youth Hostel, marked on most maps, has been closed.) Take a signposted bridleway, called Skinner Howe Cross Road, over featureless and exposed hillside to Baysdale Abbey, where a track leaves the site of the former Cistercian nunnery up a steep grassy hillside and through some patchy woodland on to Ingleby Moor (all public rights of way). The Cleveland Way can be reached by a track called Middle Head Top, from where the junction with the Coast to Coast at Bloworth Crossing is only 2 miles away. However, bear in mind two points: this is isolated and exposed moorland, and should the cloud be down navigation by map and compass will be advisable. Also, should you be walking after 12th August it is possible that the surrounding grouse butts might harbour elderly men with guns and labradors. And hundreds of dead birds. Be prepared to make detours.

It is roughly ten miles from Bloworth Crossing to Scugdale, where the Moors are left for Swainby and the Cleveland Plain. By and large these are enjoyable and uncomplicated miles, soaring up and down over the sharp northern faces of the moorland hills. The path is broad and direct, although sometimes very rough, and in places (since this is a veritable walkers' highway on some days) erosion is creeping in. Try not to exacerbate it by making new paths. If the weather is inclement you can always drop down to the flat agricultural land below and take lanes and local paths instead.

However, this is also a strenuous section. Round Hill, on Urra Moor, is the highest point on the North York Moors (454m). And although the Wain Stones (a jumble of bare rock outcrops) are lower, and the airy situation is wonderful and the views extensive, crossing them can be arduous. The steep and repetitive ups and downs – Hasty Bank, Cringle Moor, Carlton Moor – are a reminder of the taxing cliffs of the South-West Coast Path.

Unless you are continuing to Osmotherley, descend to Scugdale Beck and leave both the Cleveland Way and Coast to Coast Walk for either a muddy track (surfaced after a mile) by Huthwaite Green to Whorlton, or a quiet lane into Swainby. This picturesque village sits astride a neat brook, and at the northern end the Black Horse serves all-round refreshment. Once over the A172 take the signposted footpath through Goulton Grange to Hutton Rudby. The pleasant village centre is to the right, but in order to leave locate the road to Crathorne. Off this is Hunsdale Road, a remarkably dull string of new houses, and at the end there is an alleyway between bungalows which leads to a concrete footbridge and into fields. This path tracks the course of the River Leven, and it is supremely frustrating that you cannot legally get any nearer to its lovely wooded banks. Amid what is generally a flat and featureless plain, the river Leven has carved quite a deep and winding course. Crathorne Hall, sitting imposingly among dense broadleaved woods downstream, can be glimpsed as you wander into the village.

From Crathorne take Back Lane over the A19 and past large strawberry and raspberry fields. Looking south, the moors are still visible, but their undulating outline will gradually recede. There is a footpath through Gowsers Plantation, then across railway tracks and pasture to Picton. Where the wide, open cereal fields are under crop the paths can sometimes be overgrown, but I did not find them impassable. They lead, most usefully, to a gap in the hedge opposite the Ship public house (all-day food) at Worsall, from where there are tracks around the meandering River Tees to Rose Hill Farm. Here a wonderful, straight tree-lined avenue begins, complemented by daffodils planted by the local WI. It swings around to cross the languid, leafy River Tees, and after many, many miles of North Yorkshire you finally enter County Durham.

If you care for a short, scenic diversion, and a spot of high tea then turn right, near Dinsdale Manor, and follow the wooded path by the banks of the Tees around to Middleton One Row. It is a quiet and relaxing passage, and odd to think that this fine river – which rises high in the North Pennines – will in only a few miles spew out into the North Sea amid oil refineries and petro-chemical works.

Middleton One Row could be seen from the avenue on the opposite bank of the Tees a few miles back. The smart parade of buildings stand prominently above the river, with an attractive grassy bank falling away into undergrowth. The path you have been following emerges on the Row almost opposite the Davenport Hotel, which has plenty of tables outside from where you can admire the view over a pot of tea.

For the next few miles you will be heading west up the Tees, close to Darlington, and although there is no continuous riverside path there are some very pleasant stretches that are in the process of being linked together to form the Teesdale Way. Take the lane to Neasham and along to Hurworth-on-Tees. This crosses the river into Croft-on-Tees, from where there is a track south of the river via Monk End Wood to Stapleton. The rectory of St Peter's Church at Croft-on-Tees was the home of Lewis Carroll for twenty-five years, and he drew many of his stories from local scenery and legends. In fact the church contains many carvings that those familiar with *Alice in Wonderland* will recognise.

If you want to wander along by lane and path to Piercebridge (a very pleasant journey) then at Stapleton continue for a further tarmac mile to Cleasby, where a track leads down to the river near the A1 bridge. Here there is a fairly direct route via Holme House south of the river. If you want to walk the actual banks of the Tees for any length then you must cross Blackwell Bridge, popular with motor vehicles, and turn immediately left on to a path to Low Coniscliffe. If you fancy a rather different diversion, then the Tees Pumping Station, on Conniscliffe Road and the site of the former Darlington waterworks, shows 'the history of municipal water supply, from steam through gas to electric engines'.

There is now an excellent river bank walk of 4 miles to High Coniscliffe, a stretch also popular with local anglers, including game fishermen. High Coniscliffe has a thirteenth-century church dedicated to St Edwin, once King of Northumbria, and in fact the only church in the country so dedicated. A few minutes away is Piercebridge, which has well-preserved remains of the Romans' bridge over the Tees, and also a fort which served as barracks for soldiers travelling north to Hadrian's Wall along Dere Street. Your destination is Bishop Auckland, almost due north along Dere Street, but unfortunately the Roman road is now a modern 'B'-road, so I suggest you consider using paths and lanes north from High Coniscliffe to Walworth Gate and Houghton-le-Side, and enter Bishop Auckland from the south. Alternatively, strike out north-west from Piercebridge and link together villages such as Headlam and Ingleton through what is generally low and quiet countryside. The high cliffs and wild moors seem a long way back now.

BISHOP AUCKLAND – HEDDON (32/42 miles)

Many walkers considering the merits of the East Route will probably dismiss Cleveland and County Durham: no dramatic physical features, save industry (or the remains of it) and pockets of ugly urbanisation. But how wrong you are! Since the North York Moors ended your route has been quiet and overwhelmingly rural, and the next 25 miles or so from Bishop Auckland to the Tyne take on an altogether new dimension: railway paths.

Just as the West Route utilises the canals of Cheshire and Lancashire, once busy with industrial traffic, the network of former railway lines that criss-crossed central and northern County Durham in support of the old coal and iron and steel industries now form wonderful walkways and cycle routes. Cars and motor bikes are prohibited, and the hard, usually gravel-base tracks are easy to follow, so that you can relax and enjoy a quiet and continuous green passage to within a few miles of Newcastle city centre.

There are two ways of reaching Consett, both involving railway paths but both very different in style. One keeps to the low ground and allows a visit to the city of Durham on the way, while the other uses a small section of the Weardale Way as far as Stanhope, and then takes the Waskerley Way over the moors to Consett. Both are fine routes, but the latter is longer and will satisfy those pining for the tougher, wilder landscape of the North Pennines Area of Outstanding Natural Beauty.

Auckland Castle, in Bishop Auckland, is the former residence of the Bishops of Durham. The 'Prince Bishops' ruled the County Palatine from Norman times as virtually a separate state. They were allowed to mint their own money, levy their own taxes, even raise their own army. The city of Durham was their seat of rule, and Weardale their hunting ground – so both routes ahead will take you through their domain (which also included land in modern Northumberland and North Yorkshire).

The first of the two routes to Consett begins with the 9½-mile Brandon–Bishop Auckland Walk, which leaves Bishop Auckland in spectacular fashion by means of Newton Gap Viaduct, high above the River Wear. (Look for the sign for the A689 to Crook, and turn right at the Newton Gap public house – its sign depicts a weary rambler struggling up from the valley below.) Once over the viaduct, a breathtaking start to any walk, the track dives into quiet farmland and some wooded ravines and curves around to pass among the houses of Willington. The route runs parallel to the main road, but numerous cuttings give a pleasant detachment, with the former railway banks attracting many butterflies and insects. Dipping down to the Deerness valley, it terminates at Broompark Picnic Area. To the west the Deerness Valley Walk makes its way into what was once the heart of the local coalfield, but your route follows directly on into the next valley (the River Browney), along the Lanchester Valley Walk to Consett.

At Brandon you are only a couple of miles away from Durham, a city well worth exploring. Pride of place is of course the magnificent Norman cathedral, and if all you do is pay this a visit and wander the tree-lined paths of the Wear below, then it will be an afternoon well spent.

The Lanchester Valley Walk follows the course of the former Durham–Consett line. Despite a little bogginess close to the river it is quite straightforward, and progress between the fields of cereal crops up the open valley floor should be swift. There are shops and pubs at Langley Park, an old pit village with its own distinctive unloveliness, otherwise lunch can be taken at Lanchester. As with most of these railway paths, there are periodic picnic spots at sites of former stations, such as at Lanchester. Remains of the Roman Fort, Longovicium, can still be seen in a field by the road.

At the time of writing, the Lanchester Valley Walk ends a little beyond Lanchester, near the hamlet of Knitsley, at which point you will have to join a small lane to reach the grand railway paths junction near Howns Gill Viaduct, on the edge of Consett.

The alternative route to reach Howns Gill Viaduct from Bishop Auckland is to follow the Weardale Way to Stanhope, a distance of about 20 miles, then the Waskerley Way railway path (12 miles) north-eastwards over the moors. The Weardale Way is a 78-mile walk, from Monkwearmouth on the North Sea to Cowshill high in the lonely North Pennine hills. (It is not to be confused with the much newer Wear Valley Way, a 46-mile path that runs the administrative length of the Wear Valley District.) The Weardale Way is intermittently signposted, and indicated on OS maps, so from Bishop Auckland follow the Wear's south bank via Escomb, where there is possibly the oldest complete Saxon church in England, dating from around AD 680. Continue to Witton Castle, then cross the river and traverse the hillside to Harperley Hall. At Low Harperley Farm, cross the river once more and ascend a steep hill to reach an unfenced lane, which you join for 2 miles, before taking a bridleway over exposed moorland to Allotment House. On the way you pass what are known as the Elephant Trees, so-called because when viewed at a distance they are supposed to resemble a line of elephants linked trunk to tail. Now drop down to White Kirkley and follow tracks past quarries to Stanhope. There is accommodation and general amenities here in 'the capital of Weardale', plus the Durham Dales Centre and a 250-million-year-old fossilised tree in the churchyard.

Leave Stanhope on the painfully steep road to Edmundbyers, and after crossing a cattle grid by a converted former engine house the moors spread out, the red grouse begin appearing, and the Waskerley Way commences. This route is based on a very early railway built to carry limestone, lead and iron from Weardale to South Shields. It is raised on an embankment for a while, and later it gets bumpy and sometimes wet. A small detour is necessary near the once-busy railway settlement of Waskerley, eliminated by the use of 'Nanny Mayor's Incline', a former rope-worked system whereby the weight of the trucks travelling downwards pulled others up the 1 in 10 slope (and Mrs Mayor ran a lineside hostelry). As you make the long descent to Consett the views down the Derwent valley to Tyneside are superb, despite the windy location, although piles of old railway sleepers make excellent windbreaks.

The Waskerley Way meets the Lanchester Valley Walk just

beyond Howns Gill Viaduct (worth a short detour to visit if you have walked the latter route). Four separate railway paths meet at this important junction: the Lanchester Valley Walk, Waskerley Way, Consett and Sunderland Railway Path and the Derwent Walk. Sit at the picnic tables nearby and contemplate what a fine use these old railway lines have been put to, since you will see all manner of people out walking, running and cycling. On balance, most people prefer to cycle, but I met many walkers along the tracks, and none said that they were inconvenienced by the bicycles.

From Howns Gill join the Derwent Walk via Consett towards Newcastle. Next to the Stephenson-built stone arch bridge a giant, rusting iron ore wagon has been left on some isolated rails by the path as a memorial to the town's former industry. The huge Consett steelworks produced its last batch of steel in September 1980, and its closure was nothing short of a devastating blow on the local community. Fourteen years later there are just empty, rolling meadows.

The Derwent Walk passes through Blackhill, in Consett, to Shotley Bridge. Keeping high on the valley's southern slopes, it runs for a total of 11 miles through what is known as the Derwent Walk Country Park, and is probably the most popular of the railway paths in the area. There is plenty of mixed and attractive woodland, with visitors' centres and short waymarked walks, and it is possible that you may also encounter a few horse riders. At Ebchester there are remains of a Roman fort with bath house, constructed in AD 80 where Dere Street crossed the Derwent en route from York to Corbridge and Scotland. Then the firm, gravel track continues down to Hamsterley Mill, close to Derwentcote steel-making furnace (one of the earliest of its kind in the country and now smartly restored), and then on to Rowlands Gill, by Derwent Park Caravan and Camping Site, where the Walk joins the A694 for about 500 yards. The campsite can be rather busy at weekends and in the summer, but it has a useful shop/information kiosk, and hot showers.

The Derwent Walk officially begins/ends near a country park visitor centre next to Blaydon Rugby Football Club's ground. It comes as something of a jolt, not least because the tower blocks and offices of Newcastle city centre are almost in sight down the River Tyne. Of course there is nothing stopping you from walking right through the middle of the city and out to the North Sea at Whitley Bay or Blyth. But after so many miles of quiet countryside, small towns and villages, the shock may be too much. Plus the fact that there is a lot of Newcastle to deal with, and not all of it is nice. Instead, I suggest that you follow my directions, and in no more than an hour's walking you will have skirted the factories and houses and be back among fields and woodland.

At the small but busy roundabout above the Derwent take the B6317 signposted 'Blaydon'. To your right the A1 zooms across the Tyne on a non-pedestrian bridge, but you have to trudge past the semis and up the hill to Blaydon. Take a look at the reedy lagoons of the Shibdon Pond Local Nature Reserve, a fascinating enclave for wildlife among the human noise and bustle. From the hide you may be able to see water rail, moorhen, sedge warblers and herons. Once through Blaydon, continue over a roundabout (there are pavements all the way) and at a traffic light junction turn off to the right down a lane signed 'Ryton Industrial Estate'. Not very promising, I agree, but after only a few yards there is a footpath via the drive of the electricity station to the banks of the Tyne, and then a grassy track all the way north to Newburn Bridge. Above you looms the gigantic Stella South electricity sub-station. The twin buildings are rather old, and surrounded by the inevitable forest of pylons, but the enormous brick constructions are so unlovely that they can exert a curious fascination.

Once over the Tyne turn left and follow obvious tracks towards Newburn Leisure Centre through Tyne Riverside Country Park. Any sniff of urban Tyneside is now forgotten. The park comprises land reclaimed from the former Isabella Colliery, and a cycle path links the two ends: Newburn (in Tyne and Wear) and Prudhoe (in Northumberland). This track was known as the Wylam Waggonway and used for the transportation of coal to ships at Newburn. Remains of coke ovens and colliery houses can still be seen. Either take this track along the river bank to Wylam, then lanes back up the valley side, or else join a deserted but surfaced lane gently up the hillside to Heddon-on-the-Wall. The views back over the valley are impressive, and you will be surprised at how verdant the landscape is, dominated by the tree-lined Tyne.

If you are interested in railway history, or the industrial history of the North-East, you may like to continue the 2 miles to Wylam, since just before the village is the cottage, open to the public, where George Stephenson was born in 1781. Also at this site the oldest surviving locomotive in the world, 'Puffing Billy', was constructed. It is a fitting end to your railway path walking.

21

A COAST TO YOURSELF

Heddon – Edinburgh

HEDDON-ON-THE-WALL – BERWICK-ON-TWEED (77 miles)
Heddon-on-the-Wall is a quiet and residential outpost of Newcastle, with attractive stone cottages and a couple of pubs. But the main attraction of the village is the preserved section of Hadrian's Wall. It is no greater than a hundred yards or so long, from Turret 11b to Milecastle 12, and although neither is visible today you can make out a circular kiln built into the wall at a much later date.

From Heddon, take the B6528 for a few yards underneath the A69, then turn off abruptly along a single-track lane signposted 'East Heddon'. At once you are back in the peace and quiet of farmland, of rural Northumberland, and although underfoot it may be tarmac it is nonetheless tranquil. Head north along lanes, through Medburn and past Dissington Hall, and after Milbourne cross the A696 at the Highlander pub (restaurant), by East Newham. Take the lane opposite that is intriguingly signposted 'Ogle 1¾ miles'. This turns out to be a tiny village with little more than a phone box. Follow the lane to Shilvington, across a lovely stone bridge, and then to the ruins of Mitford's Norman motte and bailey castle before passing under the A1 and into Morpeth.

The East Route is moving inexorably back to the North Sea shore once more, since the hidden bays and beaches of Northumberland are one of the highlights of the entire route. However, it should need no pointing out that there are endless options should you wish to reach Scotland via an inland route. Consider Fontburn Reservoir and Harwood Forest, Rothbury and Wooler, the Coquet valley and the Cheviots – there is plenty of splendid walking to be had.

Morpeth is a busy county town which still retains many old buildings, including the newly restored thirteenth-century Chantry, which now houses, amongst other things, a bagpipe museum. Leave the town on a straight lane northwards, via the hamlets of Hebron, Tritlington and Earsdon, then turn east. After crossing the mainline railway there is a small opencast coal mine just past the Junction Inn. Continue along the lane through Widdrington, then take the waymarked footpath to St John's Chapel and finally Druridge Bay. The Bay boasts seven miles of glorious, smooth sand, almost a quarter of a mile wide at low tide, and incorporates a country park that has been reclaimed from what was previously an opencast mine. Despite the continued presence of mining to the north, the beach provides a tremendous return to the sea for the East Route walker. If you join the coast any further south you are likely to see more of the industrial side of Northumberland, such as at Lynemouth. But even at Druridge Bay there may be dangers. Local campaigners have been protesting for some time against the extraction of sand for the production of concrete. Now, more worrying still, the Central Electricity Generating Board have been making noises about developing a nuclear power station on land to the south of the Bay. You may like to contact Morpeth Tourist Information Centre for news of any further developments, and possibly consider joining the coast a little to the north should this appalling spectre eventually materialise.

Two miles north from Druridge Bay is the small town of Amble-by-the-Sea, which once shipped coal to London and Scandinavia. Nowadays, Braid Marina is usually home to hundreds of small pleasure boats, and a mile offshore Coquet Island houses three quarters of mainland Britain's roseate terns, as well as puffins and eider ducks. Follow the wide Coquet for a mile upstream until the bridge at Warkworth, a small place dominated by an imposing twelfth-century castle crowning a hill in a loop of the river. As at Amble, there are a few B&Bs and cafés.

Return to the wide, golden dunes, via a public right of way, then continue along the coast past a golf course for a couple of miles. If the tide is out and the River Aln is low you could consider wading across to Alnmouth, but remember your experiences on the South-West Coast Path; with a heavy pack and probably heavy legs it is wise to err on the side of safety, so take the short road detour around to the small resort. In September 1772, during the American War of Independence, Alnmouth was the victim of a bizarre attack by an American privateer, John Paul Jones. From his ship offshore he fired a cannon ball at Alnmouth Church. It missed, landed in a field, then bounced three times and ended up in the roof of a farmhouse. Jones sailed off and equally inexplicably attacked Skinningrove, further south in Cleveland.

For a greater range of accommodation and amenities Alnwick ('Annick') is only an hour's walk away up the banks of the Coquet. The town has been the stronghold of the Earls and Dukes of Northumberland for many centuries, and the superb castle fortress remains the home of the famous Percy family of Northumberland, who originally accompanied William the Conqueror in 1066.

From Alnmouth, either walk the beach or along the top of low cliffs by Foxton Hall Golf Club to reach Seaton Point. There is a nest of ugly holiday chalets at the Point itself, so you may wish to avoid this by using a small section of minor road to Boulmer. The coastal track continues along the clifftop past several inlets and sandy bays, and after Howick it is signposted all the way to Craster. Craster has contributed two products of particular note over the years: stone, from its now redundant quarry, from which many London kerbs are made; and, of course, kippers. Earlier this century up to twenty boats sailed from this relatively small port. Salt herring was barrelled and sent to Germany and Russia, and kippers transported daily to Bishopsgate Market in London. Now only the smokehouses remain. Here the herring used to be smoked for ten to fourteen hours over fires of whitewood shavings covered with oak sawdust, and sometimes there were as many as 2,500 fish smoking in each house.

The fourteenth-century ruins of Dunstanburgh Castle can already be seen clinging in a dramatic fashion to the cliffs ahead. It became a stronghold for John of Gaunt in the Wars of the Roses, when much of it was destroyed. Drop down past a golf course to Embleton Bay, where it may be necessary to divert to the footbridge rather than ford Embleton Burn, and on to Low Newton-by-the-Sea, where there is pub refreshment. The beautiful sweep of Beadnell Bay then reveals itself. Like much of the unspoilt coastline from and including Druridge Bay, it is owned by the National Trust. The designation of this part of the North-East coast as an Area of Outstanding Natural

Beauty and Heritage Coast reflects, of course, its physical beauty, but what it does not say is that this shore is among the least visited and least developed – only Seahouses has amusement arcades of any note, and they are rarely full. Those that have never walked the Northumberland coast before will be pleasantly surprised.

If the tide permits, it is probably easier and much more scenic to walk Beadnell's unspoilt sands all the way around to the small harbour, where old lime kilns are now used to store fishing nets and crab pots. The view back across the curving bay to the outline of Dunstanburgh Castle is breathtaking; this is a spot where the Walk should not be hurried. There is a large campsite, and a hotel in the village.

Beyond is Annstead Bay, popular with sunbathers and the deckchair army. The burn may be tricky at high tide, necessitating a detour to the road inland. Seahouses is usually a crowded place in the summer months, although there is not much more to it than just a single main street. There are regular boat trips out to the nearby Farne Islands, which total twenty-eight in all, although many are only large enough to accommodate the resident grey seals and sea birds that make the location famous. Seventeen different species of seabirds nest on the low islands which, with the flashing lighthouse on Inner Farne, stay in sight for some time. But it is castles that once more grab the attention, since now the majestic outline of Bamburgh Castle draws nearer as you wander north along the beach or dune paths. The fortress sits on red sandstone on top of a powerful dolerite outcrop, and was declared by Henry VI to be his royal capital during the Wars of the Roses. This, and the Ramblers' Café, off the village green, should both be on your itinerary.

Coastal access extends a little further around the coast. At Budle Point there are fine views ahead of Holy Island. To the west lies Northumberland National Park, with the Cheviot about 20 miles away. The sheltered tidal inlet of Budle Bay supports many wading birds, which scour the muddy flats for shellfish and other food. Access is permitted, but progress as far as a coastal route is difficult, and it may be more expedient to use minor roads via Waren Mill, Easington and Elwick, before contemplating the causeway across Beal Sands and a visit to the Holy Island of Lindisfarne, an important centre for pilgrims since St Aidan founded a monastery there in the seventh century. Whether you are a worshipper, historian, naturalist, or just a curious walker, the island is undoubtedly worth a detour if you have the time.

Berwick is about 8 miles away from Holy Island, although it may be a little longer depending on whether you use lanes and rights of way between the railway and the A1, or whether you forge your own route. If you choose to walk along the foreshore be very careful of the swift tides, plus the dangers of unstable sands and mudflats. Beyond Saltpan Rocks the dunes give way to rising cliffs, and there is a track that leads to Spittal and industrial Tweedmouth.

After 1,150 miles of walking you have finally joined the ends of the two most geographically extreme English counties. Even without crossing the River Tweed your achievement is already remarkable, and your current mileage is greater than many End to End walkers manage in sum total. It was obvious from the beginning that the East Route was going to involve more miles, more overall effort, than the other two more direct routes. But if you have made it to Berwick via the East of England you have had a supreme walking journey – a route of lasting quality and interest.

BERWICK – EDINBURGH (66 miles)

Berwick-upon-Tweed is a place with an identity problem. It's officially England's most northerly town and is administered by Northumberland County Council, and yet is the headquarters of a Scottish regiment, the Queen's Own Borderers; and Berwick Rangers Football Club play their matches in the Scottish League. Indeed the town was historically one of the four original Royal Burghs of Scotland, and Berwick changed hands no less than thirteen times in thirty-five years. In the High Street you are likely to hear Scottish and English accents mingling, and what with the mighty River Tweed and the red-tiled old grey stone buildings, there is a perceptible Border feel. Welcome to Scotland!

Shops and accommodation are plentiful in Berwick, and a stroll around the $1^1/2$ miles of Elizabethan walls encircling the town is recommended. To resume the journey to Edinburgh leave the town by Berwick Pier at the mouth of the river, skirt Berwick Borough golf course, and follow the coast northwards. There are some dramatic sea stacks, particularly Needle's Eye, and a caravan park at Marshall Meadows Bay. The railway runs close to the coast at this stage, but safe passage is possible along the clifftop, and at Lamberton you officially cross into Scotland. Continue past Burnmouth along the field margins of what is a very quiet and unspoilt seashore, until the greens and fairways near Scout Point indicate the imminence of Eyemouth.

Fishing (especially for shellfish) has always been the lifeblood of Eyemouth, and the port still has a busy harbour. But the sea can be a cruel master: in the great gale of 1881 half of Eyemouth's fishing fleet was sunk, and 129 men lost their lives. There are more local details, including a life-size fishermen's cottage kitchen, in Eyemouth Museum.

Leave the esplanade and take the prominent cliff path, keeping the caravan site on your left. Some distance on, the path descends to the stony shore at Linkim, with steps back on to the cliffs once more. At Coldingham Bay you can head a short distance inland to Coldingham itself, where there are B&Bs and cafés (although it can be hectic in summer). But there is also a youth hostel by the bay, and it is perhaps preferable to stick to the coast for another half mile of clifftop walking to St Abbs, a fishing village named after St Ebbe, a Northumbrian princess. Her ship was driven on to the rocky shore in AD 640, and after drying herself and looking about she decided that it was an OK place and built a monastery (like you did in those days). Unusually, there were both male and female communities at the sanctuary on the cliffs, where St Ebbe presided as Abbess until her death in 683. The unspoilt headland is a national nature reserve, and the sheer cliffs around the lighthouse abound with wheeling kittiwakes, fulmars and gulls, plus other seabirds such as guillemots and sometimes puffins. This is great clifftop scenery, and it is well worth pausing at the visitor centre (plus café) to learn more.

North of St Abb's Head the cliffs continue, and following the coastal fence along field edges it is possible to stay on or close to the coast for the whole 10 miles to near Cockburnspath. There are some fairly steep bits, and the generally rough ground will require appropriate care, especially if it is also blowing hard. A short diversion inland will be necessary to cross Dowlaw Burn. Siccar Point, 4 miles further on, holds an important place in the heady world of historical geology, for it was here, in 1788, that Dr James Hutton scratched his head and had a thought. Basically, he stared at the eroded Old Red Sandstone on top of the Silurian in front of him, and came up with the theory of geological unconformity – that erosion and sedimentation were fundamental in explaining subsequent stratification and uplifting. (Hitherto, all geological phenomena were explained in terms of Noah's Flood.)

At Pease Bay, a pretty, sheltered little place, there is a spectacularly ugly caravan park, and it is here that you join the eastern end of the Southern Upland Way for a short distance. Near Cove Harbour follow the waymarks inland under the road and railway to the village of Cockburnspath. There is a hotel, a couple of shops, a B&B, plus a campsite nearby. The Southern Upland Way runs for 212 miles across to the west coast at Portpatrick, near Stranraer, and although it is eclipsed in terms of fame and popularity by the West Highland Way, it is nevertheless a long and often tough path that wanders through some particularly remote countryside.

If you want to leave the east coast and approach Edinburgh via the Lammermuir Hills, consider following the Southern Upland Way to Abbey St Bathans (youth hostel) or Longformacus, then branching out northwards. Or you could conceivably take the trail all the way west to Melrose (42 miles from Cockburnspath) and join the End to End Central Route as it heads for the Moorfoots and Pentlands, and so to Edinburgh.

Back with the east coast, the unpleasant spectacle of Torness nuclear power station will already be evident. This, plus the close proximity of the A1 and London–Edinburgh main line, provides good reason to leave the coast for a few miles. From Cockburnspath take the minor road to Oldhamstocks, where there is a track by the burn around the back of Cocklaw Hill. (Should you feel adventurous, there is scope for heading further inland and engineering a route across Monynut Edge – this is effectively the eastern edge of the Lammermuir Hills.) Make for the path up to Doon Hill, from where there are fine views, then descend to Dunbar.

There is much of historical interest in Dunbar, 'the fort on the point', which has entertained a number of visitors either fleeing after battle (Edward II, after Bannockburn) or in uncomfortable situations (Mary Queen of Scots with Darnley, after Rizzio's murder). The customary range of facilities are available, and with luck you should enjoy them in good weather – Dunbar has been Scotland's driest and sunniest town for the past thirty years. In the

High Street you will also find the birthplace of the conservationist John Muir, a house preserved in early nineteenth-century style. Muir actually sailed for America with his family when he was only eleven, and is seen by many as the founder of America's national parks. Beyond Dunbar is the John Muir Country Park, a nature reserve of 1,760 acres which includes a delightful coastal walk for you to pursue to Belhaven. Thrift and sea aster flourish here, and eider ducks and ringed plover go about their business. Then after a small diversion around lanes, return to the sea via the rich woodland of sycamore, oak and Scots pine at Tyninghame. Peffer Sands and the Gegan are particularly unspoilt and beautiful.

The remains of Tantallon Castle, built in the 1300s but abandoned after Cromwell's destructive attentions, provide the next point of interest, although care must be exercised on the steep cliffs as you approach from the east.

On the short walk along the pavement of the A198 into North Berwick there are two arresting physical features. The first is Bass Rock, a remarkable bird-covered crag jutting sheer out of the sea. Gannets were once bred on the Rock for their eggs, though the bird's strong, tough flesh lost popularity. North Berwick Law, another volcanic plug, rises out of the fields just south of the town. This very steep protrusion of 187m has, most improbably, a gigantic whale's jawbone planted on its summit.

The tourist leaflet describes North Berwick as 'the Biarritz of the North', which is perhaps a little bit of an exaggeration, I think. Nevertheless it is a popular and likeable resort, with plenty of accommodation and good eating places, plus a campsite off the road to the east. It is also evident from the sports shops that this is important golfing country, and you leave North Berwick by the shoreline past West Links, one of ten courses in this area (including Muirfield – the Open venue). The 8 miles of sand and dune walking from North Berwick to Aberlady are superb, offering great views across the Firth of Forth to the Fife Peninsula, and on a clear day to the distant Ochils. The duneland is an escape should the tide threaten or the wind get up, otherwise the wide, firm and uncluttered sandy bays stretch around Gullane Point to Aberlady Bay. Here there is a nature reserve, and walkers are asked to keep away from nesting terns between April and June. At other times the Bay plays host to hundreds of wintering scoter and eider ducks.

Edinburgh is almost in sight. Passing buses proclaim its name, and the tops of the Pentlands, south-west of the city, gradually join the Lammermuirs in crowding in on the capital. The coast is now much flatter, and although there are short stretches of quiet footpath – such as around Craigielaw Point – the run in to Edinburgh inevitably is a pavement affair after the power station at Cockenzie. There is some rather drab seafront at Cockenzie and Port Seton, and Prestonpans is best hurried through for Musselburgh (there is a campsite on the way). Here, modern shops blend with older buildings about the River Esk, and bobbing yachts in the harbour and the old warehouses recall an older, sea-faring past. Then, 2 miles further on, as you walk along the promenade of Portobello by the old guest houses above the sands, it may at last dawn that you have finally made it to Edinburgh. Holyrood Palace and Edinburgh Castle are only 3 miles away, and although your accommodation may not be quite so grand, it is time for an evening's self-congratulation. Have a hot bath, put on some clean underwear, and go out into this fair city and celebrate the fact that since you have walked England the long way, nothing can stop you now.

APPENDIX I

Equipment and Preparation

It should hardly need to be said that any walk of over 1,000 miles requires careful planning and preparation, and a great deal of thought as to what to take – and, just as importantly, what to leave behind. Although there is a danger of actually over-preparing, to step off the London–Penzance train with no more than a few days' readiness is asking for trouble. A journey of this magnitude requires a considerable period of organisation, co-ordination and physical training, and even a certain amount of mental and emotional preparation.

First of all, ask yourself some basic questions: Is the Walk to be continuous, or to be completed in stages? What time of the year and in which direction will I be walking? Am I going alone or with anyone else? What type of accommodation will I be using? What sort of daily distance will I aim to cover? Am I restricted in any way by time or money, or rendezvous with back-up parties or other walking companions? The answers to all of these questions need to be decided before you even get the rucksack out of the loft.

Most people imagine the End to End Walk to be a long, continuous trek of many weeks' duration, and for most people it is. It gives you a chance to see and experience the country in one long and uninterrupted journey, and to appreciate both the stark and subtle changes of shape and scenery, local attitudes and accents, etc, that differ so widely throughout Great Britain. Many walkers also find that an undertaking of such magnitude allows them an opportunity to develop a fitness and physique quite unlike anything that they have experienced before – a chance to hone the body into an efficient and effective walking machine. And ultimately there is a sense of personal satisfaction in completing a marathon walk in a single, continuous journey.

But there are no rules that say you *have* to walk from End to End in one go, and in many respects it is quite a tall order for the average working person to find the time (around eight weeks, not including training) and for non-working people the money (as much as £1,000 or more to finance the project from start to finish). Perhaps it makes sense to consider another approach. A middle-aged couple I spoke to were completing the End to End Walk in regular fortnightly stages, twice a year (in the spring and autumn), resuming exactly where they had left off the time before. In this way they felt that they were still genuinely walking from one end of the country to the other, but without the huge logistical nightmare of organising a continuous 1,000-mile trip. In addition, they said that having time to anticipate the next section made the overall Walk even more enjoyable!

The time of the year that you set off depends on another fundamental question: in which direction are you going to walk? Most people tend to walk from south to north, from Land's End to John o'Groats, which is the approach of this guidebook. There are several good reasons for this. First of all, weather. The warmest should, if anywhere in the country, be in the South-West earliest of all, which should allow for the possibility of an early start. (However, it is an accepted fact that as far as the weather is concerned do not take *anything* for granted in the British Isles.) Starting earlier should allow you to enjoy the change in the seasons, whether it is lambing-time or the opening of the buds on the trees that you find of interest; and, depending on the specific dates, you should enjoy longer days on the Scottish hills. Also, the prevailing sun, wind and rain will be behind the south–north walker, and not in the face (this is usually mooted as one of the main reasons for why the Pennine Way is traditionally walked from Edale to Kirk Yetholm, and not vice versa).

Second, by starting in the South-West you leave the tougher, upland sections (Pennines, Scottish hills) until later in the Walk, when you should be fitter and stronger – but do not underestimate the rigours of the Cornish and Devon cliff paths.

Third, you can miss most of the peak holiday season in the South-West by starting just before it begins (possibly around April/May), but of course the earlier in the year that you set off the likelier it will be that B&Bs and guest houses will still be closed. Further details on this subject below.

There is also another, perhaps rather less important point. John o'Groats, due to its remote location, attracts fewer visitors than Land's End, and perhaps as a result the theme park element that Peter de Savary has introduced on the Cornish clifftop is as yet missing on the more bleak Caithness shore. Although Land's End is probably easier for more people to get to and from, it is John o'Groats, in my opinion, that is a more attractive and romantic place to finish.

However, there are other factors that come into play the longer the year draws on. Grouse shooting begins on 12th August, and deer stalking a little afterwards, and these two events can effectively put some moors entirely out of bounds until into October. This applies predominantly to Scotland, and to the Highlands in particular, but other areas such as the Pennines and the North York Moors are also affected. See the relevant sections in the text for further details.

All this said, there is no earthly reason why you should *not* walk from north to south – it will be easier to avoid the hunting season in Scotland, the weather should get progressively warmer and the terrain steadily easier. All you will have to do is read this book from back to front! At the end of the day it is down to personal preference. There are no hard and fast rules about which way and when. The Land's End to John o'Groats Walk has been attempted at all times of the year and in all weathers; so arrange the timetable that suits you best.

Naturally the availability of fixed accommodation depends on the time of year that you decide to travel, but there are other points to bear in mind as well. It is all common sense, really. For instance, an earlier start (March/April) and you will probably have to take more warm and protective clothing. But if you walk with others then the overall load can be shared, particularly if you are carrying camping gear and sleeping bags, which is what many End to Enders tend to do. For an End to End walking party, two or three is probably the best number (provided you all get on, of course). If your group is any larger it is essential that you all know each other's walking styles, preferences and limitations; and in rural areas finding sufficient fixed accommodation for any more than two or three is likely to become a problem. The pace of a group is naturally dictated by the slowest member, so make sure that you are all used to walking with each other. On the other hand, many long-distance walkers continue to prefer their own company, although it is not always easy to find single bedrooms at some B&Bs. In addition, if you are walking on your own it is essential that you are aware of your own limitations and know how to look after yourself in the event of any misfortune. This advice may seem unnecessary and rather daft when ambling over the Cotswolds or through the Fens on a hot summer's day, but if you are stuck on the Lairig Ghru in the Cairngorms in a blizzard it is wise to know how to react.

So, if you decide to take a tent, where are you going to pitch each night? Sites may be numerous along the Cornwall and Devon coasts or in the Lake District, but in other areas they are few and far between, and it may be a question of knocking at a farmhouse door and asking permission to pitch in the corner of a private field. Possibilities for wild camping similarly vary, with the most opportunities obviously in the more remote parts like the High Pennines or northern Scotland. But what most walkers seem to do is to combine camping with fixed accommodation – camp wherever possible, but when the need of a hot bath or a proper bed gets too much, then seek a B&B or youth hostel.

Youth hostels are a fairly cheap overnight stop, even if some of the hostel rules seem more appropriate to cub scouts on a summer camp than mature walkers on a serious walk; and on some long-distance paths such as the South-West Coast Path and Pennine Way there are a whole string of hostels that can be linked together (the YHA even operate what they call the Pennine Way Bureau that will book a bed in advance for you at each of their eighteen hostels along the Way). In areas such as the Pennines, North York Moors and recently Devon and Cornwall, the YHA are also introducing a number of camping barns. In addition, Britain has a growing network of independent hostels, barns and bothies that suit the low-budget traveller not averse to the spartan approach.

If you choose to use hostels and B&Bs all the way it is a good idea to consider booking ahead during popular times or in popular places. However, since daily mileage will largely depend on personal fitness and the vagaries of the weather, it is probably unwise to book any further than a few days, perhaps a week in advance.

Accommodation lists are widely available, whether nationally (such as *The Ramblers' Yearbook and Accommodation Guide*) or on a local basis. Tourist information centres are the best places for the latter, and some even operate a room-booking service. In more remote places pub landlords and the wise old lady behind the counter in the post office stores quite often have the best local knowledge of where to stay. For quality of accommodation, out-of-the-way farmhouses can be the cheapest and normally serve the biggest meals, but watch out for town centre guest houses or B&Bs in honey-pot tourist sites, where there are pink lace curtains and immaculate doormats. These places generally cater for car drivers, and are not always keen on muddy boots and dripping waterproofs. Agree on the price, and the time of breakfast. If you want an early start then say so, although this may require some careful diplomacy.

Many of the popular long-distance paths (South-West Coast Path, Ridgeway, Offa's Dyke Path, Pennine Way, West Highland Way, etc) have their own accommodation lists, which usually include not only addresses of B&Bs but also details of campsites, shops, post offices, and so on. See the main text and further reading lists for specific titles.

The number of miles that you walk in a day depends on whether you view the Walk as a gentle ramble, a serious hike, or a hasty dash. If you are limited by time off work, or personal finances, then perhaps you will have to fix a fairly high daily mileage. But do not be unrealistic or too overreaching in your calculations, since not only will it take you some time to develop a walking rhythm, but bad weather will also slow you down, and some upland or intricate stretches will inevitably be more time-consuming than you think. And blisters or a mild illness will of course lose you time. If you are arranging to meet others along the way, or stay at the homes of friends and relatives, do not set a timetable so tight that you end up hurrying and worrying days in advance. The Land's End to John o'Groats Walk is such an adventure, and there will be so many surprises and discoveries along the way, that you should be prepared to be adaptable to a certain extent. A personal schedule is certainly important – it is sensible to work out a realistic daily mileage, available time and money, etc, and to have a set destination each day – but do not get bogged down by it. If, as is advisable, you have already muddied your boots on a national trail or regional route beforehand, then you will have a good idea of the sort of daily walking timetable that suits you best.

The average daily mileage for the End to Ender seems to be between 15 and 25 miles. Of course some do slightly less, and so take longer, and others sometimes walk as much as 35 miles in a single day. Set a target that matches your own ability, taking into consideration personal fitness, the amount of gear you are carrying, the physical nature of the route you choose, the probable weather conditions and amount of daylight for your chosen season.

What to take

Now go and fetch your rucksack out of the loft. The object before you has to carry all the essential items that you will need for an eight-week walk of around 1,200 miles or so. Small, isn't it?

As any backpacker knows, the secret is to take the bare minimum. Tent, pegs, sleeping bag, insulating mat, stove, spare fuel, pans, eating utensils – and this is solely the camping gear! Above all else, ensure that you have adequate clothing. Some items, such as socks, will begin wearing out along the way, so be prepared to buy some more, or have friends send new ones to an agreed address. Waterproof clothing is vital, at any time of the year in the UK, so make sure you have reliable garments and always keep them handy. Gaiters or waterproof trousers, cagoule or cape – all this is a matter of personal preference. At the same time, if you are walking in the summer then take some sort of sunhat or cap, since heatstroke can be a serious hazard.

For any walker contemplating a marathon walk such as this, strong boots are indispensable. If you are roadwalking the whole length then a tough pair of training shoes may be more desirable, but if you choose unsurfaced paths you will need a pair of decent walking boots to cope with the huge variety of terrain ahead. And it is fairly certain that you will need a second or even third pair of boots before you complete the journey. Make sure that these are broken-in beforehand, and get someone to send them on. Out of all of a walker's bodily parts, it goes without saying that the feet are the most important of all. Treat them carefully, and shoe them correctly.

With minimal weight always in the back of your mind, consider what else you will need. Items of safety, like a torch and whistle, a basic first aid kit, survival bag, etc, should be part of any serious walker's luggage already. In addition, the long-distance walker's rucksack may also include any of the following, depending on personal preferences and interests: camera, lightweight field glasses, reading/identification book, diary or notebook, small radio . . . the list could go on, but so would the weight, and just two or three of these items would add a significant amount of weight to your load. Plus there are other pieces of equipment that are standard for any backpacker: soap, matches, water-sterilising tablets, water bottle/flask, washing kit and towel, toilet tissue, boot wax, and pumps or possibly light trainers.

A significant amount of weight and space will be taken up by guidebooks and maps. Of the latter, the Ordnance Survey Landranger series (1:50 000) is the best for the purposes of the End to Ender. Altogether you will need around forty of these maps, so unless you want to buy them for posterity or further use it is best to borrow them from somewhere like the Ramblers' Association's map library, or a well-stocked public library. (Needless to say you will have a trusty compass to hand, and some single walkers carry a spare in case they lose one.) A few of the more polished guidebooks, such as the National Trail Guides, reproduce sections of OS maps, with the actual route superimposed. These are fine if you stick to the path and are not interested in venturing off, but if you want or need to leave the route you may find yourself in trouble. As with replacement socks, boots, etc, it is best to have guidebooks and maps sent on in batches to a pre-arranged location – a friend's house or a specific post office. Then, in the same package which you have just emptied, bundle up the books and maps, etc, that you have now finished with and send them homewards. Long-distance walking professionals also have pre-packaged food sent by this means, since it saves looking for shops and spending too much money, and you can choose in advance exactly what you want to eat, especially if you are keen on special sorts of lightweight, dehydrated walkers' meals.

On the subject of food and drink, most long-distance walkers seem to consume a prodigious daily amount, which is not surprising if you are walking around 20 miles with a pack on your back over changing terrain. One breakfast or dinner followed almost immediately by another is not uncommon. Carrying your own food and cooking equipment obviously makes what, when and where you eat that much easier, but on popular long-distance trails more cafés and pubs appear to be catering for hungry walkers. Again, it is down to personal preference, but remember that what you need above all is a balanced, high-calorie diet. Pasta and rice are better than chips, for example. Make sure that you have plenty of snacks and things to munch during the day, such as dried fruit, mixed nuts, and all those things that you know are good for you but normally never touch. It is a good idea, even if you are not camping, to carry enough reserve food to see you through any conceivable emergency, and to sustain energy through successive long days. Not every B&B offers evening meals, and many rural pubs that provide food (and away from touristy areas they can be few in number) stop serving at around 8.30–9 p.m.

But everyone does it differently. The indefatigable John Merrill consumes almost nothing but bars of chocolate whilst he is walking (he has eaten ten bars in as many hours!). John explains that he prefers to keep going and avoid disrupting his walking rhythm, then eat a full meal in the evening. His other peculiar trait is to drink virtually no liquid while he walks, a habit that even he does not recommend should be emulated by any aspiring young walker. Dehydration, even when you think that you are not sweating, can occur rapidly, and it is crucial that you consume sufficient liquid throughout the whole day. In extreme temperatures a thermos flask is a sensible idea, and if conditions are particularly hot and dry then your first aid kit should include salt tablets.

A problem that you may encounter on the largely off-road End to End Walk is locating shops and banks. The three routes that I have described mostly avoid large towns and urban centres, which is why I often mention in the text whether a village has shops and services. Beware of early closing and Sundays, and if either is approaching stock up in advance. With few banks, and even fewer automatic cash machines along the route, I suggest that you consider taking out a National Savings or Girobank account, which enables cash to be drawn from post office counters.

The final weight of your rucksack depends to some extent on individual physique and whether, if you are camping, you can share the load with others. But remember – that extra kilogram can make all the difference towards the end of a long day.

If you are new to long-distance walking or backpacking, and are faced with buying major pieces of equipment such as a rucksack or boots, it is wise to do your homework first and find out exactly what is suitable for both your needs and individual build. The monthly walking magazines carry regular gear reviews and features, but for the best introduction to the subject consult *The Walker's Handbook* by Hugh Westacott; or for a more in-depth guide on what to carry (and what to do with it) read *The Backpacker's Handbook* by Chris Townsend (see further reading list).

Preparation and training

If you have just about sorted out what you are going to take, then think carefully about what you are likely to come up against day by day, and the decisions that you may be faced with. Are you going to take ferries across the estuaries of Cornwall and Devon, or have you decided to shun mechanical transport and walk every foot of the way? Is it acceptable to take a bus at the end of the day in order to reach accommodation, then return to the same spot next morning? In order to walk 20 miles a day are you going to adhere to a strict daily timetable? Some walkers force themselves to be up and off by a certain time every morning. Indeed, many experienced walkers swear by an early start, either to enjoy the best weather of the day or to avoid the crowds. If you are planning to walk upwards of 20 miles in a day then you will *have* to begin reasonably early. However, others get up at their leisure and enjoy walking late into the day, even well into the evening (this is far easier if you are camping, of course). Also, is it permissible to have rest days and simply not walk? Some End to Enders find that this disrupts their overall rhythm, but other long-distance walkers enjoy taking a day off and seeing the local sights.

Training for the event is an important matter; and if you do not do it properly the whole trip can be in jeopardy. If you regularly walk long daily distances (15–20 miles) then you should not have too many problems, providing that you can cope with the additional strain of a heavy pack. If, however, your pedestrian experience extends to walking the dog each evening or an occasional monthly ramble then you will have far more work to do before setting off. A certain level of all-round fitness is required, and swimming and cycling are as good as walking for improving this, as well as the basic need to harden your feet and strengthen your leg muscles. You are going to be walking a long way in various weather conditions over changing ground, so the obvious training is to get out and practise doing it! The ideal warm-up might be a medium-length long-distance path away from your chosen route, such as the South Downs Way or part of the Pembrokeshire Coast Path. Make sure that you are comfortable and confident with all your gear.

Getting in shape is something that you must start doing as soon as possible. Don't leave it until a few weeks before you set off. It is nevertheless a fact that unless you are a superwalker, or start the End to End immediately after finishing another long-distance trail, it will be a tough couple of weeks to begin with, as your body – and feet and legs especially – get used to the daily pounding and physical exertion. But if you are still striding out in the third week it is likely that, barring an unforeseen injury, you will complete the distance. By then you will have developed a rhythm, a routine, and your body will be developing into an efficient walking machine. Only another 600 miles to go!

APPENDIX II

Further Reading and Useful Addresses

LAND'S END – JOHN O'GROATS

– *The Big Walk* by 'A. Walker' (describes Billy Butlin's 1960 competition – unfortunately long out of print)

– *Journey Through Britain* by John Hillaby (although over 20 years old, this walking classic has inspired a generation of End to Enders ever since), Constable, 1968/Paladin, 1970

– *Hamish's Groats End Walk* by Hamish Brown (an enjoyable journey by man and dog, which also included the peaks of Wales and Ireland; packed with entertaining anecdote and information), Victor Gollancz, 1981/Paladin, 1983

– *The Great Backpacking Adventure* by Chris Townsend – see chapters on Land's End to John o'Groats and the Pennine Way (interesting and well-told accounts of long-distance walks from the master backpacker), Oxford Illustrated Press, 1987

– *Turn Right at Land's End* by John Merrill (the diary of a remarkable walk of nearly 7,000 miles around the coast of England, Wales and Scotland), JNM, 1988, from Trail Crest Publications, Milne House, Speedwell Mill, Miller's Green, Wirksworth, Derbys DE4 4BL

– *A Grandparents' Guide from Land's End to John o'Groats* by Eileen & Herbert Witherington (account of a leisurely End to End on both roads and paths by a retired couple), Wande Publications, 38 North Guards, Whitburn, Tyne & Wear SR6 7AD

GENERAL

– *The Walker's Handbook* by Hugh Westacott, Penguin, 1978/Pan, 1991

– *The Backpacker's Handbook* by Chris Townsend, Oxford Illus-

trated Press, 1991
– *The Ramblers' Yearbook and Accommodation Guide* (Ramblers' Association)
– *The Long-Distance Walkers' Handbook* (Long-Distance Walkers' Association)
– Youth Hostels Association and Scottish Youth Hostels Association accommodation guides
– *Out in the country: Where you can go and what you can do* (Countryside Commission Publications)
– *Rights of Way: a guide to law and practice* by John Riddall and John Trevelyan (Ramblers' Association/Open Spaces Society, 2nd ed 1992 – available from RA national office)
– *Rights of Way: a guide to the law in Scotland* by the Scottish Rights of Way Society
– *Heading for the Scottish Hills* by the Mountaineering Council of Scotland and the Scottish Landowners' Federation
– *Exploring Britain's Long Distance Paths*, AA, 1992 (includes useful A-Z of over 200 UK trails)
– *Great Walks of Scotland* by H. Brown, R. McOwan & R. Mearns, Printwise Publications, 1989 (24 walks that include the Lairig Ghru, St Abbs Head, Minchmoor Road, Wanlockhead/Lowther Hills and Stacks of Duncansby)

ADDRESSES

Backpackers' Club, PO Box 381, Reading, Berks RG3 4RL
Camping and Caravanning Club, Greenfields House, Westwood Way, Coventry CV4 8JH
Countryside Commission, John Dower House, Crescent Place, Cheltenham, Glos GL50 3RA
Countryside Commission Postal Sales, PO Box 124, Walgrave, Northampton NN6 9TL
Heart of England Way Association, 20 Throckmorton Road, Alcester, Warks B49 6QA
Icknield Way Association, 19 Boundary Road, Bishops Stortford, Herts CM23 5LE
Independent Backpackers' Hostels – Scotland, c/o Loch Ness Backpacker's Lodge, Lewiston, Drumnadrochit, Inverness-shire IV3 6UT
Land's End–John o'Groats Association, The Custom House, Land's End, Sennen, Penzance, Cornwall TR19 7AA

Long-Distance Paths Advisory Service, 11 Cotswold Court, Sandy Lane, Chester CH3 5UZ

Long-Distance Walkers' Association, 117 Higher Lane, Rainford, St. Helens, Merseyside WA11 8BQ

Mountaineering Council of Scotland, Flat 1R, 71 King Street, Crieff PH7 3HB

Offa's Dyke Association, Offa's Dyke Centre, West Street, Knighton, Powys LD7 1EW

Ordnance Survey, Romsey Road, Maybush, Southampton, Hants SO9 4DH

Pennine Way Association, 29 Springfield Park Avenue, Chelmsford, Essex CM2 6EL

Ramblers' Association, 1/5 Wandsworth Road, London SW8 2XX

Scottish Natural Heritage (Information and Library Services), 2/5 Anderson Place, Edinburgh EH6 5NP

Scottish Rights of Way Society, Unit 2, John Cotton Business Centre, 10/2 Sunnyside, Edinburgh EH7 5RA

Scottish Youth Hostels Association, 7 Glebe Crescent, Stirling FK8 2JA

South-West Way Association, Windlestraw, Penquit, Ermington, Ivybridge, Devon PL21 OLU

Youth Hostels Association, Trevelyan House, 8 St Stephen's Hill, St Albans, Herts AL1 2DY

FURTHER READING: CENTRAL ROUTE

Map numbers refer to Ordnance Survey Landranger maps (1:50 000) unless indicated otherwise. Where maps overlap from one chapter to the next they are listed in the first chapter only.

1 The Deserted Lanes: Land's End – Taunton

Careful attention to the OS map is the order of the day for most of this section. General accommodation guides cover the region fairly adequately; indeed, it may help to have a few addresses in advance to spare wasted journeys to out-of-the-way locations in search of a bed.

MAPS: 204, 203, 200, 201, 193, 192, 191, 190, 181

– *Camel Trail*, leaflet from Camel Valley Countryside Service, 3/5 Barn Lane, Bodmin, Cornwall PL31 1LZ

– *The Tarka Trail – A Walker's Guide* by Richard Williamson (Devon Books, 1989)

– *The Tarka Trail – an introductory guide*, leaflet from Devon County Council Planning Dept
– *The Two Moors Way* by Two Moors Way Association (available from RA national office)
– *The Two Moors Way – an introduction*, leaflet from Devon County Council Planning Dept

2 Cotswold Beauty: Taunton – Chipping Campden
MAPS: 183, 182, 172, 163, 162, 150, 151
The Cotswold Way Handbook *is invaluable from Bath onwards, including accommodation addresses and other local information, although you may like to combine it with one of the more substantial guidebooks for in-depth information of these charming hills.*
– *Avon Walkway*, leaflet from Avon County Council
– *Cotswold Way Handbook* by Gloucestershire RA (available from RA national office)
– *The Cotswold Way* by Kev Reynolds (Cicerone, 1990)
– *The Cotswold Way: a Walker's Guide* by Mark Richards (Thornhill Press, 3rd ed 1982)

3 Green Route Through the Midlands: Chipping Campden – Crowden
MAPS: 139, 128, 127, 118, 110, 109
The three guidebooks for the main part of this section are all indispensable, since waymarking can be patchy. The Gritstone Trail *is in fact more of a booklet, but the directions are clear and the map satisfactory. There are free, useful leaflets on the country parks and short trails, but OS maps are necessary for a clearer idea of direction of travel, or if you have to look further afield for accommodation, etc.*
– *The Heart of England Way Walker's Guide* by John Roberts (Walkways, 1990)
– *Heart of England Way accommodation and camping guide*, leaflet from 8 Hillside Close, Bartley Green, Birmingham B32 4LT
– *The Gritstone Trail Walker's Guide* from Cheshire County Council (1989)
– *Cestrian Link Walk* by John Davenport (Westmorland Gazette, 1983)
– Lyme Park: information from Lyme Park, Disley, Stockport SK12 2NX

– *Cheshire Ring Canal Walk No 1: Marple–Macclesfield* from Cheshire County Council
– *Sett Valley Trail*, leaflet from Hayfield Tourist Information Centre
– Middlewood Way and Etherow–Goyt Valley: leaflets and information from Stockport Metropolitan Borough Council Ranger Service or Etherow Country Park, George Street, Compstall, Stockport SK6 5JD
– *8 Walks Around Longdendale,* from Peak National Park Office, Baslow Road, Bakewell, Derbys DE45 1AE

4 The Toughest Trail: Crowden – Kirk Yetholm
MAPS: 103, 98, 92, 91, 87, 86, 80, 74
The official National Trail Guide (two volumes) and the Pennine Way Association's booklet are essential reading. The former includes strip maps of the route, but since this long and challenging section will be the roughest and most exposed so far encountered, OS map sheets are important should bad weather, fatigue or a routefinding error make you lose your way.
– *Pennine Way National Trail Guide: Edale–Bowes, Bowes–Kirk Yetholm*, (2 vols) both by Tony Hopkins (Aurum Press, 1990)
– *Pennine Way Accommodation and Camping Guide* by Pennine Way Association, from John Needham, 23 Woodland Crescent, Hilton Park, Prestwich, Manchester M25 8WQ
– *A Pennine Way Companion* by A. Wainwright (Westmorland Gazette/Michael Joseph, 1992)
– YHA Penine Way Bureau booklet, from YHA Northern England Office, PO Box 11, Matlock, Derbys DE4 2XA
– *Dales Way Handbook & Accommodation Guide* by West Riding RA (available from RA national office)
– *The Dales Way & Accommodation Guide* by Terry Marsh (Cicerone Press, 1992)

5 Through Scotland's Heart: Kirk Yetholm – Aberfeldy
MAPS: 73, 72, 66, 65, 58, 52 (and HMSO's *Southern Upland Way* includes official 1:50 000 route map)
Bartholomew: Pentland Hills Walking Map (1:42 240)
David and Kathleen MacInnes's book provides a useful commentary on a south–north Borders route from Hawick to Edinburgh, via Peebles, West Linton and the Pentlands; and Hamish Brown's

well-researched guide also covers similar ground – but has the added bonus of continuing via Linlithgow and the Forth & Clyde Canal to link with the beginning of the West Highland Way at Milngavie (End to End West Route). You may have to look to libraries or second-hand bookshops for copies of each, and both must be supplemented by OS maps. The Fife Coast Path *is a valuable leaflet for the stretch north of the Forth, after which it is back to the map. For accommodation look to the national guides and local tourist information centres.*

– *Countryside Walks in the Scottish Borders 2: Eildon Walk, 3: Newtown-St Boswells–Maxton, 4: Kelso/Kalemouth* (via Roxburgh), booklets from Border Regional Council Planning Dept, Newtown St Boswells, Melrose TD6 0SA

– *From the Pennines to the Highlands* by Hamish Brown (Lochar Publishing, 1992)

– *Walking Through Scotland* by David & Kathleen MacInnes (David & Charles, 1981) – see Ch 1: 'Borders Walk'

– *The Border Country: a Walker's Guide* by Alan Hall (Cicerone Press, 1993)

– *The Southern Upland Way: Eastern Section* by Ken Andrew (HMSO, 1984)

– *Water of Leith Walkway*, leaflet from Landscape Planning Dept, Edinburgh District Council

– *The Fife Coast Path – North Queensferry to Aberdour*, from Dunfermline District Council Environment Division (Planning), 3 New Row, Dunfermline KY12 7NN

– *Long-Distance Walks in Scotland* by Arthur Stewart (Crowood Press, 1994) – see Ch 4: Glen Almond

6 The Wilderness Miles: Aberfeldy – Inverness

MAPS: 43, 36, 35, 26 (and OS Outdoor Leisure 3: Aviemore & the Cairngorms)

Harveys: Cairngorms (1:40 000)

It is imperative that you are well-equipped for the Cairngorm crossing. In addition to the requisite maps, the general guides by Hamish MacInnes and Ralph Storer provide good route directions and all-round information, particularly if you are contemplating Glen Feshie or the Lairig an Laoigh rather than the Lairig Ghru. This is a section where pre-booking of accommodation is advisable for those without tents.

– *Walks: Pitlochry and District*, from Pitlochry Tourist Information Centre
– *Highland Walks 4: Cairngorms and Royal Deeside* by Hamish MacInnes (Hodder & Stoughton, 1988)
– *Exploring Scottish Hill Tracks* by Ralph Storer (Warner Books, 1993)
– See Stewart (above), Chapters 1: Lairig Ghru, and 5: Glen Tilt
– *Rothiemurchus Estate: Visitor Guide and Footpath Map*, from Rothiemurchus Visitor Centre, Inverdruie, By Aviemore
– *Glenmore Forest Park*, guide and map from Glenmore Forest Park Visitor Centre, Aviemore

7 The Last Lap: Inverness – John o'Groats
MAPS: 21, 17, 12, 11, 10
With no walking trails and steadily descreasing accommodation it is advisable to think carefully about the final 150 miles. There are a few SYHA hostels, but check the days that they are open. It may be tempting to simply plough on, but take care not to get stranded on the last lap. Inevitably, facilities tend to gather about the A9.
– *Walks Around Strathpeffer*, leaflet from Strathpeffer Tourist Information Centre
– *Walking and Touring Around Brora*, booklet from Brora Tourist Information Committee – available locally

FURTHER READING: WEST ROUTE

Map numbers refer to Ordnance Survey Landranger maps (1:50 000) unless indicated otherwise. Where maps overlap from one chapter to the next they are listed in the first chapter only.

8 High Clifftop Miles: Land's End – Barnstaple
MAPS: 204, 203, 200, 190, 180
The South-West Way Association's annual guide includes local details such as B&Bs and campsites, plus information on where the trail has been affected by diversions, erosion, new building work – and helpfully points out where the other published guidebooks are at fault. Although navigation may seem simple, maps are recommended (the National Trail Guide's maps may be sufficient if you are sticking with the coast all the way).
– *South-West Coast Path National Trail Guide: Padstow–Falmouth*

by John Macadam; *Minehead–Padstow* by Roland Tarr (both Aurum Press, 1990)
– *South-West Way Vol 1: Minehead to Penzance* by Martin Collins (Cicerone Press, 1989)
– *The South-West Way*, guide and accommodation list by South-West Way Association (Peninsula Press) – see addresses
– The Camel Trail: See Central Route

9 Into the West Country: Barnstaple – Chepstow
MAPS: 182, 181, 172 (and Outdoor Leisure 9: Exmoor)
Local tourist information centres will have accommodation lists, although those without a tent should not run into too much trouble in rural Devon and Somerset. Hamish Brown's route from Minehead to Chepstow is scenic and attractive, if rather wayward to begin with.
– See SW Coast Path titles above
– The Tarka Trail: See Central Route
– *Exmoor and the Quantocks – a Walker's Guide* by John Earle (Cicerone Press, 1991)
– *Walking the Summits of Somerset & Avon* by Hamish Brown (Patrick Stephens, 1991)
– *The West Mendip Way* by Andrew Eddy (Weston-super-Mare Civic Society, 1983)
– The Avon Walkway: See Central Route

10 Kingly Footsteps: Chepstow – Chirk
MAPS: 162, 161, 148, 137, 126
The solid National Trail Guide and the Offa's Dyke Association's Where to Stay *are necessities, since the land can be remote and rough in places. The latter is small, light and pocketable, and also has bunkhouse and camping information; updated every year.*
– *Offa's Dyke Path National Trail Guide*: *Chepstow–Knighton*, *Knighton–Prestatyn*, (2 vols) both by Ernie & Kathy Kay and Mark Richards (Aurum Press, 1989)
– *Where to Stay*: *Offa's Dyke Path Accommodation Guide* by and from the Offa's Dyke Association – see addresses
– *Offa's Dyke Castles Alternative* from the Offa's Dyke Association
– *Offa's Dyke Mileage Chart* from the Offa's Dyke Association
– *Walking Down the Wye* by David Hunter (Cicerone Press, 1992)

– *Wye Valley Walk Map Pack* (Chepstow–Hay) from Gwent County Council
– *Ramblers' Guide to the Shropshire Way* by Shropshire RA (Management Update, 1991)

11 North-West Passage: Chirk – Arnside
MAPS: 117, 109, 108, 102, 97
Pearson's guide is a must if you opt for towpath miles, while Gordon Emery's text includes a few B&B addresses. Cheshire County Council's guides are fairly competent, but back-up maps will help greatly. Beware outdated OS maps for the Lymm–Wigan section – recent commercial development around Risley Moss may not be shown.
– *Pearson's Shropshire Union and Llangollen Canal Companion* (1989) from J. M. Pearson & Son, Tatenhill Common, Burton-on-Trent, Staffs DE16 9RS
– *The Maelor Way* by Gordon Emery (1991) from Gordon Emery, 27 Gladstone Road, Chester
– *The South Cheshire Way* by the Mid-Cheshire Footpaths Society, 7 Ruskin Avenue, Orford, Warrington WA2 9DB
– *Mow Cop Trail* from Cheshire County Council
– *The Sandstone Way* from Cheshire County Council (1986)
– The Cestrian Link Walk: See Central Route
– *North-West Waterway Walks Vol 1: South of the Mersey* by Guy Lawson (Sigma Leisure, 1990), includes River Weaver, Trent and Mersey, Bridgewater Canals
– *North-West Waterways Walks Vol 2: Mersey Waterways* by David Parry (Sigma Leisure, 1993), includes Weaver, Bridgewater, Leeds and Liverpool Canals
– *Douglas Valley Way* by Gladys Sellers (Cicerone Press, 1991)
– *The Ribble Way* by Gladys Sellers (Cicerone Press, 2nd ed 1993)
– *Wandering in Bowland (a Walker's Guide to the Forest of Bowland*) by A.A.Lord (Westmorland Gazette)
– *A Walker's Guide to the Lancaster Canal* by Robert Swain (Cicerone Press, 1990)
– *Lancashire Coastal Way*, leaflets from Lancashire County Council
– *Walking Down the Lune* by Robert Swain (Cicerone Press, 1993)

12 England's Finest Mountains: Arnside – Carlisle
MAPS: 90, 85 (and OS Outdoor Leisure 6: English Lakes South-West, and 4: English Lakes North-West)
The two Outdoor Leisure maps should cover your journey through the Lakes, provided you do not veer too far east; and they also indicate the location of campsites. School parties and trippers may leave few beds to spare in hostels and guest houses at the height of the season.
– *Walks in the Silverdale/Arnside area* by R. Brian Evans (Cicerone Press, 1993)
– *The Furness Way* by Paul Hannon (Hillside Press, 1984)
– *The Cumbria Way* by John Trevelyan (Dalesman Publishing, 3rd ed 1987)
– Lake District information from Lake District National Park Office, Murley Moss, Oxenholme Road, Kendal, Cumbria LA9 7RL

13 The Bare Hills: Carlisle – Strathblane
MAPS: 79, 78, 71, 64 (and HMSO's *Southern Upland Way* includes official 1:50 000 route map)
Until Glasgow fixed accommodation is rather sparse, and advance planning is wise. To negotiate the city (either around or through it) I found Erl Wilkie's Glasgow's Pathways *invaluable, a well-researched and up-to-date guide.*
– *Southern Upland Way: Western Section* by Ken Andrew (HMSO, 1984)
– *Southern Upland Way Information and Accommodation*, leaflet from Scottish Natural Heritage
– *A Guide to the Southern Upland Way* by David Williams (Constable, 1989)
– *Glasgow's Pathways* by Erl Wilkie (Mainstream Publishing, 1993)
– Chatelherault Country Park: leaflets and information from Chatelherault Country Park Visitor Centre, Ferniegair, Hamilton
– Strathclyde Country Park: leaflets and information from The General Manager, Strathclyde Country Park, 366 Hamilton Road, Motherwell ML1 4ED

14 Highland Grandeur: Strathblane – Inverness
MAPS: 57, 56, 50, 41, 34, 26 (and HMSO's *West Highland Way* includes official 1:50 000 route map)
Although many WHW walkers rely entirely on the guidebook's accompanying route map, OS maps for the region are a good idea if you fancy taking in a few Munros or incorporating some scenic diversions. Inevitable pressure on the region's limited accommodation during certain months will need to be taken into account.
– *West Highland Way* by Robert Aitken (HMSO, 1984)
– *West Highland Way Information and Accommodation*, leaflet from Scottish Natural Heritage
– *A Guide to the West Highland Way* by Tom Hunter (Constable, 1984)
– *Great Glen Cycle Route*, leaflet from Forest Enterprise North Scotland Region, 21 Church Street, Inverness IV1 1EL
– *The Great Glen* (forest walks leaflet) from Forest Enterprise (above)

FURTHER READING: EAST ROUTE

Map numbers refer to Ordance Survey Landranger maps (1:50 000) unless indicated otherwise. Where maps overlap from one chapter to the next they are listed in the first chapter only.

15 Sunny South Coast: Land's End – Plymouth
MAPS: 204, 203, 201, 200
The South-West Way Association's annual guide provides the necessary local detail, including B&Bs, youth hostels and campsites, plus the state of the path and grade of walking involved. The National Trail Guide and Cicerone Press title both offer a more rounded picture, with plenty of interesting information.
– *South-West Coast Path National Trail Guide: Padstow–Falmouth* by John Macadam; *Falmouth–Exmouth* by John Le Messurier (both Aurum Press, 1990)
– *South-West Way Vol 1: Minehead to Penzance* and *Vol 2: Penzance to Poole*, both by Martin Collins (Cicerone Press, 1989)
– *The South-West Way*, guide and accommodation list by South-West Way Association (Peninsula Press) – see address list
– *The Saints' Way*, from Cornwall County Council Countryside Access (1991)

16 The English Riviera: Plymouth – Lyme Regis
MAPS: 202, 193, 192, 191 (and OS Outdoor Leisure 28: Dartmoor)
See the South-West Coast Path details above. For the Dartmoor alternative the Outdoor Leisure map is essential, showing amongst other things access land and access points to the moorland.
As SW Coast Path titles above, plus:
– *South-West Coast Path National Trail Guide: Exmouth–Poole* by Roland Tarr (Aurum Press, 1990)
– *Walking on Dartmoor* by John Earle (Cicerone Press, 1987)
– Dartmoor information from Dartmoor National Park Information Office, Parke, Haytor Road, Bovey Tracey, Devon TQ13 9JQ
– Two Moors Way: See Central Route
– *East Devon Way* from East Devon District Council (1993)
– *Wessex Way* by Alan Proctor (Thornhill, 1980 – out of print, but copies may be available locally)

17 Walking Through History: Lyme Regis – Ivinghoe
MAPS: 194, 193, 184, 183, 175, 174, 173, 165
To navigate the Wessex Ridgeway you will need to pay careful attention to the OS map as well as the text of the guide. The Imber Range Perimeter Path *booklet is useful but not essential, since the WR guide and local waymarks should be sufficient. But for the Ridgeway itself it is desirable to purchase a copy of the annual information guide, since it will soon become apparent that there are few places to stay or sites to camp actually on the trail.*
– *The Wessex Ridgeway* by Alan Proctor (available from RA national office)
– *Walk the Wessex Ridgeway in Dorset* by Priscilla Houstoun (Dorset Publishing Company/Wincanton Press 1988/1994)
– *The Imber Range Perimeter Path*, booklet from Wiltshire County Council Planning & Highways Dept or Warminster Tourist Information Centre
– *The Ridgeway National Trail Guide* by Neil Curtis (Aurum Press, 1989)
– *Ridgeway Information and Accommodation Guide*, from the Ridgeway Officer, Oxfordshire County Council

18 The Flat East: Ivinghoe – Oakham
MAPS: 166, 155, 154, 144, 143, 142, 141
This gentle, largely flat section lends itself to detours and diversions, according to where you want to visit, so OS maps are important.
– *The Icknield Way: A Walker's Guide* by the Icknield Way Association (3rd ed 1993), available from RA national office
– *The Icknield Way* (set of 3 leaflets and accommodation guide) from Bedfordshire County Council Leisure Services
– *Two Ridges Link* from Buckinghamshire County Council, County Engineer's Dept
– *The Greensand Ridge Walk* from Bedfordshire County Council Leisure Services
– *The Hereward Way* by and from Trevor Noyes, 8 Welmore Road, Glinton, Peterborough, Cambs PE6 7LU
– *The Hereward Way (Ely–Peterborough)* from Cambridgeshire County Council Rural Strategy Group
– *The Bishop's Way*, leaflet from Cambridgeshire County Council (above)

19 The Gentle Hills: Oakham – Filey
MAPS: 130, 122, 121, 113, 112, 107, 106, 101, 100
John Stead's fine little book will tell you nearly all you need to know about the Viking Way; and the National Trail Guide to the Wolds Way is the best for the next trail.
– *The Viking Way* from Lincolnshire County Council (1983)
– *The Viking Way* by John Stead (Cicerone Press, 1990)
– *Viking Way Accommodation leaflet* from Lincolnshire and South Humberside RA
– *The Wolds Way National Trail Guide* by Roger Ratcliffe (Aurum Press, 1992)
– *Walking Holidays in the Wolds* (includes accommodation list) from Humberside Tourism and Countryside Dept

20 Along The Tracks: Filey – Heddon
MAPS: 94, 93, 88 (87 & 92 – Weardale alternative; OS Outdoor Leisure 26: North York Moors West, and 27: North York Moors East)
The North York Moors National Park Office offers plenty of walking information, including the Cleveland Way Accommodation Guide. *Beyond, the local authorities publish useful leaflets and cards on the*

respective railway paths, although Charlie Emett's Walking Northern Railways *includes them all in one handy volume.*
– *Cleveland Way National Trail Guide* by Ian Sampson (Aurum Press, 1989)
– *Walking the Cleveland Way and the Missing Link* by Malcolm Boyes (Cicerone Press, 1988)
– *Cleveland Way Accommodation Guide* from Cleveland Way Project Officer, North York Moors National Park Office, The Old Vicarage, Bondgate, Helmsley, York YO6 5BP
– *The Link Through the Tabular Hills* from North York Moors National Park Office (1993) – address above
– *A Coast to Coast Walk* by A. Wainwright (Westmorland Gazette/ Michael Joseph, 1987)
– *Esk Valley Walk* and *Where to Stay* booklet from North York Moors National Park Office (1993) – address above
– *Cook Country Walk* from North York Moors National Park Office – address above
– *The Weardale Way* by J.K.E. Piggin (Dalesman Publishing, 1984)
– *Railway Walks in County Durham* from Durham County Council Planning Dept, includes Brandon–Bishop Auckland Walk and others
– Lanchester Valley Walk; The Waskerley Way; The Derwent Walk, leaflets and information from Derwentside District Council Leisure Services
– *Derwent Walk Country Park* by Durham County Council/Gateshead Metropolitan Borough Council, further details from Thornley Woodlands Centre, Rowlands Gill, Tyne and Wear NE39 1AU
– *Walking Northern Railways Vol 1: East* by Charlie Emett (Cicerone Press, 1988)

21 A Coast to Yourself: Heddon – Edinburgh
MAPS: 81, 75, 67, 66
Ian Smith's handwritten guidebook describes the whole of the Northumberland coast, including the less scenic parts further south. However, most of this largely unvisited seaboard can be negotiated using maps.
– *Best Walks in Northumberland* by Frank Duerden (Constable Books, 1990), includes coast and inland
– *Northumberland Coastline* by Ian Smith (Sandhill Press, 1988),

40 Narrowgate, Alnwick, Northumberland NE66 1JQ
– *Countryside Walks in the Scottish Borders 6: Eyemouth–Coldingham*, booklet from Borders Regional Council Planning Dept, Newtown St Boswells, Melrose TD6 OSA
– *Southern Upland Way: Eastern Section* by Ken Andrew (HMSO, 1984)
– *Southern Upland Way Information and Accommodation*, leaflet from Scottish Natural Heritage
– *John Muir Country Park Clifftop Trail*, booklet from Dunbar Tourist Information Centre